Thank you for your friendship and support of the
Charlotte Mecklenburg Library this year.
We hope you enjoy *Liberating Dixie*.

CHARLOTTE MECKLENBURG LIBRARY

FOUNDATiON

LIBERATING DIXIE

Published by Lorimer Press
Davidson, North Carolina

Printed in Korea

ISBN 978-0-9897885-1-9
Library of Congress Control Number: 2013957605
Cover art by Leslie Rindoks

ADDITIONAL ART PERMISSIONS:
Pages: 11, 98, 127, 133, 172, 193, 210, 220, 258 © Kevin Siers.
Pages: 13, 75, 90, 116, 138, 151, 159, 197, 198, 201, 217, 255 © by Doug Marlette; Permission Granted by The Doug Marlette Estate.
Page 16: © Dwane Powell.
Pages 32-33: from the Neshoba Democrat, courtesy of the author.

ADDITIONAL PHOTOGRAPH PERMISSIONS:
Page 2: courtesy of the author; Page 20: by Leslie Banks; Page 30: by Ed Williams; Page 50: by T. Ortega Gaines, courtesy of The Charlotte Observer; Page 72: by John D. Simmons, courtesy of The Charlotte Observer; Page 124: by Rebecca S. Gratz, courtesy of The Charlotte Observer; Page 136: by Don Sturkey; Page 178: by Lewis Hines; Page 206: courtesy of the author; Page 228: by Apryl Chapman Thomas; Page 250: by Deidre Laird, courtesy of The Charlotte Observer; Page 262: by Nancy Pierce; Page 271: by Nancy Pierce.

LIBERATING
DIXIE

— AN EDITOR'S LIFE, FROM OLE MISS TO OBAMA —

ED WILLIAMS

Dedicated to Hodding Carter III, Patricia Derian,
Reese Cleghorn and Rolfe Neill,
my friends and mentors;

and to Marylyn and Jonathan Williams,
who shared the good times and buoyed me up
during the hard times.

Introduction

In September 1962, James Meredith and I arrived on the Ole Miss campus in a cloud of teargas. As the school's first black student, Meredith was profoundly unwelcome, and an insurrection of historic dimensions ensued, leaving two men dead and the campus occupied by federal troops sent by President John Kennedy to restore order. *federal troops*

It was in the wake of this turmoil that I met Ed Williams, a sophomore from Hornersville, Missouri, a town of some 700 amid the cotton fields 90 miles north of Memphis. He was handshaking his way through my dormitory, campaigning for editor of the daily Mississippian. I liked him immediately, was impressed with his intelligence and forthrightness, told him I'd vote for him. I didn't, but neither did most other Ole Miss students. Up against the "Never!" insanity then permeating the state and campus, Ed's mature rationality stood no chance. How do I remember that his defeat for editor was by the largest margin ever? Because he recalls it from time to time, with amusement and absolutely no regrets.

If you know only one thing about Ed Williams, you should know that going against the tide has never bothered him in the least. I have seen him respond coolly when threatened with being "snatched baldheaded" by an enraged reader in Greenville, Mississippi, and I have seen him offer his resignation rather than endorse a publisher's chosen candidate for U.S. senator from North Carolina. (The publisher blinked, I exhaled.)

The second time that Ed ran for editor at Ole Miss he won, and he wasted little time separating himself from Mississippi's still-obstinate segregationist majority. "Apparently," he wrote, "state political leaders are becoming aware of the fact that the people who are doing the most harm to Mississippi are not out-of-state agitators, not biased journalists, not left-wing television commentators. The people who are doing the most to drag

Mississippi down are Mississippians who think they don't have to obey laws they don't like; Mississippians who attempt to live in a world of moonlight, moonshine and magnolia blossoms; Mississippians who burn churches; Mississippians who refuse to recognize the fact that two-fifths of the citizens of this state are non-white."

For most of the next half century after graduating from Ole Miss I worked either for or with Ed, first at the Delta Democrat-Times, then at our iconoclastic monthly Mississippi Freelance, finally at The Charlotte Observer. I will cement my place in geezerdom by positing ours as the golden age of newspapers. Ed is generous in crediting mentors such as Hodding Carter III and Reese Cleghorn, but he himself has been indispensable in my own serendipitous life in newsrooms.

Ed drew the title of this collection from W.J. Cash's landmark *The Mind of the South*, which he discovered as a history major at Ole Miss. "Over my career," he has written, "I hoped to help liberate the South from what Cash called the 'savage ideal,' under which 'dissent and variety are completely suppressed, and men become, in all their attitudes, professions and actions, virtual replicas of one another.' "

As this sampler of his work demonstrates page after page, Ed has challenged that savage ideal with persistence, incisiveness and wit. If you are unfamiliar with his work, you may find his range surprisingly wide for an editorial page editor, including not only political analysis, but also childhood reminiscences, historical insights and quirky humor (most memorably, his explanation of North Carolina's obsession with "Bahskeet-Baal"). His voice is clear and distinctive in such columns and editorials as "Clinton Is a Liar and a Fool," "Only Whites Think Racism Is Dead," "How Not to Go to War," "Country Club Bigots," "How America Looks to the World" and "10 Rules for Living." My personal favorites: His news coverage of the bootlegging ethos in Neshoba County, Mississippi, and his antler-rattling exchange of epistles with Sen. Jesse Helms.

It was at Harvard University, where he was a 1973 Nieman Foundation fellow, that Ed realized opinion journalism was his calling. He wrote a paper examining the Nieman Foundation's relationship with South Africa, whose apartheid government permitted black journalists to accept a Nieman fellowship only if they agreed not to return to their native land. If black fellows could not participate on the same basis as whites, Ed argued, the Nieman program should discontinue its relationship with South Africa. Pressured by the foundation and South African former fellows, the government soon relented.

"That experience set my course," he says. In 1973 he went to work for Reese Cleghorn as an editorial writer at The Charlotte Observer. As Jack Claiborne, former associate editor, recalled in his 1986 history of the Observer, Ed brought "a mischievous humor, a keen insight into Southern politics and history, and a hard-headed logic."

Ed retired in 2008 after 35 years at the Observer, including 25 as editor of the editorial pages. When he first stepped onto the escalator at 600 South Tryon Street, the newsroom was foggy with smoke from cigarettes and rackety with key strokes from Royals and Smith-Coronas; when he left, smokers had been exiled to the parking lot and computers ruled the premises with barely a beep. Along the way Ed's columns and editorials were part of Observer projects that won the Pulitzer Prize for Public Service in 1981 (brown lung) and 1988 (PTL). In 2003 he received the annual Liberty Bell Award from the Mecklenburg County Bar Association for his "willingness to take tough stands on tough issues." In 2010 he was named the James K. Batten Visiting Professor of Public Policy at Davidson College. In 2011 he was inducted into the North Carolina Journalism Hall of Fame.

Later that year Ed spoke at the dedication of a memorial to historian James Silver, who had been driven from Ole Miss after writing *Mississippi: The Closed Society*. Ed credited his former professor with showing him "how to be a man of learning and conviction who, in dangerous times, was not immobilized by fear." I suspect Ed didn't need much instruction. Regardless, however, that is certainly what he became.

— *Lew Powell*
Charlotte
September 20, 2013

Table of Contents

I.   THE NEWSPAPER LIFE   1

II. AMERICAN AND PROUD OF IT   19

III. MISSISSIPPI   29

IV. MECKLENBURG HISTORY   49

V.   TWO-PARTY SYSTEM   71

VI. PRESIDENTIAL MATTERS   85

        BUSH'S WAR (1991)   87

        BILL CLINTON   93

        BUSH'S WAR (2003)   105

        OBAMA   118

VII. SENATOR NO   123

VIII. RIGHTS   135

        RACE   137

        CRIME AND PUNISHMENT   149

        GAYS   157

        GUNS   170

IX. BUSINESS AND LABOR   177

X.   RELIGION   189

XI. FAMILY   205

XII. EDUCATION   219

XIII. ARTS AND LETTERS   227

XIV. SPORTS   249

XV. CODA   261

INDEX   272

It is useless to attempt to reason a man out of a thing he was never reasoned into.

— Jonathan Swift
Irish satirist (1667-1745)

I. The Newspaper Life

Champagne-drenched Rich Oppel (right) and Ed Williams celebrate the Observer's winning the 1981 Pulitzer Prize for Distinguished Public Service for "Brown Lung: A Case of Deadly Neglect," a series on the health consequences from cotton dust produced in the region's textile mills.

The Newspaper Life

Column in The Charlotte Observer Nov. 8, 1998

I worry about newspapers. I worry that as competition for readers' time and money intensifies we will be so market-driven that we'll perfect the techniques of packaging appealing information and forget the reason we went into journalism.

A newspaper must make a profit – as a stockholder, I applaud our success – but making money is not a newspaper's sole reason for being or the true measure of its success. I make a good deal of money for a person with a minimal interest in making money. But I'm in newspapering because I love the craft and the opportunity the job provides for taking part in community affairs.

The work has its drawbacks. People often ask how journalists can live with the pressure of dealing constantly with complex and controversial issues on deadline. It's Darwinian, I reply. Those who can't do it get out or die.

Some people think editorial writers spending their working hours in splendid isolation thinking lofty thoughts. Baloney. Opinion writing is a contact sport, especially if your name and picture appear in the paper.

Not long ago I was a pallbearer at an old friend's funeral. After we had carried the casket to the hearse, a couple of people I know stopped me to complain about something the Observer had failed to do. They are good people and the issue on their minds was important, so I didn't mind hearing them out.

Later a friend who had witnessed the encounter remarked, "You put down the casket and don't take two steps before somebody jumps on you about your work. Does that happen all the time?"

"All the time," I said. "

"Sheesh!" he said. "I wouldn't have your job."

I smiled and thought, *I wouldn't have any other.*

The Observer's Editorial Policy

A column in The Charlotte Observer Feb. 24, 1991

I received this letter last week on official State of North Carolina, Office of the Lieutenant Governor stationery:

Dear Mr. Williams :

As director of Communications for Lieutenant Governor Jim Gardner, I would like to request a copy of your newspaper's editorial policy.

The Lieutenant Governor respects the right of your newspaper to write editorials concerning him or his policy. In all fairness, Lieutenant Governor Gardner also believes your readers have the right to read his response to such editorials. In order to do this properly, please forward a copy of your newspaper's editorial policy and requirements for responding to editorials. ...

Sincerely,
Tina N. Wilson, Director of Communications

A reasonable request, I would say. In case you, too, have wondered about the Observer's editorial policy, here is my response:

Dear Ms. Wilson:

Thank you for your letter of Feb. 18, requesting a copy of the Observer's editorial policy. The Observer's editorial policy is this:

We stand for truth, justice and the American way. We like calling North Carolina home. We support the Ten Commandments, the Golden Rule and the philosophy expressed in Matthew 25:31-46. We would like to be able to love our country and to love justice.

We believe government is too important to be left to politicians. We think those who believe absurdities are likely to commit atrocities. We believe that talk's cheap, there's no free lunch, a stitch in time saves nine, the unexpected usually happens, the unexamined life is not worth living, and everybody is ignorant, only on different subjects.

We are always pleased to receive letters from Lt. Gov. Gardner in response to our editorials. ... (I have enclosed our letters policy.) We also hope the lieutenant governor will respond to our invitation to present his budget proposal through an article on our Viewpoint Page.

Sincerely,
Ed Williams, Editor of the Editorial Pages

Is The Charlotte Observer Biased?

A column in The Charlotte Observer June 10, 2001

As overseer of the Observer's opinion pages, I sometimes hear complaints that our editorials are biased. Are they?

If what you mean by "biased" is, as Mr. Webster puts it, that our editorial writers have "an inclination of temperament or outlook," I'd say "yes." Don't you?

If you mean we're so prejudiced as to be unfair or dishonest, I'd say "no."

Take, for example, Tuesday's referendum on funding proposed center-city facilities, including a new arena. The Observer's editorial board favored it. (The editorial board is made up of the publisher, editor, editorial page editor and associate editors. We opinion writers don't direct or dictate to news reporters and editors; they may or may not agree with our opinions.)

That position shouldn't have surprised anyone. Our editorials generally favor strengthening the center city. We think the N.C. Blumenthal Performing Arts Center, Spirit Square, the Convention Center, Discovery Place, the Afro-American Cultural Center and the like – all beneficiaries of substantial taxpayer investment – are good for our community.

In general, we think local government and the city's leadership – business, professional and civic – do a good job promoting community interests. (The high re-election rate of local politicians suggests that voters agree.)

The editorial board generally supports bond issues and public-private ventures that voters are asked to approve. That's because nutty stuff rarely reaches the ballot. Proposals typically go through a review process that almost always strengthens or kills the weak ones.

What I'm telling you is no secret. Our editorials reflect those views. Nor is it sinister. We have no hidden agenda.

Some critics suggest that we favor center-city projects because they increase the value of the Observer's center-city property. That would make sense if our business were real estate. It's not. The Observer owns the property that the newspaper uses, and no doubt will still be using after all of us here now are dead and buried. When property values increase, all it means for us is higher taxes.

In fact, our purpose is simple: to make this a better place. I've lived in dying or comatose cities. I prefer one that's lively and ambitious. Yes, the talk of Charlotte's can-do spirit can be tiresome, but it beats the heck out of a can't-do spirit. Citizens' civic pride, and willingness to invest talent and money in the city, help give it life.

It pays off. Look at Charlotte's history.

It was Charlotte taxpayers' willingness to invest in an airport that brought what's now the US Airways hub here and created the air connections that are invaluable to the city's economy.

It was the city taxpayers' willingness to build a Coliseum and pay for it that paved the way for our first major league sports team, the NBA Charlotte Hornets.

Mecklenburg taxpayers wanted kindergartens and footed the bill for them long before the legislature funded the program statewide. Our school board and county commissioners are showing similar vision with Bright Beginnings for needy preschoolers – an educational program the state surely will soon make available to all.

So yes, the Observer's editorial board has a bias, one shared with Charlotte-Mecklenburg: a bias toward action.

Take a look at *Tar Heel Politics 2000*, an insightful book by Paul Luebke, a UNC-Greensboro professor and state legislator. As he sees it, this state's fundamental political division isn't Democrats vs. Republicans or liberals vs. conservatives, it's modernizers vs. traditionalists.

Modernizers, he says, are bankers, developers, retail merchants, the news media and others who favor and benefit from change and growth. On the other side are those who fear change and growth, such as traditional industrialists (who abhor competition for workers) and the agriculture establishment. I'd add ideological anti-taxers and opponents of social change.

In rural areas and small towns, traditionalists usually dominate. In some cities – Winston-Salem comes to mind – the factions are locked in struggle. In Charlotte, it's no contest: This is the modernizers' paradise. When traditionalists win one here, which is rarely, it's because the modernizers split or overreached.

Though our editorial board definitely is inclined toward the modernizer view, we don't belong to that faction. Journalists aren't joiners. Our commitment to informing the public is stronger than our support for anybody's political agenda. We don't try to win arguments by silencing the opposition. In fact, I doubt you could find any argument for voting "no" last Tuesday that wasn't made prominently at some point by some writer on this page.

The newspaper I read growing up had this aphorism published daily on its editorial page: "Give the people light and they will find their own way." It may sound sappy to you, but we journalists believe that's our calling.

Working with Editorial Cartoonists
From The Masthead, Journal of the National Conference of Editorial Writers, Spring 2000

I've been working with very good editorial cartoonists, Doug Marlette and Kevin Siers, for 25 years. Here is the sum of the wisdom I've derived from the experience: It is an unnatural act for editorial page editors to work with cartoonists, a mispairing of the magnitude of a marriage between Hillary Clinton and Howard Stern (or maybe, for that matter, Hillary Clinton and Bill Clinton).

An editorial cartoonist who doesn't have great ideas that an editor would refuse to publish should seek another line of work. The cartoonist's job is to be provocative. The editor's job is to decide what a family newspaper will publish. I treat the cartoonist pretty much as a visual columnist. The standard I apply is not whether the cartoon reflects our editorial position (though I can't imagine hiring a cartoonist whose views I detest), but whether it makes a point that the general reader of our pages is likely to understand and whether it is within the rather generous bounds of taste and hyperbole that we apply to cartoons.

On cartoons I know will be controversial, I make sure I'm able to answer this question: What does this cartoon say to me that merits putting it in the paper? If I can't answer that to my own satisfaction, I'm going to have a heck of a time answering it to readers' satisfaction. Sometimes I ask the cartoonist why he thinks we should publish it. After all, he has a big stake in it, too.

In our discussion, the cartoonist and I talk about ways various readers might find the cartoon offensive. Our goal isn't to avoid offending anybody. It's to avoid offending anybody unintentionally.

Sometimes that doesn't work. A representative of a national Catholic organization threatened to denounce us in his publication as anti-Catholic because of a cartoon that centered on Mary and a manger scene. I told him that if the cartoon was offensive, surely it was offensive to all Christians, including Baptists, of which I am one, and not just to Catholics. I also told him that if he accused us in print of being anti-Catholic, his readers who already read the Observer would think he was stupid, and I offered some examples of Catholics who would say so publicly. We exchanged a couple of letters and a phone call, and ultimately he moved onto other things. My guess is that someone had complained to him and he had followed through, much the way your local power company's lawyer will send you a stern copyright warning if you use Reddy Kilowatt in a cartoon.

One time in all these years I apologized for running a cartoon. It criticized a local judge in a situation in which a prisoner was released who shouldn't have been. The cartoonist and I had our usual discussion. Then late in the day, after I'd left the office, he came up with a different version of the drawing that made the cartoon better – but in my judgment, factually inaccurate – by shifting the focus from the judicial system to a specific judge. In a column, I explained that after reviewing the facts, I'd concluded that the cartoon wrongly blamed the judge, and I apologized to him in print. (The judge then asked for the original so he could frame it with the apology.)

For editorial page editors, I offer this advice:

1. Remember, it's the editor's job to decide whether to publish a cartoon. Your cartoonist may be unhappy if you reject an idea because you think it doesn't belong in your newspaper. Believe me, he'll be a lot more unhappy if you publish it and then turn on him afterward – and he should be.

2. If you get a lot of complaints about a cartoon you don't regret pub-

lishing, don't apologize, but also don't hesitate to explain your thinking in print.

3. If after hearing the complaints you conclude that you shouldn't have published the cartoon, say so in print. It makes no sense to me to defend a decision you've concluded was wrong. Why not be straight with readers about it? Caution: If this happens to you more than once, something's wrong.

If you find yourself killing all your cartoonist's best ideas, maybe you need to (a) find another cartoonist, (b) decide whether you really want to have a cartoonist, or (c) send off for one of those exercise machines that Christie Brinkley advertises in the wee hours on cable TV to help strengthen your stomach muscles.

Provocative cartoonists may be the journalistic equivalent of lower back pain for editorial page editors, but readers love them. Admit it, so do you – when they're somebody else's responsibility.

Kevin Siers' 'Peacemakers'
A column in The Charlotte Observer Jan. 28, 1991

Many Observer readers were angered by the Kevin Siers cartoon we published Friday. In fact, mad as hell is what they were.

The cartoon shows angry people screaming and pointing at Jesus. He stands, head bowed in sadness, holding a sign that reads, "Blessed are the peacemakers."

Some callers were angry and abusive. The more restrained ones questioned the judgment of the editors and the cartoonist. The more agitated ones questioned our patriotism. One said Kevin should be assassinated. Some seemed convinced that if Jesus were on Earth today, he'd be bombing Baghdad.

A local radio call-in show host fed the furor, pumping up the anger but adding nothing to anyone's understanding.

You know, it made me wish we'd been able to hear WBT's Henry Boggan handle the topic. One of the things I've always admired about Henry is that when he deals with controversial issues, he'll often take up for the side that's unpopular with callers. Henry's genial prodding can provide an educational as well as entertaining experience. He offers listeners an opportunity to think, instead of just ranting. Such humane intelligence is rare on the airwaves, sad to say, but I'm sure it contributes greatly to Henry's popularity and staying power.

Now about the cartoon. I've written from time to time about the relationship between the Observer and its staff cartoonists, Kevin Siers and Gene Payne. The relationship is essentially this: The cartoonists come up with ideas for cartoons (I don't tell them what to draw). Kevin works in this office. Usually I talk with him as he is coming up with an idea. Gene is semi-retired (which means he's at his drawing board only about 60 hours a week). He draws at home and brings his cartoons in. I look at the completed cartoons (or one of my fellow editors does) and decide whether to publish them. About 99 percent of the time we do.

Occasionally we don't. The cartoon's point may be unclear, or it just may not seem to me appropriate for this newspaper. As I said, that happens rarely.

What do I look for in cartoons? I look for ideas that will make people chuckle or provoke them to think. I don't look for cartoons that everyone will agree with. And it's all right with me if a cartoon takes the unpopular side of an issue.

I don't try to shield you from ideas you might not like, or ideas I don't agree with. I treat cartoons the same way I treat the Tom Wicker, William Buckley, Ellen Goodman and Joseph Sobran columns that appear on this page. I want them to make worthwhile points, and make them well. I leave it up to you to like or dislike them, agree or disagree with them. I want us to provide debate, not enforced harmony.

I don't agree with all the cartoons we publish, any more than I agree with all the columns or letters to the editor. I don't think I have to. Our editorials express the views of the Observer's editors. Cartoons, columns and letters to the editor express the views of their authors. I do, however, agree with what I considered to be the point of Kevin's "peacemakers" cartoon.

First, let me say what I didn't think the point was. There are many rallies around America these days in support of our troops in the Mideast. These are not "pro-war" rallies. These people didn't decide to send our troops to fight. They may not even agree with President Bush's policy – a sizable minority of Congress didn't. But they pray for the safety and success of our

troops. They mourn for all who pay the terrible costs of war. If they saw Jesus with a sign saying "Blessed are the peacemakers," I think they'd embrace him.

Some readers saw the cartoon as maligning those people. That's not how I saw it. Look at the crowd in the cartoon. The people are angry. Their faces are filled with hate. I don't know whether you've encountered them, but I have. They're the people who say "Nuke Iraq," apparently unconcerned that innocent people would die. They're the people who say Arabs here should be locked up or sent home. They're the people who condemn Americans who oppose the war as communists and traitors.

Heaven knows, I don't claim to speak for Jesus. (Even though I'm a lifelong Baptist, I do retain some humility.) But to me, Kevin's cartoon offered a useful reminder. Jesus did, in fact, say that peacemakers are blessed. Do good to those who persecute you, he said. Love your enemy.

That's a radical message in wartime, I know, and people will argue about what it means. But it is Jesus' message, and even as our nation pursues

Love your enemy. JC

a war we consider just, we who are Christians should think about that. We can oppose Saddam Hussein without hating Arabs. We can support our troops without reviling people who challenge the wisdom of this war.

A cartoon is a two-dimensional message in black and white. You see in it what you see in it, regardless of what I saw or what the cartoonist intended. But that's what the cartoon said to me. That's why the Observer published it. And that's what I hope you'll think about.

Pols Don't Want Revenge, They Want the Cartoon
A column in The Charlotte Observer March 25, 2001

In my mail a few days ago was a letter from a reader who was "furious" about the way George W. Bush "is persistently portrayed in your 'redneck edition of the NY Times' as a bumbling idiot."

This is a "gross mischaracterization" of Bush, he continued, and "an affront to every one of us who voted for him. We, too, must be a bunch of bumbling idiots. We want this to stop immediately!"

His complaint wasn't about our news stories or our editorials. He was talking about cartoons – in particular, about ears.

He sent copies of recent cartoons to show that the Observer's Kevin Siers and syndicated cartoonists Mike Peters and Doug Marlette draw Bush with weird ears. To Siers, Bush's ears look leprechaunish. To Peters, donkeyish. To Marlette, Dumboish.

That's the nature of cartooning, of course. Cartoonists indulge in caricature, which the dictionary defines as "exaggeration by means of often ludicrous distortion of parts or characteristics."

Cartoonists are what they are: purveyors of visual lampoons. The test of fairness is not whether cartoons show Bush looking heroic as well as bumbling – to a cartoonist, you're heroic only when you die – but whether the other side is treated with equal disrespect. Surely anyone who sees how Siers draws Clinton's nose would agree that he's no respecter of personages.

I've been intrigued by Siers' rendition of Mike Easley, North Carolina's new governor. In Siers' cartoons, Easley has no chin. What does the guy have to do to get a chin, I asked. "Stick it out more," Siers replied. How? For starters, submit a state budget that doesn't rely on money from a lottery

"HE HAS THE RIGHT TO REMAIN SILENT!... HE HAS THE RIGHT TO AN ATTORNEY GENERAL!..."

that doesn't exist and tax loopholes that haven't been closed, Siers suggested.

Politicians rarely complain about cartoons, though their supporters often do. George W. Bush seems especially good at not personalizing criticism. To check my perception, I called Ben Sargent, the Pulitzer Prize-winning cartoonist of the Austin American-Statesman, who has been drawing Bush for years.

Sargent confirmed my impression. Even in the rowdy world of Texas politics, he couldn't recall Bush or his top aides ever complaining about a cartoon. I asked how he sees Bush. "He doesn't look like his father," Sargent said. "His father has flat, straight hair. George W. has hair like a Brillo pad – or like a bush. The shape of his ears is different. The smirk. Long upper lip. Tiny little eyes, close set. His eyebrows are heavy, and one is usually flying off somewhere."

To Sargent, the context of the cartoon is as telling as the physical characteristics. "It's not just how they look, it's how they act in your cartoons," he said. He often focuses on the Joe College, frat boy image that Bush projects – "his sort of goofy personality."

It may seem odd to you for a man who draws funny pictures for a living to describe a president of the United States as "goofy," but American's freedom to spoof the powerful is as old as this nation.

Jesse Helms [signature]

Few politicians have been the target of as many jibes as Jesse Helms, the senior U.S. senator from North Carolina. Yet Siers reports that almost every time he takes a poke at Helms, someone from the senator's office calls and asks for the cartoon.

A couple of years ago the Jesse Helms Center in Wingate published a hard-cover collection of Helms' favorites, titled *The Thing That Intimidated D.C.* In the introduction, Helms says cartoonists "have produced a remarkable array of memorabilia for me. ... I have scores of these cartoons on my office walls – poking fun at me, sometimes a tad bitingly. I cannot begin to count the times when as I was wondering how to handle various issues, I have walked around my office examining those cartoons and laughing at them. For me, it prevents my making the mistake of taking myself too seriously." That's a lesson worth learning.

Friends of Doug

A column in The Charlotte Observer Nov. 25, 2007

When Doug Marlette, the Pulitzer Prize-winning former Observer cartoonist, died in a traffic mishap July 10, he was riding a remarkable wave of creative energy. Not only was he doing daily political cartoons for the Tulsa World and hundreds of newspaper nationwide and drawing a widely syndicated daily comic strip ("Kudzu"), he was hard at work on a third novel. He died en route to Oxford, Miss., where he was to help a group of high school students producing "Kudzu: A Southern Musical," inspired by his comic strip.

The latest news: The N.C. Literary and Historical Association announced last week that his second novel, *Magic Time*, had won the 2007 Sir Walter Raleigh Award for the best work of fiction by a North Carolina writer.

Doug's many admirers haven't ceased calling on friends of Doug (FODs) to talk about him and his work. Here's what I've been involved with in the past month. Observer columnist Dannye Romine Powell and I talked with a Providence Methodist Church group that had read his first novel, *The Bridge*. I spoke at the opening of an exhibit of his cartoons at the University of Mississippi. I moderated a panel on Marlette and the South at the Museum of the New South. Panelists were Dr. Tom Hanchett of the

Pat Conroy

museum, former Observer managing editor Mark Ethridge III and syndicated columnist Kathleen Parker — all FODs.

Not long ago the novelist Pat Conroy, a close FOD, asked if I thought we'd spend the rest of our lives talking about Doug. We may, Pat, we may.

I met Doug, the Observer's new cartoonist, in 1972. He was a tall, skinny, excitable 23-year-old with so much creative energy he had a hard time focusing it. It didn't occur to me that he'd develop such wide-ranging talents. It did occur to me that he might be chased out of Charlotte with a mob howling at his heels, outraged by his gleeful disrespect for popular opinion on such hot topics as bombastic politicians and Vietnam.

In many ways Doug back then was an undisciplined kid. A longtime FOD, Mark DeCastrique of Charlotte, recalls that Doug would often eat at Wad's, a boisterous greasy spoon on East Boulevard. His usual lunch order was a double fried baloney sandwich. In case you've never eaten one, here's how Mark assessed it: If your doctor found out you were eating a double fried baloney sandwich, he'd urge you to smoke a pack of Camels instead.

Doug worked at the Observer for 15 years, then for newspapers in Atlanta, New York and Tallahassee. For the past few years he had worked from his home in Hillsborough. When I heard last year he was leaving to work for the Tulsa World in Oklahoma, it seemed odd to me, for it would take him away from the friends and family and region he loved. In protest, I wrote a parody of "Oklahoma" and e-mailed it to him. The last lines were,

You're leaving us for Oklahoma? Oklahoma? No way!

Doug wrote back reminding me that Oklahoma was, after all, the state that had given us Will Rogers and Woody Guthrie. The reply said something about Doug. I think down deep he felt he was, in some mystical way, in touch with the raw spirit of America, the cultural force that has given rise to patriotism and selfless courage and a fierce commitment to justice. He felt kinship, I think, with people who have inspired and interpreted that quintessential spirit – Rogers and Guthrie, Whitman, Steinbeck, Dylan – artists whose subject was the great and diverse family of America.

Doug not only had talent, he had an uncommon willingness to go beyond his own frontiers – to risk failure – rather than be content with skills he'd already mastered. His curiosity, ambition and courage would not let him stop. And he was extraordinarily generous in encouraging talented

young people to dream great dreams and work to make them come true.
His exuberant life and untimely death remind me of these lines by Edna
St. Vincent Millay:

> My candle burns at both ends
> It will not last the night;
> But ah, my foes, and oh, my friends –
> It gives a lovely light.

Hodding Carter, Maverick Editor

A book review in The Charlotte Observer June 27, 1993

I have framed in my office an editorial written by the editor of the newspaper that made me a journalist. Hodding Carter Jr. (1907-1972) published it on the front page of the Greenville, Miss., Delta Democrat-Times on April 3, 1955, under the headline "Liar By Legislation."

He wrote it after state legislators reacted furiously to his article in *Look* magazine warning that the white Citizens' Councils, founded to preserve segregation in Mississippi, could become "instruments of interracial violence" if hoodlums took them over.

Rep. Eck Windham called the article "a willful lie a nigger-loving editor made about the people of Mississippi." The House adopted a resolution denouncing it. When the news reached Carter, he was insulted and indignant. Though a friend assured him that "a Mississippi legislative majority was mentally and morally incapable of insulting anybody," Carter fired back:

"By a vote of 89 to 19, the Mississippi House of Representatives has resolved the editor of this newspaper into a liar. ... If this charge were true it would make me well qualified to serve with that body. It is not true. So to even things up I herewith resolve by a vote of 1 to 0 that there are 89 liars in the State Legislature, beginning with Speaker Sillers and working way on down to Rep. Eck Windham of Prentiss, a political loon whose name is fittingly made up of the words 'wind' and 'ham.' "

He derided the "dishonest and contemptible tactics used by the Citizens' Councils against anyone who differs with them or their methods," and concluded: "I am hopeful that this fever, like the Ku Kluxism which rose from the same kind of infection, will run its course before too long a time. Meanwhile those 89 character mobbers can go to hell collectively or singly and wait there until I back down. They needn't plan on returning."

The Hodding Carter best known today is Hodding III, the prize-winning editor, author and television journalist who was State Department spokesman under President Jimmy Carter (no relation). But the famous Hodding in the 1940s, '50s and '60s was his father, the eloquent, combative editor of a small Mississippi newspaper who stood for fundamental decency at a time when the white South's rabid racism made that a brave and uncommon act.

Ann Waldron examines the life of this Southern maverick in a fascinating biography, *Hodding Carter: The Reconstruction of a Racist*. The book is filled with compelling characters. Among them is William Alexander Percy, who invited Carter from Louisiana to create a robust newspaper in Greenville, a small, unusually cosmopolitan Mississippi River city.

Mississippi native David Cohn was the broker. While Percy's houseguest, Cohn wrote *God Shakes Creation*, in which he defined the Delta as stretching from the Peabody Hotel in Memphis to Catfish Row in Vicksburg.

Carter was editing a feisty daily in Louisiana, taking on the Huey Long machine, when Cohn met him. Impressed, Cohn hatched the newspaper idea and proposed it to Percy, a wealthy planter and poet whose home was the cultural center of the Deep South. (Walker Percy, the novelist, was his adopted son.)

Carter and his wife, Betty, the smart, charming daughter of a prominent New Orleans family, seized the opportunity. They put up $10,000; a group led by Percy matched it. In 1936, a newspaper was born.

Carter, not yet 30, was a fiercely bright, fun-loving son of a Hammond, La., farmer. As a young man, he shared the racial assumptions of his region, but he had a stubborn devotion to justice that would transform his thinking.

In Greenville he would take on Theodore Bilbo and a host of lesser-known but no less dangerous demagogues and nincompoops. He attracted bright young journalists (such as Shelby Foote, later a novelist and Civil War historian). Their work freed Carter, a gifted and prolific writer, to churn out magazine articles, novels, histories and travelogues (20 books in all) as well as courageous editorials that won him a Pulitzer Prize.

Carter's courage wasn't universally appreciated. While he knew justice required an end to forced segregation, he thought politics and custom wouldn't permit immediate, widespread integration. His stance made him anathema to most white Southerners and unpopular with many liberal Northerners as well.

His strength as a writer was passion, and his primary target was his fellow Southern whites. He shared their heritage, and many of their values, but he would not let them ignore the atrocities and indignities they inflicted on their black neighbors.

Carter, an admirer noted, "made a career of shoving the Golden Rule" down his adversaries' throats. That's not a bad epitaph for an editorialist.

II. American, and Proud of It

*Proud to Be
an American*

In 1995, 70 percent of Americans agreed with the statement, "I would rather be a citizen of my country than any other." Seventy-six percent of Americans said they were "very proud" to be citizens of their country.

American (handwritten)

U.S. 76 % (handwritten)

Ireland 77 % (handwritten)
France 35 % (handwritten)

American, and Proud of It

From a column in The Charlotte Observer July 6, 2003

A few years ago the National Opinion Research Center asked citizens of 46 countries how proud they were to be citizens of their country.

Seventy-six percent of Americans said "very proud," a degree of pride exceeded only by Ireland's 77 percent. In France, only 35 percent of respondents said they were very proud to be French.

Other surveys find similar results. Asked in 1995 whether they agreed with the statement, "I would rather be a citizen of my country than any other," 70 percent of Americans agreed and 20 percent disagreed. Compare that to Italy, where 29 percent agreed and 34 percent disagreed, or West Germany, which split 32-31.

Nation of immigrants (handwritten)

What does it mean to be French, German, or Italian? Many things, related to culture and heritage. Ask what it means to be American and the answer takes a different form. Ours is a nation of immigrants, people not bound by common ancestry, history, culture or religion. We are bound, instead, by devotion to an idea.

The idea was proclaimed to the world in 1776: "We hold these truths to be self-evident, that all men are created equal, that they are endowed by their Creator with certain unalienable rights, that among these are life, liberty and the pursuit of happiness – That to secure these rights, governments are instituted among men, deriving their just powers from the consent of the governed." That is the essence of America – a promise to secure those rights for all citizens.

We fall short daily, but that doesn't mean the commitment is not real. Look at our history. You'll see us moving, sometimes erratically but inex-

[handwritten: Frederick Douglas]

orably, toward that ideal.

Our shortcomings have been glaring. Speaking to the American Anti-Slavery Society in 1847, Frederick Douglass said, "I have no love for America, as such; I have no patriotism. I have no country."

No wonder. Douglass was born a slave on a plantation in eastern Maryland. As a boy he was sent to Baltimore, where his mistress taught him to read. He was sold and resold until, in his early 20s, he escaped to the North. Eventually he became a leader of the abolitionist movement and one of the great men of his generation.

[handwritten margin: Black leaders]

He had no love for America "as such," but he did love the America envisioned in its ideals. Now, a century and a half after Douglass's speech, a black man sits on the Supreme Court, a black man is secretary of state, and the Douglass home in Washington is a national historic site.

At almost any stage in our nation's history, this could be said of America: It is not perfect, but it's better than it was. That's why I'm proud to be an American.

[handwritten: America is not perfect but its better than it was]

On July 4, We Celebrate an Idea

An editorial in The Charlotte Observer July 4, 2005

[handwritten: King George]

In October 1775 King George III foresaw the inevitable: "The rebellious war," he told Parliament, "is manifestly carried on for the purpose of establishing an independent empire." He determined to send troops to the American colonies "to put a speedy end" to the rebellion and vowed strict punishment for the "authors, perpetrators, and abetters of such traitorous designs."

Atop the list of traitors would be the 56 delegates to the Second Continental Congress who in 1776 signed the Declaration of Independence.

To those delegates in Philadelphia, the Declaration of Independence was more a formality than a document for the ages. They had declared independence July 2 by unanimously adopting a resolution offered by Richard Henry Lee of Virginia to the effect that the colonies "are, and of right ought to be, free and independent States."

But in adopting a declaration July 4, they not only expanded on the reasons for the separation; they also endorsed a vision of government that

a vision of government

would become the American creed and inspire future generations of freedom lovers around the world. They declared:

"We hold these truths to be self-evident: that all men are created equal; that they are endowed by their Creator with certain unalienable rights; that among these are life, liberty, and the pursuit of happiness. – That to secure these rights, governments are instituted among men, deriving their just powers from the consent of the governed, – That whenever any form of government becomes destructive of these ends, it is the right of the people to alter or to abolish it, and to institute new government, laying its foundation on such principles and organizing its powers in such form as to them shall seem most likely to effect their safety and happiness."

It is fitting that the vision expressed in the document was larger than the immediate purpose required, for what many of the colonists had in mind was not merely independence from Great Britain but also something completely new: the largest republic the world had known, created overnight and based on an idea. The revolutionary pamphleteer Thomas Paine saw the new nation's opportunity clearly. In his 1776 best-seller *Common Sense* he wrote, "We have it in our power to begin the world anew."

The greatest American of the following century, Abraham Lincoln, was enthralled by the audacious spirit of the declaration. The signers, he wrote, "meant to set up a standard maxim for a free society, which should be familiar to all, and revered by all; constantly looked to, constantly labored for, and even though never perfectly attained, constantly approximated, and thereby constantly spreading and deepening its influence, and augmenting the happiness and value of life to all people of all colors everywhere."

Mr. Lincoln was right. The Declaration of Independence served its immediate purpose but served a larger purpose, too. It created a vision of a nation that America may never achieve, but must never fail to aspire to. That challenge is worth celebrating.

A Nation of Hustlers

A column in The Charlotte Observer July 3, 2004

Some years ago as a board member of the fledgling Museum of the New South I suggested an exhibit with the theme "Charlotte, City of Hustlers."

The idea didn't go anywhere, in part because of a reasonable concern that visitors might expect it to feature the ladies of the evening who at that time displayed their wares on Trade Street (prompting the center-city witticism, "If you can't trade on Tryon [Street], try on Trade").

In fact, Charlotte has always been a city of hustlers, and ought to be proud of it. The innate energy and optimism of our citizens not only gives rise to our reputation as a world capital of boosterism, it also accounts for our city's being more than a big mud hole along the Catawba.

Some cities grew because of natural advantages — a river or seaport, perhaps. Not Charlotte. Our greatest asset always has been the industry and ambition of our citizens — in a word, hustle.

It was hustlers who brought us a railroad, highways and a major-league airport. It was hustlers who made this a center of commerce and banking. And it is a reputation for hustle that has brought us many of our most productive citizens.

Cities that value hustle are a powerful magnet to strivers and seekers. Many of the men and women who helped create today's Charlotte came here from elsewhere, drawn by the city's can-do spirit.

Now an eminent historian is saying that such concentrations of hustle are more than just local phenomena. Walter A. McDougall, a Pulitzer Prize-winning historian from the University of Pennsylvania, says the key element in America's rise to the pinnacle of world power is, as he puts it, "the American people's penchant for hustling."

In his new book *Freedom Just Around the Corner* (the title is a quote from a Bob Dylan song), he says of early America, "Hustlers and speculators, merchants and developers were there from the start." It was not an accident of history but the flourishing of this trait that made modern America reflect the values of Alexander Hamilton, a "sharp lawyer," rather than Thomas Jefferson, an agrarian intellectual (who, on occasion, was a skillful hustler as well).

Hustling alone won't make a country great, but it does create the opportunities and cultural mobility that enable greatness to arise from all corners of society.

How revolutionary was the new America? McDougall writes that the pre-Revolutionary colonists "lived in a monarchy, empire and matrix of hierarchies in which everyone bowed to his betters. Privileges, not freedoms, determined one's prospects, and privileges were obtained either by patronage. Social equality was not just restricted, it did not exist."

The revolution created a republic in which people "were citizens, not subjects, individual human beings endowed with rights and responsibilities, not minions, dependents, or petitioners." The Americans "imagined something Europeans considered outrageous and, in their settings, impossible: that every man might aspire to education, wealth, prestige and power."

The new government, he concluded, "could function 'like clockwork' only so long as willing hands turned its crank, turned it forward not backward, and agreed to take turns at the handle."

The new nation offered citizens a hustler's paradise — unprecedented freedom in an environment that required them to work together for their own and their nation's benefit. On this Independence Day weekend, join me in thanking the Founders for their foresight.

Our First (and Prickliest) Ally
An editorial in The Charlotte Observer July 14, 2003

On this, the 214th anniversary of France's Bastille Day, let us toast America's long and prickly relationship with our nation's oldest ally. As the French have demonstrated of late, they can be egocentric know-it-alls who barely conceal their feeling that other nations just don't measure up. So, let us confess, can Americans.

Without France there might be no United States. When the colonies revolted against Britain, their prospects seemed dim. They sought help from France, Britain's traditional adversary. King Louis XVI was uneasy about backing rebels against a monarch. "It is my profession to be a royalist," he said. But Ambassador Benjamin Franklin, whom the French adored, generated support. France provided money and military aid.

When the rebel army trapped Lord Cornwallis at Yorktown, the combined American and French forces under George Washington and the Marquis de Lafayette outnumbered the British 17,000 to 8,000. The French fleet blocked relief of the British by sea. The British surrender ended the war.

Yet Americans were never comfortable with France. For much of their history the colonies had been surrounded by French territory, from Canada

.e mid-1700s Britain and France battled for world dom-
n Years' War [called the French and Indian War in its
r]. American colonists were relieved when the British won
ance lost its American possessions.

the revolution, the colonies' ties were stronger with Britain than
ce. When the British offered generous terms to the rebellious
, they abandoned France and made a separate peace. Historian Paul
Johnson recalls a prophetic anecdote from the time. During a celebration
of the pact, a French guest predicted that some day "the 13 United States
would form the greatest empire in the world." A British delegate replied,
"Yes, Monsieur, and they will all speak English."

In 1800 France regained control of the Louisiana territory. Americans
feared French control of the vital port of New Orleans. But Napoleon
Bonaparte, expecting war with Britain, offered to sell the territory to
America. President Thomas Jefferson jumped at the deal, and in 1803
America doubled in size, extending its western border from the Mississippi
to the Rockies.

Americans went to France's aid in World War I and II, but President
Dwight Eisenhower refused a French request for help in Indochina in 1954.
After the French lost, America stepped into the Vietnam conflict despite a
warning from France's Charles DeGaulle that "you will sink step by step
into a bottomless military and political quagmire."

Today, the French seem to regard the world with sardonic acceptance,
while Americans seem determined to remake it in our image. We consider
them cynical and dissolute. They consider us naive and headstrong. Our relationship is as prickly and important as ever. We will never be alike, but
may we always be allies. *Vive la France!*

How America Looks to the World
A column in The Charlotte Observer Dec. 1, 2002

Terrorists who fly airplanes into buildings filled with innocent people are
evil. Their deed speaks for itself.

But let us take care not to assume that just because our enemies are evil,
we therefore are good. To do so could prevent us from seeing the world as

it is and ourselves as we are.

We Americans have always considered ourselves unique – a new nation unhampered by the bonds of history, a people on a divine mission.

We believe in the singularity of America, and in many ways that belief is justified. We have provided an uncommon degree of freedom and opportunity at home. We have fought tyranny, disease and famine around the globe. What nation has done more for human progress?

If one nation is to be the world's most powerful, I'm thankful it's America. So are many around the world who have benefited from our generosity. But America is far from perfect. Sometimes, in defending our interests and supporting our allies, we have behaved as rich, powerful nations always do: We have used our power to protect our interests as we saw them.

An example: In the early 1950s, Iran's parliament nationalized the nation's oil industry and elected as prime minister the leading advocate of that move, Dr. Mohammad Mossadegh, a member of a prominent family with a law degree from Switzerland. In those Cold War days, Britain and the United States feared not only that the oil supply would be at risk, but also that Iran would be drawn into the Soviet sphere.

Allen Dulles, director of the Central Intelligence Agency, approved a $1 million fund to be used "in any way that would bring about the fall of Mossadegh," according to a CIA history. His aim: to stabilize the oil supply, bolster Iran's economy and install a government that would "vigorously prosecute the dangerously strong Communist Party."

A CIA-backed coup did topple Mossadegh, and Shah Mohammed Reza Pahlavi consolidated power. He ruled until 1978, when a revolution drove him from the country and brought on the Ayatollah Khomeini. Years earlier the shah had banished Khomeini for criticizing Iran's ties to the West. When Khomeini came to power, he denounced the United States as "the great Satan."

In 1954, the CIA helped overthrow the democratically elected government of Jacobo Arbenz in Guatemala. Arbenz had nationalized much of the land of the politically powerful United Fruit Co. He also was considered soft on communism.

After toppling the Arbenz government, the United States allied itself with the repressive, anti-communist new regime. In 1968, a State Department officer fresh from a stint as deputy chief of mission at the U.S.

Embassy in Guatemala City wrote a disturbing memo to his superiors. He warned that Guatemalans, with U.S. assistance, had imposed a vast system of violence to stamp out political opposition.

"People are killed or disappear on the basis of simple accusations," he wrote. "Counter-terror is brutal. The official squads are guilty of atrocities. Interrogations are brutal, torture is used and bodies are mutilated." He added, "In the minds of many in Latin America, and, tragically, especially in the sensitive, articulate youth, we are believed to have condoned these tactics, if not actually to have encouraged them." In fact, he concluded, they were right.

Three decades ago, a congressional inquiry found CIA involvement in planned or actual assassinations of, among others, Chilean President Salvador Allende, President Fidel Castro and Che Guevara of Cuba, Congolese Prime Minister Patrice Lumumba and Dominican President Rafael Trujillo.

Throughout Latin America and the Mideast, our nation has allied itself with brutal dictators. When political reformers in those nations say we have supported their oppressors, often they are right.

In the real world, sometimes there are few options. Our ability to oust brutal rulers is limited. Sometimes no better successor is in sight. Our relations with an oppressive dictator may keep him from being even more oppressive. And if we fight for a just cause, we inevitably kill innocent bystanders as well as enemy soldiers.

Often in world affairs, the only available choice is between two evils. Even when we choose the lesser, it is still evil. To understand how the world sees us, and how the world really is, we must accept that about ourselves.

III. Mississippi

Ross Barnett speaking at the Neshoba County Fair, August 6, 1970

Neshoba County is Bootleggerland

An article in The Delta Democrat-Times May 24, 1971

PHILADELPHIA, Miss. – The defeat of a proposal to legalize liquor in Neshoba County, where prohibition has reigned – on the books, at least – for 62 years, didn't surprise many people here last week. The referendum leaves one question: Having endorsed prohibition, will Neshoba County enforce it? In the past, the answer has been No.

Neshoba is one of 42 counties that have remained dry since Mississippi adopted a local option plan for legalizing liquor in 1966. But enforcing laws against liquor is tougher in Neshoba than in any other county, according to L. R. Mashburn, enforcement chief of the state Alcoholic Beverage Control Division.

Earlier this year, he assigned eight of the state's 32 ABC agents to Neshoba. The ABC has made more seizures of illegal whiskey here than in any other county. But a Neshoba County jury has yet to convict a bootlegger caught by ABC agents. Mashburn wouldn't speculate about the lack of convictions. He wouldn't talk about his agency's relationship with Neshoba County officials, either.

Neshoba Countians aren't so reticent, however.

A.W. "Rack" Burt was born and reared in the red clay hills of Neshoba. He runs Northside Park, a city recreational area with facilities for baseball and tennis and a lethargic, shaded stream brimming with pan-sized fish. Burt, a short, square-built man, is president of the local chamber of commerce. He thinks bootlegging has corrupted county government and encouraged many officials to ignore other laws.

"Bootleggers buy a sheriff like they would a cow," Burt said. "The supervisors are in it, too. They draw up the jury lists. They leave off people they know wouldn't stand for what's going on, and they put on a lot they know are for the bootleggers. Then a lot of good people call up their supervisor and say 'I don't have time to be on a jury. How about taking my name off the list.' So we're left with what we have."

Burt thinks legalizing liquor would make bootlegging unprofitable and do away with the sizable payoffs to officials who overlook the illegal whiskey traffic. "You take a boy out of the country and show him all that money and he forgets everything he ever said about working for the people," Burt said.

Rev. David Kendall is pastor of North Calvary Baptist Church here. He was a leader of the drys because he believes liquor means nothing but trouble, whether it's legal or illegal. "We don't have a liquor problem," he said, "we have a law enforcement problem. We don't need to legalize liquor – that just makes things worse. We need to enforce the law."

People are reluctant to believe law enforcement officers take money to ignore bootlegging, or engage in bootlegging themselves, Rev. Kendall said. "The people who kill us are the constables," he said. "They choose the juries in JP court. If the constable gets a bunch of boozeheads for the jury, that's it." He mentioned Deputy Sheriff R. C. Thrash, who is also a Philadelphia constable, as an example.

An ABC agent arrested Thrash in the county paddy wagon headed across the corner of Newton County toward Neshoba on Aug. 2. The agent and a Newton County constable said the vehicle contained five cases of whiskey, 144 half-pints in all.

Thrash's trial was postponed twice, but in October Newton County Justice of the Peace Thurman Sharp angrily refused a third delay. "The sheriff of Neshoba County came over here and tried to

AFTER CAREFULLY WEIGHING ALL THE EVIDENCE, HOW CAN I VOTE ANY OTHER WAY THAN DRY ?

AGAINST ALCOHOL

United Drys

Rev. Byron Kornegay, Chairman

DEVIL'S JUICE

TAX PAID
100 PROOF WHISKEY

TO
·MAKE YOU DRUNK
·WRECK YOUR CAR
·SEND YOU TO JAIL
·MAKE YOU A KILLER
·BREAK UP YOUR HOME
·MAKE YOU ACT LIKE
A FOOL ~ ~ ~
·DISGRACE FAMILY&SELF
·MAKE YOUR CHILDREN
ORPHANS ~ ~
· SEND YOU TO HELL

America's Greatest Curse

WHOSOEVER
IS DECEIVED
THEREBY IS
NOT WISE

United Drys

Rev. Byron Kornegay, Chairman

search my chicken houses," Sharp said. "He said I had a whiskey still. And I live in Newton County."

Neshoba County Sheriff E. G. "Hop" Barnett told me Sharp is a "damn liar."

The JP court jury found Thrash guilty of possessing liquor in a dry county and fined him $500, the maximum. On appeal, Circuit Judge O.H. Barnett reversed the conviction, citing improprieties in selection of the JP court jury.

Sheriff Barnett scoffs at the charges. Thrash is still a deputy and a constable, and he chooses persons to serve on JP court juries in Philadelphia.

In March, a public meeting concerning law enforcement drew an overflow crowd to the Neshoba County courthouse. The meeting produced a resolution taking note of "a complete and total breakdown of the law enforcement system." The group gave officials 30 days to start enforcing the law and to limit jury lists to "good, honorable and law-abiding persons."

If the officials failed to act, the group resolved to call on the governor for law enforcement help – not excluding the national guard – and to seek removal from office of uncooperative officials.

Burt said he didn't favor removing just the sheriff if no changes were made. "He's not in it alone – you'd have to get them all, supervisors, constables, JPs, the county attorney," he said.

Editor Stanley Dearman of the weekly Neshoba Democrat has given constant and thorough coverage to the liquor arrests and the rarity of convictions. He lashed out editorially at a grand jury which didn't return indictments for liquor charges brought by the ABC. "What can you expect when persons with drinking problems and relatives of persons who have dealt in illegal liquor turn up on grand juries which consider liquor violations?" he asked in an editorial.

Two delegations of Neshoba Countians have visited Gov. John Bell Williams seeking his aid in battling bootleggers. "He's a lawyer," recalled Rev. Kendall. "He got down the law books and showed up all he could do is send in the highway patrol or the national guard. He said he was willing to do that if the county wanted it." Rev. Kendall said the governor did order the highway patrol to "harass the hell" out of bootleggers along Miss. Highway 16.

Burt led the other delegation to see the governor. "He was willing to help us, he said, but I don't think calling in the national guard is the thing to do. It would give the county a lot of bad publicity, and we've had enough of that," Burt said.

The people I talked to, wets and drys, think Sheriff Barnett (pronounced like garnet) is on the payroll of the bootleggers.

Barnett was one of 18 men indicted for conspiracy in the murder of three civil rights workers in Neshoba County in 1964. He was under indictment when he won the Democratic nomination for sheriff over Deputy Sheriff Cecil Price, also indicted in the killings.

Price was convicted and sentenced to six years in federal prison. Barnett was freed when his trial ended in a hung jury.

Barnett told me he doesn't like publicity: "I don't think any publicity is good." My brief interview with him consisted mainly of questions by me, short answers or refusals to answer by him, and long silences.

He said people who say he is in league with bootleggers are "damn fanatics. There's about a dozen of them in town. People criticized me when I was sheriff before, and they criticize me now. I'm the one who has to worry about sleeping at night, not them. I know there's whiskey in the county. There's whiskey in all the dry counties. As long as the people want it, it'll be here. When they don't want it, it won't be here any more."

Barnett says he "wouldn't have the job" of sheriff again. Candidates for the post include a Baptist preacher, who resigned as pastor of his church here to run for the job, and a 33-year-old welder, who has vowed,

"I will stop every bootlegger I possibly can. The ones I can't stop, I will hound day and night until I drive them so far into the woods I cannot find them anymore."

James Silver and Sleepy Cash
From a speech at the University of Mississippi in 2011, dedicating a memorial to James Silver on the Ole Miss campus

In 1936, when James Silver, a Vanderbilt Ph.D. in hand, began his long career as a historian at the University of Mississippi, an editorial writer in North Carolina was working on a book, and his progress was painful and erratic.

Sleepy Cash, as he was known, was a graduate of Wake Forest who tried law school for a while but left because, he said, it "required too much mendacity." After a brief excursion into teaching he became a journalist. As an editorial writer in Charlotte he excoriated the Ku Klux Klan and railed against his region's anti-Catholicism during Al Smith's 1928 presidential campaign.

His greatest ambition was to write for H.L. Mencken's magazine, *The American Mercury*. He achieved it, writing several Menckenesque articles on Southern peculiarities, including the one that a decade later he was still trying to expand into a book. In 1940, at his editor's insistence he let go the manuscript. In 1941 Alfred A. Knopf published *The Mind of the South*. It was an instant classic.

So why, in a tribute to James Silver, do I mention a book by a North Carolina journalist? Two reasons. Because it was James Silver who in 1962 steered me toward the book. And because Cash's insight into the South's hostility to criticism and dissent predicted the reaction to James Silver's biting criticism of the Mississippi way of life.

A couple of years ago Mr. Cash was inducted into the North Carolina Literary Hall of Fame. He was unable to attend the induction ceremony in Southern Pines, having hanged himself in a Mexico City hotel room some 60 years earlier. So I, also an editorial writer from Charlotte, was asked to speak on his behalf.

I noted that here's what Cash wrote, back in 1940, about the growth of the reflexive hostility toward criticism that often has manifested itself in brutal ways in the South – not just in Cash's time but well into our own.

"... The final result," Cash wrote, "... is that it turned the South toward strait-jacket conformity and made it increasingly intolerant of dissent. ...

"Let a Yankee abolitionist be caught spreading his propaganda in the land, let a Southerner speak out boldly his conviction that the North was essentially right about the institution [of slavery], and he was not merely frowned on, cursed, hated; he was ... hanged or tarred or horsewhipped. At the very luckiest, he had to stand always prepared to defend himself against assault. ...

"From the taboo on criticism of slavery it was but an easy step to interpreting every criticism of the South on whatever score as disloyalty – to making such criticism so dangerous that none but a madman would risk it. ... "[I]n short, the South was en route to the savage ideal: to that ideal whereunder dissent and variety are completely suppressed, and men become, in all their attitudes, professions and actions, virtual replicas of one another."

I wasn't a buddy of Jim Silver. I didn't drink scotch with him, or swap stories. I was his student. I had some fine professors at Ole Miss, but Silver was the one who had the greatest impact on my life.

I came to Ole Miss from the flat cotton lands along the Missouri-Arkansas line on the other side Mississippi River, about 90 miles north of Memphis. When I arrived here, I felt like Henry Skrimshander, the small-town boy on his first day in college in Chad Harbach's lovely novel, *The Art of Fielding*. Like Henry, I knew no one, and all my classmates seemed to have come from one close-knit high school, or at least to have attended some crucial orientation session that I'd missed. They all traveled in packs, and when two packs converged there was always a tremendous amount of hugging and kissing on the cheek.

I wanted to be a history major. The teacher my first semester loved history, lifting weights and studying in his library carrel, but students, not so much. My second semester I had better luck: my professor was Bill Hamer, who was lively and inspiring and took an interest in me. He insisted that next semester I enroll in Dr. Silver's American history class.

I tried, but Silver's class was full. So on the first day I went to his class anyway. I told him that Professor Hamer had said I should take his class and I was determined to do so. Well, he said, the seats are full, but if you'll stick around for a couple of classes maybe someone will drop out and there'll be a place for you. I did, and there was.

The first day of class provided an indication of the kind of professor Silver was. Our first assignment was to read the first chapter of the American history textbook and find a statement that was either stupid or wrong. I read it and I didn't find anything. Silver did. There was, as I recall, a sentence saying there had been no dinosaurs somewhere or other. Silver's response was that the fact that no dinosaur remains had been found didn't mean there had been no dinosaurs, only that no remains had been found. His point was clear: Say what you know, and say it clearly. Listen to experts, but think critically.

For decades Silver had been a popular public speaker around the state. But as threats to Mississippi's system of white supremacy intensified, his steady and insightful criticism of the state's totalitarian racism became more annoying to defenders of the Southern way of life. When Silver befriended James Meredith, who integrated Ole Miss in 1962, an element of danger was added to the criticism. In reaction to anonymous threats, he slept with a shotgun beside his bed. But he was not silenced. In a speech to the Southern Historical Association in the fall of 1963, he called Mississippi "a closed society" – "totalitarian," "monolithic," "corrupt" – and condemned the state for lacking "the moral resources to reform itself." The speech became a media sensation, and he expanded on the theme in a 1964 book, *Mississippi: The Closed Society*. The burden of vilification and danger wore on him and his family. In 1965 he accepted an attractive offer from Notre Dame, and never returned to teach in Mississippi.

Silver the professor helped shaped my appreciation of history. But more valuable to me was the lesson taught by Silver the man. I was at an impressionable age, trying to figure how to live. He showed me how to be a man of learning and conviction who, in dangerous times, was not immobilized by fear.

A Justice's Questionable Ethics

An article in The Gulfport Daily Herald Oct. 9, 1971

JACKSON – State Supreme Court Justice Tom Brady is keeping his seat on the bench while running for governor. By doing so he is violating the canons of judicial ethics of the American Bar Association.

Brady has been an ABA member "about 35 years," he said, and he plans to remain an ABA member. "When faced with the choice of violating the canons of ethics or allowing disaster to occur in Mississippi, I chose to violate the canons," the 68-year-old Brady explained.

[The potential disaster he referred to the possibility that Charles Evers, mayor of Fayette and brother of the slain civil rights leader Medgar Evers, might be elected governor. Brady, while a circuit court judge in 1955, had written *Black Monday*, a book calling for, among other things, creation of a forty-ninth state for Negroes and abolition of public schools.]

What happens when a judge violates the ABA canons of judicial ethics? In Mississippi, nothing.

The state supreme court, when it adopted the canons of ethics to govern Mississippi jurists, deleted the ABA prohibition on involvement of judges in non-judicial politics and substituted a state law which governs races for judgeships and doesn't mention anything else. That gives judges free rein in non-judicial politics, and many have taken advantage of it.

John Stennis was on the bench when he first campaigned for the U.S. Senate. Russel Moore retained his Hinds County circuit judgeship while campaigning throughout the state in the George Wallace for president effort. This year, Marshall Perry of Grenada ran for governor while serving as circuit judge, and now Brady sits on the supreme court bench and runs for governor.

ABA Canon 30 prohibits this. It says if a judge decides to seek a non-judicial office, "he should resign in order that it cannot be said that he is using the power or prestige of his judicial position to promote his candidacy...."

If the state bar forbade such political activity, few judges would risk it, since the bar could take punitive action. A lawyer must belong to the state bar to practice in Mississippi, so the bar wields tremendous power.

But membership in the American Bar Association is voluntary. "We don't give lawyers a license to practice, and we can't take it away," said Frederick Beck, staff director of professional standards for the ABA in Chicago. "We refer complaints to the state grievance committee."

Since state bar associations aren't required to adhere to ABA ethics, those ethics are merely "an aspirational standard," Beck said. There's little chance of action against violators.

Bar association leaders in Mississippi don't seem concerned with involvement of judges in politics.

Hugh N. Clayton of new Albany, a member of the ABA House of Delegates, pleaded ignorance. "The House of Delegates is the legislative, not the judicial or executive branch of the American Bar Association," he said. "I've never had any experience with those matters."

William Henley of Hazelhurst, another member of the ABA House of Delegates, said he has "no opinion at all" on Brady's apparent violation of ABA Canons. "I wouldn't be in a position to answer your questions without knowing more about it," he said.

Lester Summers of New Albany, president of the state bar association, flatly refused to discuss the propriety of judges engaging in non-judicial politics. "The timing is not right for a statement on that," he said.

Joseph Meadows of Gulfport, president of the Young Lawyers Section of the state bar association, did comment, however. He made it clear that his remarks are not directed at Brady and do not represent a position of his organization. "I think the judiciary should be kept as much apart as possible from the political arena," he said. "I think this question merits study, and it's my feeling that there should be a change."

While bar association leaders show little interest, some lawyers do have strong opinions. But they're reluctant to express them publicly, for fear of offending a judge who may later decide their cases.

"I don't mind telling you what I think if you won't use my name," said one prominent Jackson lawyer. "I don't think a judge should run for another office without resigning first. Suppose a judge should call on an attorney for support. That attorney would be hard put to turn him down. Judges have to avoid even the appearance of impropriety, I think."

Another lawyer, assured of anonymity, said "No lawyer is going to blow the whistle on a judge. A judge is pretty much the guardian of his own ethics unless he does something shocking."

Another situation involving Brady is a case in point. In 1970, he and Sen. James O. Eastland were co-chairmen of a drive to raise $1.25 million to support the all-white schools run by the Citizens Council here.

A letter to several "distinguished community leaders" asked them to serve on the sponsors committee for the Council School Development Fund Campaign.

The last paragraph in the letter said, "We feel sure you will accept a place on this distinguished panel of community leaders. However, if for any reason you are unable to serve, please call ... immediately. If we do not hear from you... , we will take it for granted you will participate."

Next came the signatures: Sen. James O. Eastland, Honorary Chairman, and Justice Thomas P. Brady, Campaign Chairman.

The Mississippi Rules of Judicial Ethics apparently prohibit such activities. Rule 25 says, "A judge should avoid giving grounds for any reasonable suspicion that he is utilizing the power or prestige of his office to persuade or coerce others to patronize or contribute either to the success of private business ventures or to charitable enterprises. He should not ... use the power of his office or the influence of his name to promote the business interests of others; he should not solicit for charities. ... "

If Brady's participation did indeed violate state rules of judicial ethics, nothing was done about it.

EDITOR'S NOTE: *In the general election, Democrat Bill Waller won with 77 percent of the vote, followed by two independent candidates, Evers with 22 percent and Brady with 0.85 percent.*

Fannie Lou Hamer
From an article in the Gulfport Daily Herald Oct. 31, 1971

Mrs. Fannie Lou Hamer, a founder of the Mississippi Freedom Democratic Party, is running against incumbent Robert Crook for a state Senate post from Bolivar and Sunflower counties.

Mrs. Hamer has no experience in government, but says that makes no difference. "The only way you can learn to be a senator is by being a senator," she said. "If you've got to be a senator to get to be a senator, then we wouldn't have no senators, because wasn't nobody born a senator."

'My Parents Didn't Swing by Their Tails'
An article in Mississippi Freelance February 1970

If man evolved from a lower order of animals, Rep. Ney Gore of Marks must be the direct descendant of the asp.

In state House of Representatives debate, Gore spews sarcasm, punctures windbags and makes usually voluble legislators stay seated.

When Gore told reporters his House Judiciary B Committee would report favorably on House Bill 49, he ventured a wry smile in apparent contemplation of the battle he saw ahead.

> H.B. 49: "An act to repeal sections 6798 and 6799, Mississippi Code of 1942, which provide that schools supported by state not to teach that man ascended or descended from the lower order of animals, and penalties for violation thereof."

Gore, a 48-year-old lawyer, looks like a Prussian. His hair is trimmed to a uniform length of one-quarter inch and, speaking normally, he sounds like an officer tongue-lashing an errant subordinate.

He is, in short, ably suited to lead a debate which from its outset promised to unleash the greatest volume of chest-thumping theological bombast and unadulterated fundamentalist buffoonery heard in the legislative halls since Mississippi enacted its monkey law in 1926.

The law resulted from a wave of anti-Darwinism which swept the Bible Belt in 1925 in the months following the trial of biology teacher John T. Scopes in Dayton, Tenn. The Scopes trial pitted the renowned iconoclast, Clarence Darrow, against the Great Commoner, William Jennings Bryan. Bryan won the verdict but lost the battle for public opinion when Darrow's piercing questions picked apart a fundamentalism based on equal parts of faith and foolishness. A week after the trial, Bryan was dead.

There ensued a great rush of would-be successors to Bryan as a national leader of the anti-evolution movement. One was George

Washburn, who, four months after Bryan's death, declared that God had commissioned him to succeed Bryan and organize the Bible Crusaders of America.

The Mississippi legislature demonstrated a great lack of interest when Reps. Hickey of Lee County and Evans of Leake County introduced an anti-Darwin bill during the opening days of the 1926 session. But a crew of Washburn's Bible Crusaders came to Jackson and made believers of the legislators.

The chief crusader, T.T. Martin, told legislators, "Go back to your homes and face your constituents and tell them that you bartered the faith of your children for gold; go back to the fathers and mothers and tell them that because you could not face the ridicule and scorn and abuse of Bolsheviks and Anarchists and Atheists and Agnostics and their co-workers, you turned their children over to a teaching that God's word is a tissue of lies and that the Saviour who said it was God's word was only the illegitimate son of a Jewish fallen woman."

Some legislators paid no attention to Martin's warnings. In the House, Rep. W.T. Wynn of Greenville expressed regret "that in the past few years Southern states have passed laws that tended to cut down the liberties of free speech and free thinking. We complain about the centralization of power by the federal government and yet we come here and try to pass laws declaring what shall and shall not be taught in the public schools of the state."

Rep. B.B. Hall of Amite County, a Baptist minister, called the bill "foolish and untimely." "It doesn't make any difference to Christianity whether evolution is true or not," he said.

Leading foe of the bill was Rep. E. K. Windham of Prentiss. He proposed an amendment requiring that "Any person suspicioned of teaching the theory shall be arrested, brought before an ecclesiastical court and, upon conviction, sentenced to be burned at the stake, it being the purpose of this bill to restore the Spanish Inquisition." The amendment was ruled out of order.

Rep. Barrows of Lincoln County cautioned legislators of the fruits of teaching evolution. "I can cite you to a young lady, who before she went away to a state supported school where she learned the theory of evolution, was as fine and Christian a girl as lives. Since she went to that state supported school she has returned to her home and is now teaching her three-year-old flesh and blood that there is no God."

Rep. Anderson of Tippah County drew cheers from the packed gallery with his argument that "Evolution is ignorance. Any person who believes in it is ignorant, just as ignorant as the pagan who tried to account for existence without giving God credit for creation."

The House passed the bill 76-32, but Windham held it on a motion to reconsider. The next day, he had a few words for the Bible Crusaders. They "came to the Capitol under the guise of serving their God, and tried to force legislation upon the people of Mississippi," said Windham. "That they found it profitable is indicated by the fact that they took rooms in the finest hotel in the city, paid for by collections taken from people at mass meetings at which they preached against teaching evolution. My opinion is that the God of Rev. Martin is the almighty American dollar."

Windham and his allies changed no minds, however. The bill's advocates easily tabled the motion to reconsider and sent the bill to the Senate.

Senate opponents of the bill were no less outspoken and no more successful. Sen. Walton Shields of Greenville moved to postpone action on the bill indefinitely. "Had this legislature been in session several hundred years ago, similar legislation would have been introduced to prevent the teaching of the fact that the earth revolves around the sun," he said.

Sen. Hardin Brooke of Meridian said he needed no legislative act to establish "the sacredness of my mother's religion." Sen. W.A. Winter of Grenada tried to substitute a bill prohibiting the teaching of disrespect for the Bible and that the United States has an inferior form of government, a move to kill the anti-evolution aim of the bill. He was voted down.

The Senate gave its approval 29-16. Gov. Whitfield signed the bill, and Mississippi had its monkey law.

The House debate last month demonstrated that after 44 years, hardly anyone had anything new to say.

Gore disappointed the few spectators by keeping his sarcasm in check and limiting his arguments to two basic propositions: the teaching of evolution as a theory is in no way contradictory to Genesis, and federal courts have ruled similar law unconstitutional, so the Mississippi law is meaningless.

"Such laws have been stricken down by the Supreme Court in other states," Gore said. "In Arkansas, it cost the state $100,000 to prosecute the lawsuit, and they lost it.

"But my point is this: This law is a restriction on man's mind, man's thought, man's beliefs, which the state should not arrogate to itself. I don't have to direct your minds back to the Middle Ages and its efforts to control man's thoughts. This idea is a carryover from that time."

W.T. McCullough, chairman of the board of deacons at his Baptist church in Pope, disagreed. He asked legislators to "consider the cause of the Darwin theory. He was an atheist. He wanted to give a reason why we're here. ... I think if you depend on evolution you have to rule out any consideration that man has a soul. I don't think man came up from a lower species.

"The thing I'm worried about is when a child goes to college and runs into an egghead professor who thinks he knows everything. He hears those eggheads talk about evolution, and he believes it. It's not against the law to teach it as theory – it's against the law to teach it as fact. If you can't teach religion in the schools, I don't think you should be able to teach atheism, either."

C.L. Bullock of Gulfport took a different view. "Speaking as a Baptist, I believe the Bible is the inspired word of God. That's sufficient for me. But I believe when Jesus said 'Follow me,' it was not a command, it was an invitation. I don't believe it needs to be enforced by civil edict. ... When I say as a Baptist that I believe in separation of church and state, I don't say it out one side of my mouth and then say I believe religion should be enforced by state law."

Ben Owen, a Columbus lawyer, said "I think any law that infringes on teaching of the truth is wrong. Truth is science, and science is what we are prohibiting by this law."

James Harvey Turner, a farmer from Carthage, gave personal testimony. "My parents didn't swing by their tails. A few of them swung by their necks. I can't be a party to any bill that would make a monkey out of the Creator."

Betty Jane Long, a Meridian lawyer, said she saw "no purpose in this debate except a little publicity. The law is already in court, and it will be decided there." She offered an amendment to make the law apply only to elementary schools, but the speaker ruled the amendment out of order.

Walter (Buck) Meek, a Eupora lawyer, capped the debate with an arm-waving hellfire 'n' damnation denunciation of "apostles of atheism" who are spreading the evolution doctrine. "These college students are bringing this action to do away with Christian laws. It seems today like if you were born before World War II, you just ain't with it. ... These are Christian statutes on our books, and they're trying to take a little bit more of them out of the state of Mississippi. Christianity is still in power in this state!"

He concluded, "Nobody in this country wants to stand up against the teachings of atheism. Let me tell you, Mississippians, you're not alone in trying to hold the line against this law. Let's remove the guilt from our hands. Let it be done by a federal judge. We need all the divine help we can get!"

Meek yielded momentarily for a question from the floor. "Don't you think this is a part of a national move by forces of atheism to destroy our country?"

The pandemonium in the House had increased as Meek spoke. Someone was blowing a duck call into one of the desk microphones, and the House rang with cries of "You tell 'em, Buck!" and general hurrahing from several representatives who were unable to take the debate with anything approaching a serious attitude.

Bullock regained the floor for a question and said "Come, let us reason together. I want you to be calm. ..."

"I'll answer your question," shouted Meek, "but I won't promise anything about my demeanor!" Cheers rang out again.

Rep. J.G. Moss of Raymond brought the madness to an end by moving the previous question on all pending matters, which limits foes and friends of the repealer to five more minutes of debate.

Gore was the only speaker. "This is not the first occasion in my life I've been called an infidel or atheist or communist, and I don't expect it to be the last occasion when such appellations are applied to me. But it's the first time anybody ever said I tried to make a monkey out of God.

But when I consider the source, this name-calling is of complete inconsequence to me.

"This is not an attack on organized religion. There's only one question at issue. Not the truth or falsity of Darwin, or the truth or falsity of Christianity or Judaism. The only question is whether it's right for society to attempt to legislate thought processes or beliefs. I don't say Darwin should be taught. I don't say it should not. I do say if it's a sound scientific theory there shouldn't be a law saying it can't be taught."

The legislators, unimpressed, voted 69-42 against the repeal attempt. "If there'd been a secret ballot, the results would have been different," Gore said.

As several of the debaters noted, the matter is in the courts. Five professors and five undergraduates at Mississippi State University have filed suit in the U.S. District Court in Oxford asking the court to declare the anti-evolution law unconstitutional. Two high school teachers and a high school student from Greenville later joined the suit.

A few days after the legislative debate, a Hinds County court ruled in another attack on the law that the Mississippi statute forbids only teaching of evolution as fact. Teaching that evolution is a valid theory is legal, the court ruled.

No one has ever been prosecuted under the Mississippi law – it's generally regarded as a vestige of the general lunacy of the '20s, like goldfish swallowing. When the MSU students involved in the federal suit filed charges against a professor for teaching evolution in violation of the law, an Oktibbeha County grand jury refused to return an indictment.

The ridiculous thing, of course, is that today – 4,306 years after the biblical Great Flood, according to computations by one of Bryan's Bible experts – any legislature anywhere is wasting time worrying whether Darwin conflicts with Genesis. But the Mississippi legislature has always had an infinite capacity for the ridiculous.

HOW THEY VOTED

What's MF given you this time that no one else thought you'd care about? A breakdown of the monkey vote by religion, of course. Here it is:

For repealing the monkey law: 12 Baptists, 10 Methodists, 7 Episcopalians, 6 Presbyterians, 4 Catholics, 1 Church of Christ, 2 with no religion listed.

Against repeal: 36 Baptists, 21 Methodists, 4 Presbyterians, 2 Catholics, 2 Episcopalians, 2 Church of Christ, 2 with no religion listed. (One of these listed membership in the John Birch Society, but didn't say whether he considered that his religion.)

Ross Barnett
A column in The Charlotte Observer Nov. 19, 1987

I remember Ross Barnett as a wonderful phrase-maker. In those more trusting days, nobody thought he might just be good at delivering phrases crafted by witty writers, as John Kennedy was then and Ronald Reagan is now.

Barnett was governor of Mississippi when I was a student at Ole Miss in the early 1960s and a popular speaker for the rest of his life. I can see him now, standing on tiptoes behind a lectern, head back, right arm stretched skyward, poised to swoop like a diving hawk as he pounded home his point about Teddy Kennedy ("that grrrrrrrreat driver, that grrrrrrrreat swimmer") or the meddlesome federal government.

I still get a lot of laughs telling stories about ol' Ross. There was the time, for instance, when some Parchman prison trustys assigned as servants at the governor's mansion took off to Arkansas on an unauthorized trip that they obviously hoped would be one-way. It may be that they took some of the governor's silver with them; I can't recall.

Ross's comment: "If you can't trust a trusty, who can you trust?"

Then there was the time Ross had flown to make a campaign speech in the Delta. He got out of the small plane and walked into the propeller, which was rotating slowly, thank heavens. When he came out of the hospital, Ross said he had learned that "the front end of an airplane is like the back end of a mule" – that is, you've got to keep an eye on both of them.

The islands of Quemoy and Matsu, off the China coast, figured in one of the debates between John Kennedy and Richard Nixon during the 1960 presidential campaign. The islands were controlled by Chinese anti-communists in exile on Taiwan, and the mainland Chinese bombarded them during the late '50s and occasionally in 1960.

State House reporters asked Ross what he would do about Quemoy and Matsu. "I'd appoint 'em to the Game and Fish Commission," he said.

Ross Barnett died a few days ago at the age of 89. He had been a trial lawyer and a successful one, winning huge (for a poor state) verdicts in damage suits against power companies and other opponents with deep pockets. A friend of mine concluded that Barnett, the shrewd lawyer, had played the dumb ol' country boy before so many juries that he had finally become a dumb ol' country boy.

People can sit around all night telling Ross Barnett stories and leave the impression that he was at worst a good-hearted, amiable buffoon, but that's only part of the story. He was also a committed racist. He believed that blacks were inferior, that segregation was the will of God as well as the law of Mississippi. His rabble-rousing resistance to the idea that the Constitution applied in Mississippi provoked a bloody insurrection on the Ole Miss campus when federal officials tried to enroll James Meredith, a black native Mississippian, as a student. Two people died in the riot. The next day, federal troops occupied the campus to end what I have always considered the last battle of the Civil War.

Barnett was a pleasant companion and in some ways a good and caring man. But he was an eager servant of the force that for centuries poisoned his region – racism.

Perhaps it seems unfair to blame political leaders such as Barnett, Orval Faubus of Arkansas and George Wallace of Alabama for reflecting the passions and prejudices of their time. For me, the fact that they were not alone in their bigotry is no defense. One measurement of excellence in political leaders is how well they grasp important opportunities and help shape their times.

Remember, Ross Barnett was governor of Mississippi at the same time Terry Sanford was governor of North Carolina. The difference in the two men says a lot about the differences in the two states.

IV. Mecklenburg History

BATTLE OF
CHARLOTTE
···
ornwallis's army cap-
tured Charlotte after a
fight here with Davie's
troops. Sept. 26, 1780.

Mecklenburg County was a hotbed of rebellion against British rule. In 1780, 150 patriot volunteers briefly stood off 2,000 British troops in the Battle of Charlotte, memorialized by this plaque on Tryon Street. When the British left a few days later, Gen. Cornwallis called Charlotte a "hornet's nest" of rebellion.

Meck Dec: History or Hoax?

A column in The Charlotte Observer May 20, 2007

Mention the Mecklenburg Declaration of Independence and listeners split into two camps:

Believers: They point to ample evidence – including statements from participants – that 27 freedom-loving men met in Charlotte on May 20, 1775, and reacted to news of battles in Lexington and Concord, Mass., by declaring their independence from King George III.

Naysayers: They believe those soon-to-be revolutionaries adopted a set of resolves for self-governance on May 31, but years later confused them with a May 20 declaration that never existed.

The debate is fierce, ideological and unlikely to end unless someone finds an original copy of the declaration – and in more than two centuries, no one has done so. But the naysayers, while they offer good arguments, must prove a negative – that despite eyewitnesses who say otherwise, there was no declaration. That's difficult, for while it's easy to imagine some people involved in a self-serving mass delusion, it's harder to imagine when the people are Presbyterian elders.

It is certain that those men wrote the Mecklenburg Resolves, a plan for governing themselves. At issue is whether they also wrote a declaration of independence from the king.

While that matters for the historical record, it doesn't matter as an indicator of the spirit of the people.

In the late 1700s Mecklenburg was fed up with the British, and for good reason. Many of the leading citizens were of Scots-Irish descent and had come here to seek opportunity and escape British oppression. Yet in Mecklenburg, they still were under the king's thumb. Though Presbyterians, they were taxed to support the Anglican church. Presbyterian ministers could be fined if they performed marriages. When leaders of the new Charlotte Town asked to start a college, the king refused, saying it would be merely "a seminary for the education and instruction of youth in the principles of the Presbyterian Church." When the provincial government did authorize a school, it required that the president be Anglican.

The result of such indignities? Col. Banastre Tarleton, an officer under the British Lord Cornwallis, looked back in 1787 and wrote, "the counties of Mecklenburg and Rohan [Rowan] were more hostile to England than any other in America."

But could these men have created a declaration that echoed with some phrases and sentiments also found in the document written by Thomas Jefferson and a committee in 1776?

There's no reason to think they couldn't. They were hardly rustic bumpkins. Presbyterians put a high value on education. Four of the 27 reported signers of the Mecklenburg Declaration had studied at the College of New Jersey (now Princeton), a seedbed of the revolution. (Princeton's John Witherspoon was the only clergyman and only college president to sign the Declaration of Independence.)

So was there a Mecklenburg Declaration of Independence? I can't settle that argument. But no matter what historical facts remain unresolved, the spirit of those brave, freedom-loving people was clear, and that's worth remembering today.

How Did Charlotte Get to Be?
A column in The Charlotte Observer April 27, 1997

Ignorant of local history? Don't be ashamed. This quiz will prepare you to wow your friends with your knowledge of how things came to be here.

Q. Why did settlers settle here?

A. Charlotte is where a lesser trail crossed the Great Trading Path, a major commercial thoroughfare during pioneer days that probably followed a trail first worn by animals as the shortest route across the high ground to water.

It was a significant Indian trading trail, and Nations Ford was a popular point for crossing the Catawba River.

Q. What is the significance of the two dates on the North Carolina flag, April 12, 1776, and May 20, 1775?

A. April 12, 1776, is the date the provincial congress adopted the Halifax Resolves, authorizing N.C. delegates to the Continental Congress to concur in a resolution declaring independence. May 20, 1775, is the date of the Mecklenburg Declaration of Independence, which purportedly declared Mecklenburg's independence from England, well in advance of Thomas Jefferson's more famous declaration. No copy of it survived, however, and many historians are skeptical about it.

Q. Why is there a Mint Museum?

A. Because in 1799 young Conrad Reed discovered a 17-pound shiny rock about the size of a shoe in Cabarrus County's Little Meadow Creek, 25 miles east of Charlotte. The family used it as a door stop, and his father eventually sold it for $3.50. A Fayetteville jeweler later extracted $3,500 worth of gold from it. By the early 1800s, Mecklenburg County was caught up in America's first gold rush. In 1835, Congress authorized a branch of the U.S. Mint in this bustling town of 2,000 in the heart of gold mining country. The present Mint Museum incorporates the old Mint building, moved from West Trade Street.

Q. Why is there a Charlotte Observer?

A. How nice of you to ask. Industrialist D.A. Tompkins did it, taking over a failing daily in 1892 and turning it into a robust newspaper "to preach the doctrine of industrial development." There was a need for the South to get away from a single crop (cotton) as income, he said. The Observer now is the largest newspaper between Washington and Atlanta, with 235,000 daily and 305,000 Sunday circulation.

Q. Who was Charlotte's first great real estate developer?

A. E.D. Latta. In 1881 he was running a clothing manufacturing factory at

Fourth and Tryon. He bought the horse-drawn streetcar company, then built a powerhouse and laid tracks for an electric streetcar system. In 1880, he formed a construction company and bought a thousand acres of rural land for $100 an acre and called it Dilworth. He built a lake and amusement park at what is now Latta Park to lure people on the 12-mph trolley ride from the city. A great promoter, he used the slogan "Buy a house with rent money." People did.

Q. The nation's fourth-largest (NationsBank) and sixth-largest (First Union) banks are headquartered here. Why are N.C. banks so big?

A. Nationally, banking began as a highly protected industry. Not here. North Carolina has permitted statewide branch banking since the early 1800s, so N.C. banks, serving a state with a healthy and diverse economy, grew large and competitive. When interstate banking became possible, N.C. banks were primed to compete in other states.

Q. Why is there a University of North Carolina at Charlotte?

A. Because many local citizens who believed Charlotte needed an outstanding public institution of higher learning fought a successful political battle to create it. It began with 250 students in 1946, administered by the public school system as an extension school for veterans. Bonnie Cone, a math teacher, became its director, at a salary lower than she'd have made teaching math full time. She helped coordinate the local effort that ultimately gained university status. By early next century, UNCC is expected to have 20,000 students and offer doctoral degrees in several fields.

Q. Why are big-league sports here?

A. Because in 1986 businessman George Shinn, a self-described "stubborn little cuss," and other investors aided by sports marketer Max Muhleman convinced the National Basketball Association that hoops-crazy Carolinians from miles around would support a Charlotte-based team. Many scoffed, including a Phoenix writer who said the only franchise Charlotte had a chance to get was one with golden arches. The Hornets' regional success paved the way for the award of a franchise for the NFL Carolina Panthers.

N.C. Demanded a Bill of Rights

An editorial in The Charlotte Observer Dec. 17, 1991

In 1788, North Carolinians weren't satisfied with what would become the U.S. Constitution. They liked the division of powers and the system of checks and balances, which seemed likely to frustrate would-be tyrants. But the Constitution offered no specific protections for state or individual rights. So, even though 11 states had already ratified it, North Carolinians meeting at Hillsborough refused to do so.

The omission wasn't accidental. As James Iredell argued in the Hillsborough debate, "A bill of rights, as I conceive, would not only be incongruous, but dangerous," because "No man, his ingenuity be what it will, could enumerate all the individual rights not relinquished by this constitution."

Opponents such as Judge Samuel Spencer of Anson County were not convinced, however, that a document that didn't mention such rights would protect them. "I know it ought to be so, and should be so understood," he said, "but sir, it is not declared to be so."

North Carolina's commitment to individual rights was not new. When the state drew up its own constitution in 1776, that was uppermost in many minds. Indeed, Mecklenburg officials instructed the county's delegates to push for a state charter that would "set forth a bill of rights containing the rights of the people and of individuals which shall never be infringed in any future time. ... "

Two hundred and fifteen years ago today, the state constitutional convention adopted a Declaration of Rights that "ought never to be violated on any Pretence whatever," including the right of assembly, no excessive bail, freedom of worship and of the press and a right to bear arms "for the Defence of the State." Later the delegates adopted a constitution.

By April 30, 1789, 11 states had ratified the federal Constitution and the United States of America was born – but only after Congressman James Madison, the Virginian who was chief architect of the Constitution, had agreed to sponsor amendments to it. On June 8, he offered the 10 amendments that would be known as the Bill of Rights, justifying them in part as an "accommodation" to encourage North Carolina to join the union. Six months later, North Carolina did so. And 200 years ago this month, the Bill of Rights was added to the Constitution.

Nothing is more fundamentally American than the guarantee that some individual acts are beyond the government's control. From the beginning, North Carolina has been an unremitting advocate of that idea. In this, the 200th anniversary of the ratification of the Bill of Rights, let us reaffirm that commitment.

Uptown or Downtown?
A column in The Charlotte Observer June 27, 1999

Some time ago I was talking with an old friend about changes in Charlotte. During his banking days he had helped recruit businesses to come here from other states. Now he has mixed feelings about his success. "If I'd known they all were going to be Republicans, I'm not sure I'd have done it," grumped the man, a lifelong Democrat. Well, that's how it goes. Promote change, and you may get more than you want.

I thought of that as I read Lauren Markoe's report in Tuesday's Observer on the debate about what to call Charlotte's central city. For years the area's promoters called it "uptown" and glared with disapproval at anyone who did otherwise. Now, a new generation of promoters wants to call it "downtown" and considers "uptown" a no-no – the civic equivalent of calling the main business street Tyrone.

Rob Walsh, who flew in from New York – what, 15 minutes ago? – to run what is now Charlotte Central City Partners, finds uptown "a bit pretentious" and favors this pledge: "I will not in any language, speech or brochures use the word uptown, so help me God."

I admire his conviction, but I'm not sure God would help. It was God, after all, who made it "up." As Charlotte native Jack Wood, a retired clothier, explains, the center city really is at the central business district's highest elevation – thus, uptown. "Don't let these new arrivals change what we established for generations," he urged.

Logic does not always prevail in such matters, of course, and some old-timers disagree that "uptown" ever was universally used.

So confusion reigns. As you enter the central business district on North Tryon, a sign welcomes you to Uptown Charlotte. As you drive along I-277 near Ericsson Stadium, a sign directs you to Downtown. My guess is that the newcomers will win this argument, simply because "uptown" sounds odd to so many – well, newcomers.

Whether we old-timers like it or not, newcomers are likely to change Charlotte again, just as they've been doing ever since the Spratts and Polks and their Scotch-Irish kith and kin came down the Great Wagon Road to settle Charlotte Town more than 250 years ago.

Some years ago I received a letter from a reader who was incensed that in editorials we had supported recruiting a big brewery from another state to relocate in North Carolina. They'll just bring in out-of-staters to work here, he fumed. What we need are jobs for North Carolinians.

I replied, "They'll live in North Carolina, shop in North Carolina, educate their children in North Carolina and pay North Carolina taxes. What does that make them – Martians?"

It makes them North Carolinians – immigrants, to be sure, but so were we all at some point in our family history.

As to calling uptown downtown, that's fine with me. Calling up down may seem a bit Orwellian to some, but for a city that calls a crossroads (Trade and Tryon) a square, that isn't much of a challenge.

Chicagoans Ignorant, but Probably Educable

An editorial in The Charlotte Observer June 19, 1989, when Sears, Roebuck & Co. was rumored to be considering moving its headquarters from Chicago to Charlotte

The "Application to Live in North Carolina" circulated at the Sears office in Chicago was an amazing compilation of regional slurs. Sample questions:

Do you own any shoes? If so, how many?

Does your wife weigh more than your pickup?

Are you married to any of the following:

( ) Sister ( ) Cousin ( ) Sow ( ) Don't know her name.

Nobody here worries much about that sort of thing. We already knew big-city folks could be just as prejudiced and parochial as inhabitants of the most isolated rural backwater.

A few things Chicagoans might not know about North Carolina:

1. When Chicago was still Indian territory, North Carolinians were helping write the U.S. Constitution (and refusing to ratify it without a Bill

of Rights) and founding a great university.

2. North Carolina has done much to make Illinois habitable. Joe Cannon, who as an Illinois congressman was longtime speaker of the U.S. House, was born in Greensboro. The Stevenson family, which has provided progressive political leadership for Illinois, moved there from North Carolina. Then there's Chicago's most popular citizen today – Michael Jordan, of Wilmington and Chapel Hill.

3. When residents of Chicago suburbs were stoning Dr. Martin Luther King Jr. and hosting Nazi marches, Charlotte was providing a national model for human relations.

4. While Chicago's public schools are widely considered the worst in the nation, Charlotte business and school leaders have pledged to make Charlotte-Mecklenburg schools one of the premier urban, integrated public school systems in America.

5. When Carl Sandburg, the Illinois-born poet who defined Chicago ("hog butcher of the world"), looked for a place to settle, he chose North Carolina. (Truth is, his wife wanted to raise goats and couldn't in Chicago. Now what kind of city is that?)

We Southerners are accustomed to having uninformed Northerners think all manner of bad things about us. When they move here they often continue to gripe – years in a cold, harsh climate do that to you, we guess – but most of them don't move back north.

If Sears does move here, we'll welcome its employees as friends and neighbors. Chicago is a wonderful city, but we know they'll soon be happy to be here. Their ignorance, after all, need not be a permanent affliction.

Charlotte's 20th Century
From a column in The Charlotte Observer Nov. 21, 1999

The 1890s were years of great beginnings for Charlotte.

In 1891, Edward Dilworth Latta broke ground for the city's first suburb, urging residents to "Buy a Home in Dilworth with Rent Money." He connected Dilworth to the city by Charlotte's first electric trolley. In a few years Charlotte's horse-drawn streetcars would be history.

In 1892, industrialist D.A. Tompkins announced plans for the Atherton

Mill in the same area, part of the great campaign to "Bring the Cotton Mills to the Cotton."

The Belk brothers, successful retailers in nearby Monroe, opened their first store here in 1895, promising in a Daily Observer ad that customers at the East Trade Street location would find the "Cheapest Store on Earth." One leading merchant – Joseph Baruch, uncle of famed financier Bernard Baruch – predicted those "country-town merchants" wouldn't last six months in Charlotte.

At the turn of the century, James B. Duke and his older brother, Ben, were talking with Walker Gill Wylie and William States Lee about damming the Catawba River to produce electricity.

Charlotte was never shy about its aspirations, though outsiders often judged it to be over-reaching. In 1798, for example, George Washington spent a night here and dismissed the rustic village as "a trifling place." He underestimated its potential.

A year later, 12-year-old Conrad Reed of nearby Concord was fishing in a creek and spotted a shiny rock about the size of his mother's flatiron. For a couple of years the family used it as a doorstop. Curious about the heavy stone, his father took it to a Fayetteville jeweler who determined it was gold.

Soon the gold rush was on. In the decades before the California gold strike of '49, Charlotte was the mining capital of the United States. The gold find was so rich that the U.S. Mint, which had no branches outside Washington, opened one here.

By the end of the century, Charlotte had been transformed from Washington's "trifling place" to a thriving city. In 1900 its population was 18,091, second in the state only to Wilmington's 20,976.

Just after the turn of the century, Observer editor Isaac Ervin Avery offered this tongue-in-cheek portrayal of a city en route to world classiness: "Charlotte has passed through the transition state and has become a sure-enough city. ... You may dodge a creditor for days without remaining in hiding, the country mules do not shy at automobiles or silk hats ... and no one thinks about fainting when a Charlotte woman goes off to get a Ph.D. vocal degree and comes home singing in a high Dutch or broken Eye-talian."

What a century this has been. Charlotte has launched Billy Graham and Jim Bakker, Charles Kuralt and Hugh McColl Jr. It was one of the first big Southern cities to elect a black mayor, Harvey Gantt. The city is home to the nation's biggest bank. Our local government is consistently recognized as a national model. We've grown to a city of 512,000 in a metropolitan region of 1.8 million. Our streets, filled at the beginning of the century with horses, now hold enough automobiles to earn a reputation for traffic jams. Ah, progress.

Charlotteans of the 20th Century
A column in The Charlotte Observer Jan. 2, 2000

After talking with historians and reading their books and discussing possible standards of evaluation, I concluded that picking a few people who during the 20th century did most to shape Charlotte is like picking the dozen best songs or best baseball players: A few may be obvious, but beyond that it's personal preference. With that in mind, here are my Charlotteans of the Century – a baker's dozen people who helped make this the prosperous, progressive city it is today.

Zechariah Alexander Sr. (1877-1954) was a sergeant major in the Spanish American War as white N.C. Democrats worked to regain political power. They succeeded in 1902 with a constitutional amendment disfranchising blacks. Alexander believed, a relative later wrote, "The only way to be free of intimidation was to work for yourself. If the Negro community supports you, then you are free to speak out against injustice." That became his goal.

He sold insurance until in 1909 he took a job in a funeral home which he later bought. Over the years, as barriers fell, the Alexander family became a powerful influence on city politics. Alexander's son Fred in 1965 became the first black elected to City Council this century and in 1974 was one of the first two blacks elected to the state Senate this century. Son Kelly Alexander Sr. was chairman of the state NAACP and of the organization's national board.

William Henry Belk (1862-1952) was orphaned in 1865 when Sherman's raiders drowned his father, a farmer, after he refused to reveal the location of the family's gold mine. Young Belk was educated at home by his mother and took a job in a Monroe dry goods store at age 14. Eleven years later he was running the store. The next year he opened his own store in Monroe. He called it the "New York Racket" because it "sounded big." It was profitable from the start. Soon his brother, John Montgomery Belk, a physician, joined him and they opened a store in Chester. In 1895 the Belks opened a Charlotte store on Trade Street. A skeptic predicted "those country town merchants won't last six months in Charlotte."

Today, Charlotte-based Belk Stores is the biggest privately held department store chain in the United States and the family has produced three generations of civic and political leaders, including former Mayor John Belk.

Julius L. Chambers was born in Mount Gilead and graduated from N.C. Central University in Durham before enrolling at the University of North Carolina law school, where he became the first black editor in chief of the law review and graduated first in his class in 1962. From 1964 to 1984 he was a partner in a Charlotte law firm and one of the nation's premier civil rights lawyers.

In his first year in Charlotte, he went to court to reshape racial relationships on many fronts: job discrimination, school desegregation, racial bias in public accommodations and public hospitals. In 1971 he argued the landmark Swann vs. Charlotte-Mecklenburg case in the U.S. Supreme Court, winning the court's unanimous approval for use of busing to integrate public schools. His work often made him the target of racist anger. In early 1965 his car was bombed as he spoke at a civil rights rally in New Bern. In November 1965 his Charlotte home was bombed as he and his family slept. In 1970 and again in 1971, his father's auto repair garage in Mount Gilead was set afire. And in 1971, his Charlotte law office was destroyed by fire. He left Charlotte in 1984 to head the NAACP Legal Defense and Education Fund in New York. In 1993, he became the first alumnus to serve as chancellor of N.C. Central University.

Bonnie Cone, an S.C. native and Coker College graduate with a master's degree from Duke University, was teaching math at Central High School in 1946 when Charlotte became home to one of 14 centers across the state that would offer college-level courses to veterans returning from World War II. Charlotte had no state college at the time. Cone signed on as a part-time math teacher and the next year became the center's director. She was president when it became Charlotte College and was a skilled advocate in its rise to become a major university. Many people helped, of course, but Miss Bonnie was in the forefront because, as a Charlotte Observer editorial noted, she is "uncommonly smart, persistent and gifted in sensing how to put people in a position in which they wanted to say yes." She always will be known as the mother of UNC-Charlotte, an institution whose growth and development are vitally important to our region's future.

Ben E. Douglas (1895-1981) was born near Statesville and educated in Gastonia. He earned a Silver Star and a battlefield commission in World War I and came to Charlotte in 1926. In 1935, he won the first of three terms as mayor and embarked on a remarkable program of public works that would make him, as one historian observed, "the builder of modern-day Charlotte." He doubled the size of the city's water system and pushed for funding of the first municipal airport, which now bears his name. He was instrumental in founding Charlotte Memorial Hospital (forerunner of Carolinas HealthCare System), the building of Memorial Stadium and the city's first public housing developments. Later, as a member of the state highway commission, he found money to build Independence Boulevard, a major thoroughfare today. One longtime City Council member said Douglas "had more vision about this city than any other man I ever knew."

Harvey Gantt grew up in public housing in Charleston, S.C., and in 1963 became the first black student at Clemson University. He earned a bachelor of architecture degree with honors and moved to Charlotte to join the firm of Odell Associates. As his career flourished, he became active in neighborhood and civic activities. In 1974, he was appointed to City Council to fill the unexpired term of Fred Alexander, who was elected to the N.C. Senate. Gantt was elected to the at-large seat in 1975, 1977 and 1981. In 1983, he became the first African American to be elected mayor of majority-white Charlotte, and was reelected in 1985. The state's Democrats twice nominated him to oppose U.S. Sen. Jesse Helms, but Helms won both races. President Bill Clinton in 1995 appointed Gantt to chair the National Capital Planning Commission.

Billy Graham, born in Charlotte and reared on his family's Park Road dairy farm, grew up to be the world's most famous modern Christian evangelist. Since a Los Angeles crusade in 1949 thrust him into national prominence, Graham, now 81, has preached to live audiences in 185 countries totaling more than 200 million people. He has written 18 books, advised every president since Harry Truman, appeared on the covers of *Time* and

Newsweek and for 32 consecutive years has ranked high in Gallup's annual poll of the "Ten Most Admired Men in the World." Honored for his life work at a Charlotte Chamber dinner last year, Graham said he's the same person who sold Fuller brushes as a lanky farm boy. "Only now," he said, "I'm trying to sell people on the idea of coming to know Christ."

Edward Dilworth Latta (1851-1925), an S.C. native, studied in New Jersey and, after his father's death, became a salesman in a New York clothing store. In 1876, he opened a clothing store in Charlotte, then sold it to go into real estate. He bought a thousand acres south of the city and named it Dilworth in honor of his grandmother. He built a lake and an amusement park, bought the streetcar line, electrified it and in 1890 began selling lots in what would become Charlotte's first streetcar suburb. Soon his park had a merry-go-round, a theater and a pavilion that hosted horse races and football games (Davidson vs. UNC in 1905) and traveling attractions such as "Buffalo Bill's Wild West Show" with Annie Oakley (1901). Latta hired noted architect C.C. Hook as a consultant on home design and the Olmsted Brothers, famous Boston landscape architects, to lay out much of his development. The suburbanization of Charlotte had begun with a vision and standard of quality rarely equaled here.

Hugh McColl Jr. grew up in Bennettsville, S.C., in a family that owned a small-town bank. After graduation from UNC-Chapel Hill and a brief active duty stint in the Marines, in 1959 he came to Charlotte to work for American Commercial Bank. The bank's CEO, Addison Reese, had a burning ambition: to build a bank that would overtake Winston-Salem-based Wachovia as the state's dominant financial institution. Reese and his brilliant successor, Tom Storrs, recognized and rewarded McColl's passion for competition and his skill at taking risks that paid off. With McColl as the point man, Storrs launched a successful mission to expand into Florida. When Storrs retired in 1983, McColl was his successor. Soon came expansionist forays into Texas, Atlanta and ultimately San Francisco, where a 1998 merger with BankAmerica created Bank of America, the nation's largest, a coast-to-coast institution with McColl at the top.

McColl's global vision for his bank didn't diminish his devotion to its home town. Under his leadership, the bank has spawned substantial development in Charlotte's center city, building new office towers and underwriting arts and cultural facilities. As McColl's vision and competitiveness reshaped the banking industry, his commitment to the health of his city reshaped and revitalized Charlotte.

Cameron Morrison (1869-1953) was a lawyer, mayor of Rockingham and state senator before moving his law practice to Charlotte in 1905. When he was elected governor in 1920 few North Carolinians expected him to become one of the state's greatest governors. But he had a big agenda. He pushed through the legislature the historic Highway Act of 1921, providing for a $50 million bond issue to begin construction of a 5,500-mile state highway system that would be a key to the state's economic development. He won dramatic increases in funding for public schools. He called for an $8.5 million bond issue to finance construction of a state-owned port terminal on the coast and to establish a state-owned ship line between N.C. ports and seaports of the industrial Northeast. Many state leaders denounced the proposal as "socialistic." Voters rejected it in a 1924 referendum.

Morrison's record as a progressive was mixed. He supported the anti-evolution crusade in 1924, banned high school textbooks that discussed Darwin's theory, and either opposed or was indifferent to women's suffrage and child labor laws. But his visionary pursuit of major improvements in transportation and education helped shape modern North Carolina.

Sue Myrick has demonstrated two of Charlotte's distinctive political characteristics: hospitality to immigrants from the North and willingness to elect women to high office. Democrat Martha Evans, a Philadelphia native with a Boston University degree, blazed that trail in the 1950s. She moved to Charlotte in 1946 and broke City Council's male-only tradition by winning a seat in 1955 and '57. She ran two strong but unsuccessful races for mayor and later became the first woman to serve in both houses of the N.C. legislature. Republican Myrick, an Ohio native, came here in 1971 and won a City Council seat in 1983. She sought the Republican mayoral nomination in 1985, lost, won it in 1987 and skillfully focused suburban discontent about traffic to upset incumbent Harvey Gantt and become Charlotte's first woman mayor. After two terms she sought and lost the Republican nomination for U.S. Senate, then was elected to Congress in 1994, '96 and '98.

Gladys Avery Tillett (1892-1984), daughter of a state Supreme Court justice, helped organize the student government at the State Normal and Industrial School (now UNC-Greensboro) and was its first president.

Gov. Locke Craig, while speaking there, nodded to her and said, "Well, I know this young lady, this lovely young lady, is not for votes for women." She listened quietly, patting her face with a handkerchief embroidered "Votes for Women." Later she and her friends burned him in effigy. In 1917 she earned a political science degree from UNC and married Charles Tillett of Charlotte, a lawyer also devoted to progressive politics. She worked for ratification of the 19th Amendment to the Constitution, giving women the right to vote. She helped found the Mecklenburg League of Women Voters and was an active Democrat. In 1943 she was the first woman to be an assistant to the chairman of the Democratic National Convention. In 1944 she became the first woman to address the convention.

Daniel Augustus Tompkins (1851-1914), an S.C. native and engineer, came to Charlotte in 1883 as an agent for Westinghouse Machine Co. Soon he formed his own company to build cotton oil mills, electric plants and cotton mills. He owned mills, too, including the Atherton here. In 1892, he bought The Charlotte Observer, and with partner and editor J.P. Caldwell of Statesville used it in his crusade to promote Charlotte and a New South with an economy based on locally owned industries. By 1910, his company had built some 250 cotton oil mills, 150 electric plants and 100 cotton mills. The Atlanta Constitution wrote in 1911, "He perhaps has done more to stimulate the cotton mill development of the South than any living man." Tompkins was an industrialist of his time and place: racist and outspokenly opposed to wage and hour laws, compulsory public education and laws limiting child labor. But his vision and vigorous promotion helped create a New South.

Chalmers Davidson, sui generis
An editorial in The Charlotte Observer July 3, 1994

Chalmers Gaston Davidson did not found Davidson College (though a long-ago relative did have a hand in it), but he would not have felt more of a proprietary interest in it if he had been present at the creation. It was a large part of his life, and he returned the favor, enriching the institution and the lives of generations of students.

Dr. Davidson was a 1928 graduate of the college (*summa cum laude*) who earned advanced degrees at Harvard, then returned to his alma mater in

1928. He stayed 58 years, serving as professor of history, library director and archivist.

He knew the history of the college and community so well you'd think he'd lived through all of it. He had strong opinions, some of them supported by facts, others by only his strong will, and he argued for both with equal vigor and wit. He was a prolific writer, an elegant and irrepressible raconteur, a model of dignity and decorum, a man for whom the term "gentleman of the old school" was invented. His death June 25 at age 87 left an emptiness in the landscape, as though a mighty oak had fallen, or a stately building had crumbled under the wrecker's ball.

Chalmers Davidson was rooted in the history of his place in a way fewer and fewer Americans are. We are a mobile people, better at making new attachments than at nurturing old ones. Dr. Davidson knew that, and didn't much like it. In fact, there was a lot he didn't like about modern life, and he spoke right up about it. He championed numerous losing causes at the college, opposing coeducation, the abolition of compulsory chapel and the dropping of the dress code (coats and ties) for men. Once the issue was settled, however, his position was clear: He was devoted to Davidson, no matter how (in his opinion) foolish were its accommodations to modern ways.

The past, he knew, had lessons worth learning and values worth maintaining. He believed in a Davidson way of life, "based on things of the mind, tempered by manners and morality." He cherished learning, tradition, morality and manners, and sought to instill those values in his students.

He was *sui generis*, an entirely distinctive character. Life with him was a rewarding, if not always agreeable, adventure. Life without him will be a little poorer, a little shallower, a little less firmly rooted in the traditions and values he held dear.

Charles Crutchfield, broadcasting giant

An editorial in The Charlotte Observer Aug. 21, 1998

Charles Crutchfield lived with vigor and passion, and sometimes he ran smack into troubles a less self-assured person might have avoided. But that was the man. When he thought he was right, he forged ahead; when he saw he was wrong, he apologized. He cared deeply, he eagerly sought the next challenge and he had a memorable impact.

Mr. Crutchfield started in radio as a teenager and bounced around the Carolinas before landing at WBT in Charlotte in 1933. He helped make it one of the nation's premier stations. He was an innovator: John Crosby, former radio critic for the New York Times, credits him and Arthur Godfrey with being the first to abandon the stilted "announcer voice" and adopt the "sincere," personal approach that broadcasters use to this day.

Mr. Crutchfield saw the potential of television early. In 1963, he became president of Jefferson Pilot Broadcasting, parent company of WBTV, and led that station to regional dominance.

He believed his position in the community provided an opportunity not only to make money but also to make a difference. He was a visionary civic leader. He was convinced that allowing bedroom suburbs around Charlotte to become independent towns could subject this city to white flight and economic difficulty, so he pushed legislators not to allow it. Though he stumbled in saying blacks were "not mentally or economically qualified" to run a big city, he apologized and explained he meant unqualified by education and experience. In 1971, as Chamber of Commerce president, he led the effort to bring black leaders into the mainstream of civic affairs. He explained, "Building a strong urban center involves more than buildings and physical activities. It involves all elements of the community and the removal of false fences which have been built between people." He was an early advocate of city planning to make Charlotte a place where people of all incomes and races could live together.

He disagreed with U.S. Judge James McMillan's order to use busing to integrate Charlotte-Mecklenburg schools, but his company spent thousands of dollars to air commentaries by such leaders as Billy Graham and to bring in celebrities such as football hero Bart Starr to calm public anxiety over school integration.

He was a sharp critic of what he saw as liberal bias among Dan Rather and other reporters at CBS, his station's network. He wrote to a CBS executive that "some people who work in your news shop come very close to being news prostitutes and should be removed."

He backed Richard Nixon "right up to the time I saw him get on the plane and say goodbye," he later recalled. "I just couldn't believe I could be fooled to that extent by anybody."

We often disagreed with Mr. Crutchfield, but we never questioned his integrity and we always admired his commitment to making the world a better place.

Dean Colvard, master builder
An editorial in The Charlotte Observer June 29, 2007

Dean Colvard, the UNC-Charlotte chancellor emeritus who died Thursday at age 93, didn't just seize opportunities, he created them.

UNC President Bill Friday expected that when he brought him here in 1966 as UNCC's first chancellor. As dean of the agriculture school at N.C. State University and later chancellor of Mississippi State University, Dr. Colvard had shown uncommon ability to unite people behind good ideas and turn potential into reality. He had proven to be a man of vision and courage.

He grew up on an Ashe County farm, but knew his future would be beyond his rural homeplace. He believed education would take him there. He was salutatorian of his small class and the first of his family to go to college. He won scholarships to Berea College in Kentucky, the University of Missouri and finally to Purdue University for a doctorate. After Purdue, he came home to teach at N.C. State. When he became agriculture dean, he boosted enrollment, improved the curriculum and won recognition for distinguished service to agriculture.

In 1960, Mississippi State picked him to be its president. Under his energetic leadership, enrollment grew from 4,500 to 7,300, an ambitious campus development plan was launched and a new fund-raising program brought in millions. He also showed courage and conviction rare for Mississippi leaders of that era. In 1963, MSU's all-white basketball team won the conference championship. Dr. Colvard defied racist politicians and sent the team to play an integrated Loyola of Chicago team in the NCAA tournament.

UNCC had been a four-year college only three years when Dr. Colvard arrived. There were 1,800 students, no dorms, 80 faculty members. The 1965 graduating class had 20 members. When he retired in 1978, UNCC had a $60 million physical plant, a faculty and staff of 400, a graduating class of 1,800 and a vision of greatness.

Under Dean Colvard, UNCC's ambitions matched and helped shape those of our region. UNCC and the Charlotte region still benefit from the example set by his wise leadership.

Wade Stroud: fine officer, fine man
An editorial in The Charlotte Observer June 29, 1987

Charlotte Police Capt. Wade Stroud approached his death the way he lived his life: with courage, confidence and humor. When he died last week, he left a lot of good memories and a vacancy that will be hard to fill.

Death was no stranger to Wade Stroud. He had faced it as a police officer, when gunfire came his way. He had lost a son, a member of the Outlaws motorcycle gang, to violent death. Stricken with lung cancer, he saw his own death coming long before it arrived.

"The doc told me my attitude was going to have a lot to do with how I got along," he told an Observer reporter 10 months before he died. "I told him, 'You do your part, Doc, and I'll handle the attitude.' I was surprised that it didn't affect me any more than it did, but it helps to know where you're going. If I worried I was going to hell, I suspect I'd have a different attitude."

Wade Stroud was one of the finest homicide detectives around. He earned the respect of his fellow officers and the gratitude of this community. His skill, courage, modesty, humor and devotion to duty made him a model worth emulating – not only as a police officer but as a man.

John Belk's legacy
An editorial in The Charlotte Observer Aug. 19, 2007

John Belk was a business titan who ran one of the nation's most successful department store chains. As mayor (1969-77) he used his considerable clout and prodigious energy to further his ambitious vision for the city he loved. When he died Friday at age 87, Charlotte lost one of the most distinguished leaders in its history.

It was easy to underestimate Mr. Belk. He was an unlikely politician. As a speaker he was prone to statements so baffling they became known as Belkisms. Writer Alex Coffin collected some in his 1994 book, *Brookshire & Belk: Businessmen in City Hall.* "We ought to decide where our problems are and implement our own," Mr. Belk once said. And, "You can't be unreasonable about something until you get the facts." And, "I can see a cloud in the distance and want to make sure I'm near the hen house."

But when Mr. Belk wanted something done, there was no misunderstanding it. He used his personal and political power in the late 1960s and '70s to promote rebuilding of the declining center city. He was instrumental in locating a new Civic Center there. He helped persuade what's now Bank of America to build its headquarters at The Square. Some of his initiatives were controversial, but under his leadership Charlotte made a civic investment that averted the hollowing out experienced by so many cities and laid the foundation for today's impressive skyline. He was one of the strongest supporters of what is now an international airport, one of the Charlotte region's most valuable economic assets.

Wherever he went, he was a gregarious booster of the city. When there was a ribbon to be cut or ground to be broken here, John Belk could be counted on to do it.

He was a proud alumnus of Davidson College and its most generous donor. He established the prestigious John Montgomery Belk Scholarships to help the school compete for the nation's best students.

Mr. Belk was the latest, perhaps the last, in a line of leaders from the city's business elite to serve as mayor. His commitment and personal power enabled him to push through programs that helped shape a prosperous, progressive city. His tenure preceded the advent of partisan politics and district representation, which he opposed. He may have been the last mayor who could lead and expect City Council to follow without too much fuss.

John Belk had the vision to see what his city needed and the power to make it happen. Today's Charlotte is, to a great degree, his legacy.

V. Two-Party System

JOHN D. SIMMONS

Barack Obama (lower left) carried North Carolina in the 2008 presidential election, making him the first Democrat to win the state since Jimmy Carter in1976, though Bill Clinton came within 20,000 votes of doing so in 1992.

1800 Political Feud Turned Deadly

A column in The Charlotte Observer, Dec. 3, 2000

The 2000 presidential race has had rough spots, but its worst moments are political pattycake compared to the 1800 race, when an electoral vote tie threw the election into the U.S. House of Representatives. That struggle not only ended in a political deal, it led to a fatal duel.

George Washington was twice elected president (1788 and '92) without opposition. When he declined a third term, his vice president, John Adams, was elected, narrowly defeating Thomas Jefferson, who as runner-up became vice president.

There were no political parties when Washington was elected, but by 1800 rival factions had organized as the Federalists (Washington and Adams) and Democrat-Republicans, called Republicans (Jefferson, Madison, Monroe), though the party evolved into today's Democrats.

Republicans considered Adams too fond of a king-like presidency and too distrustful of popular government. They also favored strong states' rights and a weaker central government. The parties split over the French Revolution, too. Republicans supported the revolution; many Federalists wanted to go to war with France.

In 1800, Jefferson challenged Adams again. Adams' running mate was C.C. Pinckney of South Carolina. Jefferson's was Aaron Burr of New York.

The election of 1800 introduced widespread bipartisan name-calling into presidential politics. Federalists called Jefferson a revolutionary, anarchist and unbeliever. Federalist editors printed salacious verses saying he fathered children with Sally Hemings, one of his slaves. Some Federalists said he would establish a military dictatorship. The fundamentalists of the day claimed he would round up all Bibles and replace them with one he had written. A Connecticut clergyman wrote, "I do not believe the Most High will permit a howling atheist to sit at the head of this nation."

Republicans called Adams a spendthrift and a madman and derided his support for the Sedition Act, which authorized fines or jail for journalists critical of high officials (including Adams). Federalist Alexander Hamilton split the party by calling Adams mentally incompetent and criticizing his policy of neutrality with France. (Hamilton himself was forced to admit paying blackmail to conceal an "amorous connection" with a Mrs. Reynolds while he was Washington's treasury secretary.)

In presidential elections, voters don't elect candidates, they elect electors, who gather and vote for candidates. The U.S. Constitution gave each state a number of electors equal to its members of the U.S. House and Senate and gave each elector two votes. The candidate with the most votes would be president; the runner-up would be vice president.

But the writers of the Constitution had not anticipated party tickets. The electors assembled in their states' capitals and sent their votes to Washington. Republican electors dutifully cast one vote for Jefferson and one for Burr. Though Jefferson defeated Adams, the party-line vote produced a tie between Jefferson and Burr, throwing the election into the House. (To fix that problem, in 1803 the Constitution was amended so that electors cast one vote for president and one for vice president.)

Republicans had won a majority in the House, but the newly elected representatives hadn't taken office, so Federalist lame ducks would determine which Republican would be president.

Burr, an ambitious man, did not withdraw, and some Federalists preferred him to Jefferson. Republican governors in Maryland and Pennsylvania threatened to call out their militia to make Jefferson president. The Federalist press predicted civil war.

Some Republicans believed Jefferson was unelectable and urged Burr to try to win. Others saw the defeat of Jefferson as a way to slap down the powerful Virginia faction (four of the first five presidents were Virginians).

Chief Justice John Marshall – Jefferson's cousin – opposed him for fear he would overthrow the independent judiciary.

But Hamilton strongly opposed Burr and worked hard to defeat him. In letters to House members, he called Burr unprincipled, a profligate and a voluptuary (Burr's numerous sexual adventures were no secret).

The stalemate continued for six days, until the lone Delaware congressman was assured that Jefferson would not abandon the national debt, scrap the Navy and purge all the Federalist political appointees. His support gave Jefferson the presidency on the 36th ballot, with Burr as vice president. Adams was so upset that he refused to stay in Washington for Jefferson's inauguration.

The Burr-Hamilton feud continued. Burr ran for governor of New York in 1804 and lost. Soon afterward, he read an insult from Hamilton published in a newspaper and challenged him to a duel. When they met, both men fired their pistols. Hamilton missed, perhaps intentionally, but Burr's shot hit home. Hamilton died of his wound the next day.

Has Observer Endorsed Republicans?
A column in The Charlotte Observer July 18, 2004

A reader called recently to ask me to settle a bet: Had the Observer ever endorsed a Republican for president? Yes, indeed, I said. We endorsed Eisenhower in 1952 and 1956 and Nixon in 1960 and 1968.

Since few of you, I'd bet, spend much time on newspaper history, maybe you'd enjoy a brief romp through the Observer's past.

The Observer dates to 1892, when industrialist D.A. Tompkins and journalist Joseph P. Caldwell bought The Charlotte Chronicle and renamed it. Tompkins wanted a paper to promote his vision of a New South in which industry replaced agriculture as the economic mainstay.

The Observer supported what political scientist V.O. Key called the "progressive plutocracy" that ran our one-party (Democrat) state. (Republicans were not forgiven for The War.)

When Democrats nominated prairie populist William Jennings Bryan for president in 1900, the Observer took a step sure to alienate many readers: It didn't endorse him. Caldwell wrote that Bryan was "not a fit man for President; in charge of the craft he would run it upon the rocks."

After William McKinley beat Bryan, the Observer resumed its support for Democrats, a position it maintained, sometimes uncomfortably, until we liked Ike in '52.

Over the years the Observer became a voice for pro-growth progressivism, especially on social and racial issues.

In our endorsement of Nixon in '68, we raised an issue that would affect our future choices. We noted with disapproval "the alliance Nixon made with Sen. Strom Thurmond and others of his party's reactionary right wing in winning the nomination."

Thurmond, South Carolina's dominant 20th-century politician, was a key player in the political realignment of the South. He broke with the Democrats in 1948 after hearing young Minneapolis Mayor Hubert H. Humphrey tell the party's national convention, "It is now time for the Democratic party to get out of the shadow of states' rights and walk forthrightly in the bright sunshine of human rights."

When the convention adopted a strong civil rights statement, many Southern delegates walked out. Soon the State Rights Party was formed. The Dixiecrats, as they were called, nominated Thurmond for president. He told the nation "there are not enough troops in the Army to force Southern people to admit the Negroes into our theaters, swimming pools, and homes."

In 1964 he became a Republican. In early 1968 he and others met with Nixon in an Atlanta motel room and made a deal that would convert Dixie's conservative Democrats into Republicans.

Nixon pledged to ease the federal pressure for integration, maintain a strong military and control federal spending. He'd rein in textile imports and appoint "strict constructionists" to the U.S. Supreme Court. With those assurances, Thurmond backed Nixon and pulled many conservative Democrats with him. In '68 Democrat Hubert Humphrey won only one state from the Old Confederacy, Texas.

The Democrats helped, of course. The party had become a hodgepodge of argumentative interest groups, often represented by leaders whose beliefs about politics and culture alienated traditional voters across the nation as well as in the South.

But Nixon had allied the Republicans with Southern politicians we had opposed when they were Democrats, especially on civil rights. In 1972 we didn't recommend him or Democrat George McGovern. Since the heirs of the Dixiecrats have gained veto power over the GOP choice, we've endorsed Democrats.

No party is a monolith, of course. Politics is always evolving. Our state and may others have more than one variety of Republicanism. Here I identify the factions with two leaders: Jim Martin, the former congressman and two-term governor, and Jesse Helms, the five-term U.S. senator.

Helms personifies what our 1968 editorial meant by the "reactionary right wing." While Martin agreed with Helms on some social issues, they weren't at the heart of his appeal. Martin pushed for greater investment in education and roads and favored higher taxes to pay for it. He rejected racism and drew strong support from environmentalists.

We've often favored Republicans with such views: Jim Holshouser for governor in '72, Martin in 1984 and 1988 and Richard Vinroot in 2000, plus many seeking other state and local offices. As the parties and issues evolve, so do our choices.

Dissent is Good for the Parties

An editorial in The Charlotte Observer Aug. 29, 2004

Dick Cheney spoke less as vice president of the United States than as the father of a lesbian daughter when he commented on gay unions Tuesday at an Iowa town hall meeting. He said "freedom means freedom for everyone" to enter "into any kind of relationship they want to." His comments were further evidence of the dissent at the top of the Republican Party from some stands on social issues expressed in the party's platform.

Mr. Cheney's comments broke no new ground. During the 2000 vice presidential debates he had said much the same thing. "The fact of the matter is we live in a free society," he said then, "and freedom means freedom for everybody. We don't get to choose, and shouldn't be able to choose and say, 'You get to live free, but you don't.' And I think that means that people should be free to enter into any kind of relationship they want to enter into."

Earlier Lynne Cheney, the vice president's wife, expressed similar feelings and said states should have the final say over the legal status of personal relationships. That put her at odds with President Bush, who advocates a constitutional amendment that effectively would ban gay marriage.

The Cheneys' statements are a reminder that the Republican Party leadership is far from monolithic on social issues, and in the Bush White House dissent from the party's dominant view is accepted, not punished.

When the University of Michigan's student admissions policies were challenged in court, Secretary of State Colin Powell and national security adviser Condoleezza Rice expressed support for affirmative action in college admissions.

Gov. George Pataki of New York, Gov. Arnold Schwarzenegger of California, New York City Mayor Michael Bloomberg and former mayor Rudolph Guiliani all support abortion rights. The fact that they're to speak at the Republican National Convention prompted some socially conservative Republicans to urge the president to add speakers who support the party platform on those issues.

Some critics say having a platform that says one thing while some party leaders say another is deceptive politics. We disagree. Give the dissenters credit. Too many Republicans – and too many Democrats – put political consistency and party loyalty above honest debate over difficult issues. America would be better governed if more issues were determined by debate reflecting the independent thinking of informed representatives rather than by allegiance to a party line.

Liberals' Choice: Evolve or Else

An editorial in The Charlotte Observer Nov. 18, 1980

Sen. Paul Tsongas's indictment of political liberalism should be required reading for American liberals. The 39-year-old Massachusetts Democrat, himself a liberal, concludes that liberalism is in trouble for two good reasons:

1. Liberals too often become prisoners of their ideology, clinging to programs that sound progressive and humane but in fact don't work, or don't work well enough to justify their cost.
2. Liberals still talk in the rhetoric of the New Deal even though more than half the people in America today have been born since the death of Franklin Roosevelt.

A Gallup Poll taken after the election found that voters' rejection of liberal candidates Nov. 4 did not signify a national turnabout on such social issues as the ERA, gun control, abortion and the death penalty.

The election did indicate that voters agreed with Ronald Reagan's answer to a question he asked while debating President Carter: Do you really think the nation is better off than it was four years ago?

It is ironic that, though Republicans are often accused of looking backward, it is Democrats who are doing so today. Mr. Carter's campaign was largely an attempt to portray Mr. Reagan as a relic of the Cold War and remind voters of the accomplishments of Presidents Roosevelt, Truman and Johnson. Mr. Carter's vision of America's future was not the dominant message of his campaign.

Everywhere, Democrats were on the defensive. Republicans were the party of change. As only a party out of power can, the GOP offered painless remedies for the nation's ills, from inflation to joblessness to the need to refurbish America's reputation around the world. The next four years will not be painless, however. Conservatives, now in power, will find that taking optimistically was easier than governing effectively will be.

It is effectiveness, not repeal of 40 years of progress, that voters want. The tendency among too many liberals has been to assume that what's good for business is bad for America. A healthy economy, however, is as important to liberals as to conservatives; the policies liberals represent can't be achieved without it. The Democrats' economic failure was the major reason for their downfall.

Americans do not want a return to the 1880s. They want the government to continue to lessen the problems of unemployment, old age, ill health and poverty; to ensure on-the-job safety and keep the environment clean; to safeguard equal opportunity. They want a firm, but not a belligerent, foreign policy.

The Democrats created the issues that Republicans won on. The Republicans no doubt will return the favor. What liberals should do now is put aside their paens to FDR and do what he did: Look at the major challenges of today and tomorrow, and develop workable ways to meet them.

N.C.'s Feuding Republicans
An editorial in The Charlotte Observer March 29, 1987

Sen. Jesse Helms and Gov. Jim Martin may be the best of buddies, as they unfailingly profess, but the feud between Congressional Club Republicans and the Martin Republicans these days is almost as hot as the ones between rival televangelists. Since the TV preachers dominated the news during last week to the exclusion of virtually everything else, here's an update on the N.C. GOP.

Last week in Raleigh, the Martinites took control of the Wake County GOP out of the Club's hands for the first time in years. And the Clubbers, as graceless in defeat as they customarily are in victory, stalked out in a huff and threatened to sue.

What happened? The Clubbers arrived at the convention, found themselves in the minority and tried to stall the proceedings until sensible people (that is, Martinites) would get fed up and go home – past midnight, if necessary.

The Martinites saw what was going on and countered by voting to remove the Clubber who was presiding over the convention and replace him with a Martinite. Then they elected a county leadership and slate of delegates to the state convention that does not include Carter Wrenn, Tom Ellis and other Club stalwarts.

Then Mr. Wrenn complained that the convention was rigged and said the Club may sue to overturn its results. Rigged? That's Clubspeak: If the Club manipulates the rules and wins, it's because the Club is well-organized;

if the Club's opponents manipulate the rules and win, it's because the convention is rigged.

The Republicans have accomplished one thing we never thought possible: They have made the Democrats the party of harmony and decorum.

For GOP, How Important is Purity?

An editorial in The Charlotte Observer April 11, 1977

Will Griffin's resignation as chairman of the Mecklenburg Republican Party may make possible the selection of a chairman who will have fewer problems than Mr. Griffin in unifying the party.

Mr. Griffin, long a hard worker for the GOP, created some problems for himself by his brusque treatment of Republicans less conservative than he in the week following his election. But the party's problems go beyond the identity of the county chairman.

The Republican Party is afflicted with the same dysfunction that struck the Democratic Party in places where George McGovern's more zealous supported ousted party regulars in 1972. The winners, heady with success, are willing to make few compromises or tolerate any divergence of opinion.

The problem with this kick-the-losers strategy is that after a new group takes over a party organization, it needs the people it ousted to help win elections.

State Sen. Carolyn Mathis, Rep. Marilyn Bissell, Councilwoman Pat Locke and other Republicans may not fit the strict-conservative mold some Mecklenburg Republicans would like for their party, but the fact is that they were able to win enough Republican, Democratic and independent votes to get elected. It is difficult to see how Republicans can advance their party by ousting moderates who can win elections and replacing them with conservatives who possibly can't.

The question Republicans must ask themselves is whether electing candidates to office, in the hope of affecting government policies, is the party's goal. If the goal, instead, is to turn the party into a fraternal order in which everyone recites the same oath and adopts the same creed, the GOP has little chance of doing more than electing a small chorus of naysayers while the Democrats govern.

While Mecklenburg's most conservative Republicans may have the organizational skill to take over the party, they have not demonstrated that they have the inclination or the ability to form the broad coalition necessary to win elections – any more than have Mecklenburg's most liberal Democrats.

Congressman Jim Martin, one of Mecklenburg's most successful Republican politicians, expressed that need for a broad appeal in an article he wrote for the Observer last December. Voters can be liberal on some issues while conservative on others, he noted. "Perhaps 25 per cent of the electorate can pass our test of faith if we insist on allegiance to every item in the Republican platform. Far better, 55 per cent can be mustered if we find more persuasive ways to convince independent voters that for the most part ... we are better able to serve their view. ... "

Mecklenburg and North Carolina need a strong Republican Party, not because its candidates or programs are necessarily superior but to keep lackluster Democrats from winning important offices and adopting uninspired programs by default. In its present shape, the GOP is not playing that vital role, and government is the worse for it.

Democrats Addled, but Not Dead
A column in The Charlotte Observer Dec. 8, 2002

Woe, the poor Democrats. After losing the popular vote but winning the presidency, George W. Bush risked his reputation by making the '02 congressional races a national issue. He crisscrossed the country to campaign for Republicans he needed to get his programs through Congress.

His risk paid off. Now his party controls both houses of Congress as well as the White House. Only a decade ago, the Democrats controlled all three. So the question arises: Are the Democrats dead?

No. Addled, but not dead.

A few years ago E.J. Dionne Jr., a Washington Post columnist whose work appears on this page, wrote a book titled *They Only Look Dead: Why Progressives Will Dominate the Next Political Era*. I agree with his premise. The big question is whether the Democrats or the Republicans will be the progressives.

In 2000, Al Gore beat Bush in the popular vote with a campaign that prompted some Democrats to think class warfare is the key to success. They miss an important point: Few Americans care how rich the rich are. What Americans do care about is how the folks who aren't rich are doing.

Right now, many of them are not doing very well. Why? Globalization of commerce is threatening many American jobs. Corporate failures are robbing workers of their pensions, and corporate cost-cutting is endangering their health insurance. President Bush's tax cuts for the rich aren't touching the most important issue for American workers – the heavy burden of payroll tax deductions. Stock market shenanigans by corporate executives and dishonest stock analysts are putting workers' 401(k) investments at risk. A nutty tax structure is imposing on more and more middle-class taxpayers a charge intended for the rich.

In politics, death is only temporary. Bill Clinton brought the Democrats back to life by embracing issues that had belonged to Republicans. He backed welfare reform and a balanced budget. He was tough on crime and favored the death penalty.

Bush did some image-shifting, too. He preached compassionate conservatism and made school reform – an issue dear to middle-class parents – a priority.

Now Bush is riding high in the polls for two reasons. The first is that national security is a major concern, and Americans traditionally trust Republicans more on that issue. The other is that on domestic policy Bush has a few commitments – tax cuts, deregulation and the war on terrorism – but on lesser issues he has no inclination to stick with a losing hand.

Examples abound. First the Bush administration pushed military tribunals to handle national security cases. Now it's clear that such tribunals will be used rarely. First he seemed ready to invade Iraq with no regard for world opinion. Then he took his case to the United Nations and now he's courting international support. And just last week he dumped his ineffective economic team to free himself for a new approach to an issue he's vulnerable on.

Bush's oratory may be clumsy, but in making political decisions he has been uncommonly nimble. Still, he may find, as Clinton did, that when a president's party controls Congress, it creates risks as well as opportunities.

Some GOP congressional leaders have priorities that the president doesn't share. If they pull the party out of the political mainstream, they may open the way for a Democratic resurgence. Smaller government sounds fine, but what if that means crooked corporations get away with murder? Deregulation? Great, but what if the environment suffers? Bush is pro-life, but what if Congress makes abortion a hot issue?

There was a lot of talk about the image Nancy Pelosi, the liberal San Francisco Democrat, may create as the party's new leader in the House. But who knows, Tom DeLay, the Texas firebrand who's the most powerful Republican in the House, may be more of a threat to Bush than any Democrat could be.

So that's the picture. The Democrats in disarray, as usual, but the issues are there for a winning Democratic platform – jobs, affordable health care, middle-class tax cuts, support for families. But Republicans see those issues, too. The political future will belong to the party that convinces voters it has the programs and the will to handle them.

VI. Presidential Matters

President Bush talks with the troops in Saudi Arabia, November 22, 1990.

Bush's War: 1991

Taking a Democracy to War (1991)
An editorial in The Charlotte Observer Nov. 28, 1990

When there's talk of war, what's a democracy to do?

President George Bush is taking all the steps necessary to go to war over Kuwait – a lot of harsh talk, a series of U.N. resolutions, a big troop buildup. There are strong arguments for using force to push Iraq out of Kuwait, if peaceful efforts fail. But there are at least equally strong reasons for believing that U.S. involvement in a ground war in the Mideast would damage this nation's long-term interests in the region.

In a democracy, such differences of opinion should be the subject of public debate. But wait a minute. Does President Bush really want to attack Iraq, or he is just making war talk to show Saddam Hussein how seriously the world takes Iraqi aggression? The public can't know. Public debate over the president's policy might harden Saddam Hussein's resolve and decrease the likelihood that our saber-rattling will make him free Kuwait. That, in turn, might make war more likely.

That's one of the problems of government by, for and of the people. Kings and emperors can take their nations to war; presidents, thank the Founding Fathers, can't, unless the people – through their representatives in Congress – agree to go along.

The Vietnam experience shouldn't teach Americans that there's nothing beyond our borders worth fighting for. Access to Mideast oil, for example, has long been recognized as one of this industrial nation's vital interests. The Vietnam experience should teach us, however, that when our nation is considering a faraway fight, both our leaders and we citizens should know why we're fighting, what our chances are of success and under what conditions we'll bring our troops home.

Unless there is an attack on U.S. forces or territory, America is a hard nation to take to war. It should be.

Operation Desert Storm Begins

An editorial in The Charlotte Observer Jan. 17, 1991

President George Bush repeatedly warned Saddam Hussein that refusal to withdraw from Kuwait would mean war. Saddam Hussein scoffed. Now the war has begun, with swarms of aircraft from the anti-Iraq coalition soaring through the night sky to rain death and destruction on Iraq.

In the war's early hours, communications were sketchy. It was impossible to get a clear idea of what was happening. There were no solid reports about the extent of damages to Iraq.

Information was scarce about what losses the anti-Iraq coalition might have suffered. All we could do was pray for a quick victory with a minimal loss of life.

Many have questioned the wisdom of going to war, but there is no question about the justice of the cause. Saddam Hussein rules his nation by terror. He has twice invaded his neighbors. His unprovoked attack on Kuwait was horrifying in its brutality. His lust for power and conquest seemed boundless.

While it is true that the U.N. coalition launched this attack after months of uneasy inaction, it is Saddam Hussein who must bear responsibility for this war. Karl von Clausewitz, the German philosopher of war, observed wisely that the aggressor is always a man of peace; nothing would please him more than to march into a neighboring country unresisted. It is the victim, and the victim's friends, who must choose to fight. Though he died a century and a half ago, Clausewitz could not have described the present situation better.

Still, America fights this war at great risk – not only to the sons and daughter, fathers and mothers, who are doing battle, but to the nation's long-term interests as well. Would further reliance on the embargo have made Iraq yield without so much loss of life? Will a war, even a victorious war, stir the anti-American passions of the volatile region? Will it embolden the Islamic fundamentalists who threaten the rule of pro-Western Arab leaders? Will Israel be drawn into the conflict? Will the hostilities unleash a worldwide plague of Arab terrorism? Will the Mideast with a weakened Iraq be a safer place?

These are the risks President Bush must have considered in his months of pondering the options. Ultimately, he judged those risks to be less than the danger of allowing Saddam Hussein's aggression to go unchallenged.

We can only pray that events will prove his judgment sound, and that history will record the war with Iraq as a wise action, as well as a just one.

Not Another Vietnam

An editorial in The Charlotte Observer Jan. 18, 1991

"I've told the American people before that this will not be another Vietnam. And I repeat this here tonight," said President George Bush in an address to the nation Wednesday night.

President Bush is right. Though war protesters have seized upon the metaphor, the war in the Mideast is not another Vietnam. America's effort in Vietnam was doomed for three reasons: We didn't know how to fight that war, it was not altogether clear why we were fighting, and we didn't know how to define victory. None of the three is true in the war against Iraq.

This is a war we know how to fight. The Iraqis have a uniformed, organized military force, armed with modern weapons, trained by Soviet experts and defending an open terrain. This is the sort of war U.S. troops have been preparing to fight for decades, though the training anticipated the terrain of Europe, not the Persian Gulf. But this is a war where the enemy is identifiable, modern weapons are effective and modern techniques are applicable. None of that was true in Vietnam.

It is clear why we are fighting. Though many Americans would have preferred to use economic and diplomatic means rather than force, Saddam Hussein clearly is a ruthless and ambitious despot who must be prevented from annihilating his neighbors and dominating his region. It is true that the United States made many policy errors in the months preceding Iraq's attack on Kuwait. While contemplating that history may be instructive, dwelling on it does not solve the problem presented by Saddam Hussein. He rules Iraq by terror and bloodshed. He defiantly brandishes chemical

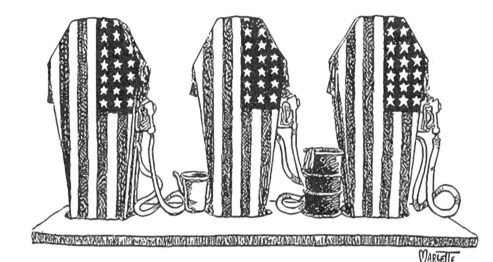

MARLETTE

and biological weapons outlawed by the civilized world. He has attacked two neighbors, including tiny Kuwait, and threatened Saudi Arabia and Israel. The United States is obligated by treaties and interests to stand by its allies. Although many Americans question the wisdom of Mr. Bush's policy, few question the need to constrain Saddam Hussein.

President Bush has defined victory clearly: This war will be over when Iraq has withdrawn from Kuwait, that nation is again ruled by Kuwaitis and Iraq has complied with the relevant U.N. resolutions.

The war is not just our cause. Our effort in the Gulf, unlike our effort in Vietnam, has the overwhelming support of the community of nations, expressed in numerous U.N. resolutions. And it has the support of most of the Arab nations, who recognize Saddam Hussein as the only Arab leader to attack another Arab nation.

There are reasons to argue about U.S. policy, and that debate will continue even as our men and women fight. Hardly anyone who protests Mr. Bush's policy is in any sense anti-American. The vast majority are patriotic Americans who believe this war is not in the best interests of this nation or the world. They are not betraying our fighting men and women; they want them to be safe at home.

The freedom for this debate to continue even in wartime is one of the reasons America is worth fighting for. Here, protesting the government's policy will put you on television. In Iraq, it will put you in a shallow grave.

George Bush's Finest Hour
An editorial in The Charlotte Observer Feb. 28, 1991

The war is over. The allied coalition has won a clear, swift military victory, putting Iraqi forces to rout and forcing Saddam Hussein to remove his troops from Kuwait, the tiny neighbor he invaded seven months ago.

What Iraq plans to do in regard to other U.N. mandates is unclear. But the fighting is over if Saddam Hussein wants it to be over. There is time now to deal with the other matters, and the possibility of continued sanctions if Iraq proves reluctant.

This is George Bush's finest hour. He said from the first that Iraq's aggression would not stand. He created an international coalition pledged to making Iraq pull out and pay for its rape of Kuwait. Saddam Hussein tried to split the coalition by attacking Israel, appealing to Muslim unity and offering numerous cease-fire proposals that fell short of complying with the U.N. resolutions. But the coalition's resolve remained firm and its mission remained clear: to remove Iraq from Kuwait. The Arab partners in the coalition resisted Saddam Hussein's appeal to Arab unity, correctly branding it ethnic demagoguery from a desperate tyrant who, after all, had started the war by crushing an Arab neighbor.

The allied military forces used brilliant strategy and overwhelming force to pound Iraqi troops relentlessly from the air until the outcome of the land battle was a foregone conclusion. The performance of the military coalition, made up mostly of U.S. forces, was extraordinary.

President Bush proved an exemplary war leader. Through the United Nations, he shaped clear and achievable war aims. He left the military operations to military commanders, and followed through on every deadline he set for Iraqi action. He held the coalition together in support of the war aims until Iraqi resistance collapsed.

Do not be misled, however, by the blessedly small allied death toll. This was a costly war, horribly destructive of life and treasure. The extent of devastation to civilians and cities in Iraq is not yet known. Nor can we yet estimate the carnage in Kuwait. Reports of mass killings and monstrous actions against civilians were rampant in the final days of battle. The extent to which Kuwait was destroyed during the struggle to liberate it is as yet unknown.

War – even a just war in which a vicious aggressor is defeated – is an awful enterprise. This military success does not erase the diplomatic failures that preceded it. Nor should the swift victory suggest that the Mideast's problems are solved. Securing peace and stability in the region will be much more difficult than winning the war.

Nevertheless, the war has been won, the aggressor has been vanquished. President Bush chose his course and completed it masterfully. The free world's thanks go to the brave men and women who did the fighting. We are proud and grateful for their courage and skill. Our prayers go to the families who lost loved ones, no matter whose side they were on.

May the high cost of even this swift victory remind us of the horror of war, and renew our commitment to devote our intelligence, energy and resources to finding peaceful means of securing freedom and justice in the world.

Bill Clinton

Clinton for President (1992)
An editorial in The Charlotte Observer Oct. 1992

Any presidential election is a referendum on the incumbent. This year, the polls consistently have shown that voters don't think George Bush deserves another term. We don't either.

If Mr. Bush had shown half the vigor and commitment in confronting domestic problems as he showed in confronting Saddam Hussein, he'd be a shoo-in for reelection. Instead, he has seemed a prisoner of the status quo. Although he talks of leading America into a new world order, he offers no compelling vision of how to do it.

Mr. Bush is in trouble because the U.S. economy is in trouble:

- He has presided over the three largest annual budget deficits in history. The federal debt is a record $4 trillion and growing.
- There are fewer private-sector jobs now than when Mr. Bush took office.
- The economic growth rate under Mr. Bush has been the lowest for any administration since Herbert Hoover's.
- Last year, the real median family income was $1,600 lower than in 1989. The wealthiest 1 percent of Americans now control more wealth than the bottom 90 percent; wealth is more concentrated than at any other time since the 1920s.

Mr. Bush could not have prevented all these problems, but his response to them gives no reason for confidence.

In his area of greatest interest, international affairs, Mr. Bush has done better. He was masterful in leading the multinational coalition against Saddam Hussein. As the Cold War ended, some critics say he stuck too long with Mikhail Gorbachev; perhaps, but the situation was far from clear. If Mr. Bush missed some opportunities to make the situation better, he also avoided the risk of making it worse.

Voter interest in foreign policy, however, pales beside voter alarm over the economy. Mr. Bush understandably has tried to shift attention to issues he considers more favorable to him: experience, trust and character. Here again, his record undercuts his efforts:

- His experience with Iraq also includes strengthening Saddam Hussein almost until Hussein attacked Kuwait.
- New information about Mr. Bush's role in the Iran arms-for-hostages deal, and the breaking of his "read-my-lips" no-tax pledge, raise doubts about his trustworthiness.
- Mr. Bush's current attempts to tarnish Bill Clinton's character raise questions about his own. Mr. Bush and his surrogates are trying to make voters think of Bill Clinton as at best unpatriotic, at worst an undercover agent of the pre-Gorbachev Kremlin. This has alarmed even some Republicans, who fear that by embracing the tactics of the paranoid right, Mr. Bush may strengthen the party's increasingly strident neo-McCarthyite fringe.

H.L. Mencken observed years ago that "The whole aim of practical politics is to keep the populace alarmed (and hence clamorous to be led to safety) by menacing it with an endless series of hobgoblins, all of them imaginary." Mr. Bush seems likely to create enough hobgoblins between now and Nov. 3 to make every day seem like Halloween.

Bill Clinton presents an attractive alternative. As governor of Arkansas, he is well-schooled in the agony arising from a lack of good jobs. He has shown that he knows how to get things done with limited resources, how to run a government and how to unite opposing factions behind a plan for action.

In June, a *Newsweek* survey of governors voted him America's best governor. His most prominent cause has been education: He is a leader of the national school reform movement, and he co-chaired President Bush's national education summit in 1989.

Though Republicans portray him as a tax-and-spend liberal, the record says otherwise. Like former governors Jim Hunt of North Carolina and Dick

Riley of South Carolina, he is a Southern progressive: pro-business, moderate to liberal on social issues and neither fiscally loony nor a captive of party extremists.

We recommend Gov. Clinton after considering three major concerns:

1. The next president must make fiscal responsibility a high priority. The Democrat-controlled Congress has been a willing partner with the Reagan-Bush White House in running up horrendous deficits. We think, however, that giving one party the responsibility for fiscal sanity will be better than dividing the responsibility and enabling each party to blame the other for the mess.

2. Mr. Clinton promises to take on America's biggest challenges: health care, jobs, education. Democratic presidents with such ambitions sometimes have pursued them by mandating one national approach for everybody. On some problems that works. On others, it is costly and ineffective. Private enterprise, with the proper incentives, often can do better than a government agency. On many issues, states need money but not mandates. Bill Clinton knows this. As a governor, he has had a crash course in the burdens of federal mandates.

3. Gov. Clinton has little experience in international affairs. Three factors reassure us. He is a good student. He has surrounded himself with capable advisers. And many of America's international problems (such as the economy) are rooted in domestic problems (such as poor education and unfocused government policies) that Gov. Clinton seems amply prepared to deal with.

Another point in Gov. Clinton's favor is his choice of Sen. Al Gore as his running mate. Sen. Gore strengthens and balances the ticket primarily by his qualifications and not just by his political appeal to a particular geographic area or constituency.

Four of the last eight vice presidents have ended up in the White House, two by succession and two by election. Four years is long enough for Americans to have to live with someone of such obviously limited abilities as Dan Quayle a heartbeat from the presidency.

Changing horses in midstream may be risky, but it's even riskier to cling to a horse that has no sense of direction and is sinking fast. We think Bill Clinton can do better.

Clinton for President (1996)

An editorial in The Charlotte Observer Oct. 27, 1996

Bill Clinton seems to be, alas, many of the things his critics say he is. Yet he is, we think, the right choice for president.

Our reason is simple. It goes back to the cry that House Republicans raised in 1995 when they were new to power and behaving like unruly students who had taken over the schoolhouse. The cry was essentially this: If we had a Republican in the White House, we could do everything we want.

That struck us as scary, for what many of them had in mind was a series of ill-considered, unwise changes that would have substantially weakened protections for the environment, for workers and for consumers, given big tax cuts to the well-to-do, made draconian changes in public welfare, and on, and on.

Resistance in the Senate no doubt would have moderated some House actions, but the strongest barrier to Republican congressional excess was the Democrat in the White House.

More change is needed in Washington. But change should come after full debate and consideration of the effects. The nation is at peace and the economy is healthy. Mr. Clinton offers the best opportunity to maintain a steady course.

Bob Dole, the alternative, promises to radically alter the present course with, for example, a 15 percent tax cut, which he promises he would accompany with a balanced budget. Mr. Dole's sudden fondness for supply-side economics – a cure-all he had scoffed at for years – made him appear opportunistic. We doubt that his plan would work without much deeper cuts in social programs than most Americans want. And, worse for Mr. Dole, many voters doubt that he believes it would work.

Mr. Dole's ideas have not caught on with the public, so the real race for president has not been between Bill Clinton and Bob Dole but between Bill Clinton and Bill Clinton.

That's some contest. In his one term, the public has seen at least three Bill Clintons: the liberal Democrat, the fiscally conservative New Democrat, and now the moderate Republican. For Mr. Dole, the inconsistency of embracing supply-side economics is a shocking departure; for Mr. Clinton, inconsistency is a way of life.

So why endorse him? Because in a rapidly changing world, the federal government has an important role to play – a role many Republicans in Congress and Mr. Dole seem unwilling to accept, if not unable to see.

The next president and Congress, hamstrung by the national debt, won't launch great programs, but they will face many challenges. For starters, Medicare and Social Security must be rethought and reworked.

Even more challenging, we think, will be problems created or worsened by the changing world economy. Some 42 million Americans are without health insurance now. That number will grow. Many workers who have steady jobs are seeing their employer-provided benefits shrink or vanish. Under pressure from competitors and investors, many corporations have abandoned any sense of loyalty to hard-working, long-term employees. Competition from abroad may erode the economic security of the middle class. The revolution in public welfare may leave many Americans with neither work nor public assistance – a potential disaster for poor children. Many families will need help that won't be provided by simply reducing their tax bill.

In an era of big commerce, big financial institutions and global competition, individual citizens are at the mercy of forces they cannot hope to influence. The interaction of those forces is creating challenges for America that won't be solved by the invisible hand of the free-enterprise system. The federal government should not be the nation's nanny; but in the face of national needs, it should not be paralyzed and impotent because of ideology or lack of imagination.

Mr. Clinton is rightly known as the Kerri Strug of the political flip-flop, but on some difficult issues he has chosen a tough course and stuck to it. He generated the Democratic support needed to approve the North American Free Trade Agreement and the General Agreement on Tariffs and Trade, policies that will create some problems but are in this nation's long-term interests. In Haiti, he stopped the bloodshed and brought at least temporary stability. He helped Mexico through a financial crisis and intervened in Bosnia to stop the carnage. To the dismay of many congressional Democrats, he joined Republicans in making a balanced budget a top priority. He outraged many Democrats by supporting fundamental changes in the welfare system. We think some of those changes went too far, but fundamental overhaul was needed. Now the 50 states will be free to devise better

KEVIN SIERS ©1998 THE CHARLOTTE OBSERVER

ways of dealing with poverty and need. The federal government must be ready to help if states can't meet their obligations to the needy.

Mr. Clinton's empathy with ordinary citizens is often caricatured, but it is an asset for a national leader. In challenging times, Americans want someone in the White House who is not too obsessed with global strategy to care about the lives, and needs, of ordinary people.

Our greatest concern about Mr. Clinton is not what we know but what we don't know. If he is re-elected, investigations will swarm about him like mosquitoes in a swamp. Who knows what, if anything, they will turn up?

In the best of all worlds, we'd prefer someone of Gen. Colin Powell's unquestioned rectitude in the White House. The election is not, however, simply a referendum on Mr. Clinton's reputation. It is a choice between different visions about the role of the federal government in national life. Looking at the vision offered by Mr. Clinton, and comparing it to the one put forward by Bob Dole, Newt Gingrich and the Republican Party platform, we favor the re-election of Bill Clinton.

Clinton No Model of Virtue

An editorial in The Charlotte Observer Feb. 6, 1998

Hardly anyone who voted for Bill Clinton was under the impression that he was a model of virtue. His record was distressingly clear. He tried marijuana but "didn't inhale." He agonized over how to avoid the draft while preserving his political future. His history of philandering introduced us to Gennifer Flowers and made a top adviser fret about other possible "bimbo eruptions" during the '92 campaign. Mr. Clinton has a cherubic smile, but there's a streak of deviltry in him.

Republicans knew this and tried to use it against him, but the voters weren't buying. Why? Not because character doesn't matter, but that, to many voters, other things matter, too – and perhaps matter more.

Many ordinary citizens feel the top politicians are out of touch with the realities of everyday life. Many people saw in Mr. Clinton a politician who felt their pain and understood their hopes and believed government could help them. When asked, "Which candidate has admirable character," many voters answered, "Bob Dole." But when asked, "Who understands and cares about you," more voters answered "Bill Clinton." They looked at what the candidates offered and voted for Mr. Clinton.

Americans are cynical about politics, and it's easy to see why. Look at what we've learned about our leaders. The mistresses of FDR and possibly Ike. The sexual athleticism and possible mob connections of JFK. Lyndon Johnson's corruption. Richard Nixon's illegal abuse of power. Sexual harassment in Congress. Bipartisan fund-raising outrages. And on, and on. And now the Clinton stories.

Americans don't look to politicians for moral examples. Instead, many voters hold a utilitarian view of government. They ask how politicians would serve them. In 1992 and 1996, Bill Clinton did not persuade Americans that he was a man of flawless character. He persuaded them that as president, he'd do his best to understand their needs and develop policies to meet them.

Voters did not issue Mr. Clinton a deportmental blank check, however. His approval ratings are high now, but the polls suggest that many people simply have suspended judgment until the facts are in.

So there the matter stands. The people who from the beginning considered Mr. Clinton unfit for office still do, and are appalled that their fellow citizens disagree. Judging from the polls, those fellow citizens thus far simply care less about flaws in the man who holds the job than they do about his success in getting the job done.

Clinton is a Liar and a Fool

An editorial in The Charlotte Observer Aug. 18, 1998

Bill Clinton is a brilliant politician, a philanderer, a liar and a fool. He had a sexual affair with a former White House intern and lied about it, not only in a sworn legal deposition but also to his friends, his family and the American people.

For months he let his supporters defend him though he was living a lie. His dishonesty caused them anguish and cost some of them heavily in legal fees. In the process he damaged his presidency and betrayed Americans who entrusted him with the nation's highest office.

Finally, in a brief speech that was contrite but also combative, legalistic and vague, he admitted his deceit and apologized for it.

What next? Most Americans who voted for Mr. Clinton knew, or at least suspected, he'd had sexual relationships outside his marriage and lied about them. While that no doubt mattered, in the voting booth other things mattered more. They elected him, re-elected him and, polls show, strongly support his policies.

When the rumors about Monica Lewinsky surfaced, many Americans had no trouble believing them, and no more trouble putting them in the context of what they wanted from a president. Mr. Clinton was damaging himself and his family and friends, but he stood for many things the public considered important, and the nation was in good shape. Voters separated their approval of his performance in office from their disapproval of his private behavior.

The Lewinsky matter, however, didn't stay private. Because Mr. Clinton denied it in a sworn deposition, the affair was drawn into Kenneth Starr's investigation of possible obstruction of justice arising from other matters. The inquiry took the nation into areas of a president's life where most Americans clearly did not want to go – and surely will not want to go again.

Mr. Clinton's desire to put this matter to rest is understandable, but the court of public opinion won't render the final judgment. Mr. Starr soon will report his findings to the House of Representatives. It may cover not only the Clinton-Lewinsky affair but such other matters as:

- The Clintons' involvement in two failed Arkansas businesses, the Whitewater Development Co. and the Morgan Guaranty Savings and Loan.
- Possible White House misuse of FBI files.
- Possible obstruction of justice in the Lewinsky matter, in the handling of Vince Foster's papers after his suicide, and in the payment by companies close to the president of hundreds of thousands of dollars in consulting fees to Mrs. Clinton's former law partner while he was facing a prison sentence and Mr. Starr was pressuring him to cooperate in the investigation.

Mr. Clinton's conduct has been deplorable. Whether he should be impeached, however, is a judgment that must await Mr. Starr's full report.

Bill Clinton is an intelligent, talented and tragically flawed president. He is quite skilled – and, unfortunately, quite experienced – at wriggling out of embarrassing situations. He has shown he can look Americans in the eye and lie. For his sake, and for our nation's, let's hope when he looks Americans in the eye from now on, he'll tell the truth.

Sad Spectacle? Yes. Tragedy? No.
An editorial in The Charlotte Observer Dec. 16, 1998

There's a simple reason why the American people think the U.S. House is nuts to impeach President Clinton. It is this: The public retains a sense of proportion that has been lost by politicians and pundits who are hell-bent on impeachment. The public knows that for a president, there's a difference between lying about an illicit sexual affair and, for example, illegally misusing the CIA, FBI and IRS to try to conceal crimes and punish political enemies. Both acts are wrong, but only one involves the grave threats to the nation referred to as "high crimes" by the Constitution.

Yet the Republicans, unable to defeat Mr. Clinton at the polls and regularly embarrassed by him during political confrontations, apparently will try to do through the impeachment process what they couldn't do through the political process. Some will do so because they consider it their constitutional duty; for others, it will be an act of political malice.

We are in the midst of a sad spectacle: sad because of the inexcusable behavior that left Mr. Clinton disgraced and vulnerable; and sad because of the zeal with which his political opponents seek a punishment that does not fit the crime.

A sad spectacle, yes. A national tragedy? We think not.

What if, as seems inevitable, the House approves one or more articles of impeachment? The case will go to the Senate, beginning what many observers fear could be a long and costly national nightmare.

But will it? The Senate trial could, and should, be brief. The arguments are clear. No one anticipates new evidence. The senators' first responsibility will be to decide whether the charges against Mr. Clinton, if true, constitute a "high crime." We'd bet more than a third of them would say no, and the matter would end there. Or they might opt for some form of censure.

Or suppose, contrary to expectations, the Senate voted to oust the president. We think that would be a constitutional travesty the nation would come to regret. But however foolish and wrongheaded, it would not be devastating to our country. America has lost better presidents under worse circumstances. Abraham Lincoln died with the nation bitterly divided only five days after Gen. Robert E. Lee's surrender. Franklin D. Roosevelt died while World War II raged on.

The ouster of Bill Clinton would be nowhere near as jolting. America is prosperous and at peace. Far more people oppose impeachment than are loyal to Mr. Clinton. Al Gore, a man of similar political views, is amply prepared to assume the presidency.

We hope the House will either vote down impeachment or agree on a punishment more appropriate to the crime. If it doesn't, then let the process proceed. Whatever happens, the nation will survive.

Why Not Censure?

An editorial in The Charlotte Observer Feb. 11, 1999

Nowhere does the U.S. Constitution give the Senate authority to censure –

that is, condemn or reprimand – a president. Nowhere does the Constitution forbid it, either, and there's precedent for it. If the senators want to censure Bill Clinton for actions they determine don't merit his removal from office, they should do so.

Opponents of censure offer several arguments against it. Some say it sets a dangerous precedent that could alter relations between the executive and legislative branches. Others say it is an empty action, carrying no real penalty.

They are right. It is not the business of the Congress to rate the president's actions like a panel of judges flashing scores at an ice skating competition. Nor does a censure resolution carry any tangible penalty.

What censure would do is recognize that extraordinary times may demand extraordinary actions. Even if Mr. Clinton's misdeeds do not merit his removal from office or lead to criminal charges, he certainly has failed in a significant and appalling way to live up to his responsibility. If the senators feel contempt for his actions, as most Americans do, there's no reason they shouldn't express it as a group. Yes, such a "sense of the Senate" expression should be used sparingly; but twice in two centuries (the first was against Andrew Jackson) would not be excessive.

No, a censure resolution wouldn't impose a penalty on the president. That isn't its purpose. Assuming the Senate does not vote to remove Mr. Clinton from office, a sharp, clear censure resolution could dispel any conclusion that the senators therefore found him not guilty.

Other senators argue that impeachment and trial put a sufficient stain on Mr. Clinton's record, rendering censure unnecessary. That is a reasonable argument, but voting not to oust him carries an imprecise message. A censure would make it clear that the senators agree there was ample and compelling evidence of reprehensible actions, even if they did not conclude those actions required his removal from office.

Mr. Clinton's reckless, dishonest behavior justifies a strong rebuke from the Senate and from the American people. The senators surely will state their conclusions individually. If they can muster the majority needed to express it in the form of official censure, they should do so, and resolve this sordid matter in a way that cannot be misunderstood.

After the Vote

An editorial in The Charlotte Observer Feb. 2, 1999

Washington insiders are betting that unless Monica Lewinsky, Vernon Jordan or Sidney Blumenthal says in a deposition that "I lied because the president promised to appoint me to the Supreme Court if I'd cover for him," the U.S. Senate won't kick Bill Clinton out of office.

If they're right, what happens next?

What should not happen, in our opinion, is a Senate "finding of fact" concluding that Bill Clinton's actions were crimes. Certainly the president tried to mislead everybody at every turn, but whether his offenses amount to crimes is a matter for a court to decide, not a body of 100 elected officials who are at least as interested in politics as justice.

Yet that's what some senators propose as they discuss voting on "findings of fact" about Mr. Clinton's actions. They want to find him guilty of the crimes alleged in the House indictment even as they vote not to remove him from office.

The senators should reread the Constitution – especially the parts about separation of powers. The Senate has one duty in this process: to decide whether to remove the president from office. Anything else the senators do will be an ad hoc response to the current situation.

That's fine if it means a resolution of censure, sternly criticizing Mr. Clinton for his misdeeds. While that would impose no legal penalty, it could be a powerful bipartisan expression of contempt for Mr. Clinton's contemptible actions.

It's not fine if the senators attempt to usurp the role of the courts by saying that the president is guilty of perjury or obstruction of justice.

Why? Because the Senate has not conducted a full and fair trial, and could not do so. All the senators have so many conflicts of interest that they would not be allowed to serve on an impartial jury. Neither their rules of evidence nor their process would meet a court's standards for a fair trial.

The senators should vote for or against removal and, if they wish, adopt a censure resolution, but they should not make a pseudo-legal ruling on Mr. Clinton's guilt. To do so would be a politically motivated constitutional travesty. Leave criminal trials to the judiciary.

Bush's War: 2003

A Just War Against Terrorism
A column in The Charlotte Observer Sept. 30, 2001

Some of my fellow Christians are pacifists. I'm not. I can't imagine a military action more justified than an effort to defeat terrorists whose declaration of a holy war against America and Americans led to the slaughter of thousands of innocent people in attacks on the Pentagon and the World Trade Center.

Some religious people who rightly oppose violence seem to me to be confused about the appropriate use of force. Theologians since the time of St. Augustine have drawn moral distinctions to define the just use of force. They recognize that humans are imperfect, driven by lust for power into the abuse of others. This is particularly true of groups, including nations, that in their quest for power and wealth disregard principles of common justice.

The United States is no less vulnerable to this temptation than any other nation, and often has succumbed to it. But the fact that our history is not pure does not make our quest for justice in this instance less compelling.

The principles of just war require us to have just cause for action and to act in a just way. Clearly, the attacks that were aimed at civilians and succeeded in killing thousands of them provided a just cause. Pursuing it justly requires that we focus on the planners and agents of this massacre, not on innocent civilians, and that we use force as a last resort.

No war is without sin. In a recent discussion of a potential U.S. military response, a questioner asked if attacking the terrorists was morally permissible if we killed even one innocent person. A Catholic bishop turned the question around. He asked, what if not attacking for fear of killing a small number of innocent civilians allowed terrorists to launch another attack that killed thousands of innocent civilians? As the bishop suggested, the principles of just war require a consideration of proportionality. We must ask ourselves what is likely to happen if we do attack, but we also must consider what is likely to happen if we don't.

The ideals of love and justice are easy to espouse in the abstract, but not so easy to live up to in a world where reality creates hard choices. Is it loving and just to refrain from using force if doing so permits terrorists to slaughter defenseless civilians?

Consider what Reinhold Niebuhr, the great Protestant theologian of the mid-20th century, said to religious nonparticipants in the war against tyranny: "Your difficulty is that you want to try to live in history without sinning," he said. "Our effort to set up the Kingdom of God on earth ends in a perverse preference for tyranny, simply because the peace of tyranny means, at least, the absence of war."

Failure to use force to oppose terrorism not only would seek peace at the expense of justice, it also would fail to stop the violence. It would only permit the agents of violence to execute their plans without fear or danger.

But people of conscience must understand that improper use of force in pursuit of justice can lead to injustice, too. How it is done, with what goals and in what spirit, makes all the difference.

I consider force to be morally neutral. It can be used for good or bad purposes. Surely no one would consider it wrong to use force to protect yourself or your family against unprovoked attack. I think that applies equally to the use of force to protect innocent fellow Americans against attack.

The fact that use of force is morally permissible does not mean it is mandatory. Force should be the last resort. President Bush's efforts to combat terrorism by pressuring governments not to offer terrorists support or refuge, and his commitment to crippling them by cutting off their sources of money, are both politically sensible and morally sound.

But will such measures deter the terrorists associated with Osama bin Laden? I take the terrorists at their word. They call America their enemy. They vow to kill Americans. They define their mission as a holy war. They are not subject to the pressures that might dissuade a government from hostile actions.

The use of force in the volatile Middle East can produce unforeseen reactions, many of them bad. That does not mean force should not be used, only that it should not be used thoughtlessly.

The best case for use of force has been made by the terrorists themselves.

If you think love and justice forbid the use of force against murderous terrorists, imagine that you are one who lost loved ones at the World Trade Center.

Don't Rush into War (2003)

A column in The Charlotte Observer March 16, 2003

The Bush administration, so focused and well-organized on most matters, has approached the problem of Iraq with all the control and directness of an elephant on roller skates. It will take a diplomatic miracle to create a broad coalition to confront Iraq's threat to stability in the Middle East.

The cause of the American clumsiness was the Bush team's inability to unite behind a workable approach to the problem. First the administration seemed eager to go it alone against Iraq. Then the president decided to seek international support through the United Nations, while making it clear he reserved the right to invade Iraq no matter what the U.N. decided. U.S. troops began massing near Iraq. When Germany and France presented problems, Defense Secretary Donald Rumsfeld insulted and alienated America's traditional European allies one by one. His actions inspired the thought that the best national security use for duct tape might be a strip across his mouth.

So here we stand, troops battle-ready, diplomacy in disarray, and Saddam Hussein hoping that once more international indecisiveness will let him off the hook.

The urge to act swiftly is strong. Military experts fear a long wait would erode our armed forces' readiness and make war a riskier enterprise. But even at this late date, President Bush should keep working to forge an international commitment to disarm Iraq.

The danger posed by Saddam is not a Bush hallucination. The Iraqi tyrant has twice invaded neighboring nations. He has developed weapons of mass destruction. Though his oil-rich nation has no need of nuclear power, he has long sought to develop nuclear capability. If he'd had nuclear weapons when he invaded Kuwait, that misadventure might have ended far less favorably.

To save his skin in 1991, Saddam agreed to rid Iraq of weapons of mass destruction and to accept U.N. inspections to make sure he did so. He didn't keep his commitment, and the U.N. imposed a trade embargo on Iraq. The embargo did great harm to his people, but Saddam failed to keep the promises that would have lifted it.

Eventually his resistance led to withdrawal of U.N. inspectors, leaving Iraq free to build and stockpile weapons outside the gaze of world authorities. Iraq readmitted U.N. inspectors only when President Bush put the threat of U.S. military force behind the U.N. mandates. If the threat of force is removed, why would anyone doubt Saddam would see it as another victory and continue to rebuild his arsenal?

Any decision to invade Iraq must be based on a number of difficult judgments. Does Iraq under Saddam pose too great a threat to world peace and order to ignore – or will it, if freed of U.N. restrictions?

Would a U.S.-led attack on Iraq ignite a widespread hostile reaction in the Islamic world, setting off a wave of terrorism aimed at America and its allies?

Would post-Saddam Iraq secure order, justice and economic opportunity for its citizens, or would simmering animosities lead to wars among political and religious factions that could be prevented only by a long military occupation by the United States and its allies?

Bush is satisfied that the gain of disarming Iraq and ousting Saddam is worth the risks. I have far less information than he, but to me the risks seem so great that the United States should not proceed before building an international coalition to deal with Saddam and with Iraq after he's gone.

Is Saddam really so great a threat? President Bill Clinton, who bombed Iraqi weapons sites in 1998, thought so. In 1998, he explained why.

Clinton said, "What if he fails to comply [with U.N. orders] and we fail to act, or we take some ambiguous third route, which gives him yet more opportunities to develop his program of weapons of mass destruction? Well, he will conclude that the international community has lost its will. He will then conclude that he can go right on and do more to rebuild an arsenal of devastating destruction. And some day, some way, I guarantee you he'll use the arsenal."

Clinton was right. Bush is right. The international community must stand up to Saddam.

Yes, hot weather is coming in Iraq, but it doesn't last forever. It is more important for President Bush and the United Nations to do this right than to do it soon.

How Not to Go to War

A column in The Charlotte Observer March 23, 2003

The national unity that comes when America sends its sons and daughters to war does not mark the end to the struggle at the highest levels over how this nation will conduct itself in world affairs. At most, it's a pause to allow the principal antagonists to focus on the battlefield.

On one side are the multi-nationalists, represented in President George W. Bush's Cabinet by Secretary of State Colin Powell and outside the White House by George Bush the elder and his closest foreign policy associates.

On the other side are the lone wolves, represented in the current administration by Vice President Dick Cheney, Defense Secretary Donald Rumsfeld and his assistant Paul Wolfowitz and a passel of neo-Reaganite editors and writers such as William Kristol centered at *The Weekly Standard*, a lively Washington-based political affairs magazine.

The fundamental difference of opinion is this: As the richest, most powerful nation on Earth, should the United States set its own course in world affairs, breaking tradition, voiding treaties and scoffing at consultation and compromise as a way of doing business? Or should America wear its power more modestly, working as a member of the community of nations to seek multinational accords as a way of conducting its affairs?

America is so powerful it could function either way, and each way offers its own costs and benefits. What America can't do, without seeming petulantly hypocritical, is attempt to function both ways. Yet that's what America did in the run-up to the war with Iraq. As a result our leaders appeared arrogant, insincere and adolescent.

Here's an example. The lone wolf crowd always wanted to topple Saddam Hussein. There are reasons aplenty to want him out, heaven knows. It was how they wanted to make it happen that made them unusual. They wanted to just link up with any nation that offered to help and then do it by force. Never mind the United Nations. Never mind that Saddam posed no direct threat to the United States. Never mind the possible repercussions for other nations in the region, or the excitement an invasion would provoke among terrorist groups. Never mind any obligation to persuade allies that attacking Iraq was wise, or to reassure other nations that there was some standard other than Uncle Sam's whim to determine whether America might invade them.

On Iraq, the lone wolves eventually won the president's support. But he kept one foot in the multilateralist camp, too. He sent Colin Powell to try to win U.N. support for invading Iraq. Cheney made it known he thought going through the U.N. was silly.

Powell did win unanimous support for a forceful but vague ultimatum to Iraq. But President Bush made it clear that he reserved the right to invade Iraq no matter what the U.N. Security Council did. Freed from the expectation that what they did made any difference, members of the Security Council behaved in a way that justified Vice President Cheney's dismissal of them.

The United Nations isn't a world government. It provides a forum for member nations, and a mechanism to enable them to work together to meet global needs. Our nation should not entrust its national security to a group governed by other nations' political needs and international grudges.

But sometimes even the world's most powerful nation needs friends. This nation's No. 1 international priority – the war on terrorism – demands an unprecedented degree of close and careful international cooperation. And in the pursuit of international terrorists, France – a foe of America's efforts on Iraq – has been an invaluable ally. On such important matters as the global environment, the worldwide pursuit of justice and international relief of hunger and suffering, the United Nations plays an invaluable role.

If the United States becomes known as a nation that's interested in working with others only if it can have its own way, it may find others less willing to provide help when America needs it. A strong nation willing to bully others may get its way even when it's wrong. A great nation protects its own vital interests while working with others to advance the common good. America is the world's strongest nation. I hope it can also become the greatest.

After Saddam, Then What?
An editorial in The Charlotte Observer March 23, 2003

Don't be misled by the early days of the war with Iraq. There's little doubt about the eventual outcome – the United States and its allies will win – but Saddam Hussein and his elite troops can make that victory incredibly costly if they're determined to do so.

Saddam has assembled his best and most loyal fighters in Baghdad, apparently preparing for a bloody last stand. He has never shown concern for the suffering of his people. There's no reason to think he'll do so now. He may put innocent and defenseless Iraqis in harm's way so he can portray his attackers as monsters. As his end draws near, his last hope may be that world opinion, shocked by the horror of war, will save his life.

Despite the difficulties ahead on the battlefield, the shaping of post-Saddam Iraq will be even more challenging. President Bush hopes to make post-war Iraq a model for the region – an orderly democratic state with a strong economy and opportunity for all. Such an Iraq would offer a welcome contrast in a region where the typical nation is ruled by a corrupt, authoritarian regime, where population growth is outstripping economic opportunity and political unrest is growing. But creating a new Iraq won't be simple or easy.

In the north, the Kurds have flourished under the protection of the U.N. no-fly zone. Many of them will want an independent Kurdistan – a possibility neighboring Turkey, with political unrest among its own Kurds, strongly opposes.

In the impoverished south, Saddam's Baathist regime has fiercely persecuted the Shiite Muslims. He massacred tens of thousands in putting down their 1991 uprising. For many Shiites, the top priority may be revenge. The Shiites will need substantial economic relief before they can focus on political arrangements.

Many talented Iraqi exiles, committed to a democratic Iraq, want immediate access to political power. But it has been decades since most of them lived in Iraq, and newly liberated Iraqis are unlikely to see their claim to power as legitimate.

The Iraqi army offers both problems and potential. Some of Saddam's closest supporters should face criminal trials, but among the military ranks are many of the well-trained and experienced Iraqis needed to run the nation. Will Iraqis accept a government that includes many who were so recently their oppressors?

Decades under Saddam have provided Iraq neither the structures nor the traditions that prepare a nation for democracy. As one observer noted, since 1968 the only political activity that wouldn't get you killed was unswerving allegiance to the Baath party.

What next? Should the U.S.-led coalition establish a military government and arouse memories of colonialism? Or move swiftly toward a democratic government in a diverse nation with no democratic tradition? Or put the U.N. Security Council in charge?

The mission now is simple: Defeat Saddam. There'll be nothing simple about creating post-war Iraq. Yet the ultimate test of the success of the allies' mission is not what happens to Saddam, but what happens to Iraq.

Why We Stood up to Saddam
A column in The Charlotte Observer Feb. 4, 2007

My Sunday school class at Myers Park Baptist Church is discussing what constitutes a just war, with a focus that will include Iraq.

In the murderous chaos that envelops Iraq, it's easy to forget what drew us into the war. Everyone remembers the weapons of mass destruction that were not found. But there was more. I looked back at columns and editorials I wrote in 2003 to refresh my memory. Here are some of the facts.

In December 2001, two French human rights organizations published a report titled "Iraq: An Intolerable, Forgotten, and Unpunished Repression." It reported that in 2000 the Iraqi regime launched a campaign of public beheadings of women accused of prostitution, or of opposing the regime themselves or having relatives who did so. The report documented about 130 women beheaded and warned the true number could be much higher.

John Burns, who reports for the New York Times from Iraq, addressed pre-war Iraq in his essay in "Embedded: The Media at War in Iraq" (The Lyons Press). Though President Bush made weapons of mass destruction and possible links to al-Qaida his principal arguments for invading Iraq, the war could have been justified "on the basis of human rights alone," Burns wrote. "This was a grotesque charnel house, and also a genuine threat to us. We had the power to end it and we did end it."

Remember the events that preceded the war?

In the late 1980s, Saddam Hussein's regime launched a campaign that led to the disappearance of tens of thousands of Kurds in northern Iraq (Kurdish authorities give the number 182,000 for 1988 alone). Saddam's forces razed Kurdish villages, launched poison gas attacks and slaughtered men, women and children or buried them alive in mass graves.

The Iraqi government built a nuclear reactor that an Israeli air attack destroyed in 1981 to prevent Saddam from using it to create nuclear weapons.

In 1990, Saddam invaded Kuwait. The first President Bush organized an international force to drive him out. In 1991, in return for a cease-fire, Saddam promised to disarm and admit U.N. inspectors to ensure he'd done so. Yet for more than a decade he misled and harassed inspectors and eventually expelled them. The U.N. imposed an embargo to pressure him to cooperate.

The embargo, intended to restrain Saddam, did more harm to the Iraqi people. A senior U.N. official estimated that 500,000 Iraqi children under age 5 had died of malnutrition and disease under the embargo. Those lives would have been saved if Saddam had cooperated with the United Nations.

The international community sought to make adequate food and medicine available to the Iraqis under the oil-for-food program, but the Iraqi regime blocked proper distribution. After the 2003 invasion, coalition forces found military warehouses full of supplies meant for the Iraqi people but diverted by Iraqi military forces.

Mark Bowden, author of *Black Hawk Down*, wrote about Saddam in 2003 in *The Atlantic Monthly*. "I really do think that Saddam poses a serious threat to the United States and the rest of the world," he wrote, "not that he will attack Israel or the United States directly, but if he possesses or develops nuclear weapons of mass destruction, I have no doubt that he will find a way to get those weapons into the hands of groups like al-Qaida and others who will use them. I think that in the interest of self-defense it's really important that we do something to end his regime."

In 1998, Bill Clinton said unless Saddam was stopped he'd believe the international community had lost its nerve and he could safely rebuild his arsenal. Clinton said, "In the next century, the community of nations may see more and more of the kind of threat Iraq poses now – a rogue state with weapons of mass destruction, ready to use them or provide them to terrorists. If we fail to respond today, Saddam, and all those who would follow in his footsteps, will be emboldened tomorrow by the knowledge that they can act with impunity."

History will judge America for what we've done there. History would have judged us for doing nothing, too.

Bush's Disastrous Foreign Policy
An editorial in The Charlotte Observer May 18, 2008

George W. Bush apparently believes his view of foreign policy is right and history will thank him for it. He clings to this view despite the fact that America's power in the world is diminishing, world opinion of America is increasingly unfavorable, and our nation's disdain for international alliances is mystifying to our allies and dispiriting to Americans who know the value of such alliances in pursuing our global interests.

Remember how the free world rushed to support America after Sept. 11, 2001? The European Union declared the attacks were "not only on the United States, but against humanity itself and the values of freedom we all share." The EU ministers said, "There will be no safe haven for terrorists and their sponsors" and pledged to "work closely with the United States and all partners to combat international terrorism." The NATO nations' ambassadors said the alliance would "stand ready to provide the assistance that may be required as a consequence of these acts of barbarism."

What did the Bush administration do? It said, essentially, no thanks, we'll handle it ourselves.

London's conservative Financial Times later wrote, "A disdainful refusal even to respond to a genuine offer of support from close allies, at the time of America's most serious crisis in decades, spoke volumes about its attitude to the alliance."

In March 2003, America invaded Iraq. By that summer international support for our nation had plummeted. A poll by the Pew Research Center reported that more than 70 percent of citizens in such generally friendly countries as France, Spain, Russia and South Korea thought America didn't take into account the interests of others. A majority in India, Brazil, Russia and South Korea saw us as more dangerous than Iran.

World opinion shouldn't dictate U.S. policy. Yet the Declaration of Independence, our nation's first statement of its values to the world, recognized the importance of "a decent respect for the opinions of mankind." America knew from the start that global relationships matter.

In a speech Thursday to the Israeli Knesset, President Bush touched on his foreign policy approach by creating a straw man to malign his critics. He said they would "negotiate with the terrorists and radicals" and be rewarded with "the false comfort of appeasement." Democrats, wary of being branded as gutless appeasers, reacted sharply, which no doubt pleased the president and his supporters. As long as the debate centers on whether Democrats are gutless appeasers, the spotlight isn't on President Bush's record.

Here's the record. The Bush administration has squandered international support, snubbed many allies and blundered into a war that is draining our treasury, eroding our values, killing our troops and strengthening our adversaries in the region. Our nation has failed to control its addiction to foreign oil, neglected to use its influence to help resolve the Israeli-Palestinian stalemate and virtually ignored environmental concerns that may be the biggest threats of all.

The president's commitment to deterring terrorism has been commendable; his methods often haven't. Overall, he won't leave America's standing in the world better than he found it.

Fire Donald Rumsfeld
A column in The Charlotte Observer Dec. 12, 2004

Were you as outraged as I was by Defense Secretary Donald Rumsfeld's response to the soldier who asked why troops were being sent into Iraq in vehicles that lacked adequate armor?

Specialist Thomas Wilson, a member of the 278th Regimental Combat Team of the Tennessee National Guard, took Rumsfeld to task Wednesday at a town hall meeting in Kuwait, where his unit was preparing to deploy to Iraq. "We do not have proper armored vehicles to carry with us north," he said.

Rumsfeld's response: "You go to war with the Army you have, not the Army you might want."

That's nonsense. You go to war with the Army the Pentagon provides. And the man in charge of providing is Donald Rumsfeld.

Rumsfeld added that the Army was "breaking its neck" to get armor protection to the front. That turns out to be nonsense, too. Armor Holdings, the company that makes armored Humvees, says it could step up production immediately, but has been waiting since September for the Pentagon to put in its order for more armored vehicles.

More than half the roughly 1,200 U.S. military deaths in Iraq have resulted from roadside bombs or ambushes from rocket-propelled grenades. A lack of armor on older vehicles has been blamed for many of the deaths.

Rumsfeld seems to be in denial.

Before the war, Army Chief of Staff Gen. Eric Shinseki said it could take "something on the order of several hundred thousand soldiers" to stabilize Iraq.

Deputy Defense Secretary Paul Wolfowitz called that estimate "wildly off the mark." Rumsfeld derided it in almost the same words – "far off the mark."

Rumsfeld was right that a small, mobile army could topple Saddam Hussein. But he failed to anticipate that such a limited force could not stabilize Iraq. Now terrorist bombers seem to have free run of the place. Shinseki looks prophetic.

Iraq's interim president, Ghazi al Yawer, summed up the feelings of many Iraqis some months ago. "We blame the United States 100 percent

for the security in Iraq," he said. "They occupied the country, disbanded the security agencies and for 10 months left Iraq's borders open for anyone to come in without a visa or even a passport."

Then there was Abu Ghraib. A blue-ribbon panel investigated and concluded that U.S. forces were unprepared for the chaos that followed the war and for handling the large numbers of soldiers, terrorists and criminals who were detained there. "We believe there is personal and institutional responsibility right up the chain of command as far as Washington is concerned," said former Defense Secretary James Schlesinger, chairman of the four-member panel.

There was no shortage of pre-war warnings of post-war chaos. They came from Iraq experts, generals, the State Department and the CIA. Pentagon officials didn't listen – and didn't plan. Trudi Rubin, a Philadelphia Inquirer columnist who has been to Iraq several times since the U.S. invasion, says Wolfowitz predicted to her that post-war Iraq would resemble post-World War II France. He expected the opposition headed by Iraqi exile Ahmed Chalabi to come back and establish a democracy. He believed there was little likelihood of post-war violence. Wrong, wrong, wrong.

Pentagon planners were so dismissive of the possibility of extended conflict that they sent tens of thousands of U.S. reservists to Iraq without adequate body armor or armored vehicles. The problem was brought home to our area by news from the 343rd Quartermaster Company, based in Rock Hill. On the morning of Oct. 13, members of the unit didn't show up for a convoy to northern Iraq because they said their trucks were ill-prepared and unarmored. They said their complaints to their commander were ignored. They could have been court-martialed for disobeying orders. Instead, the Army handed down only lighter administrative punishments.

Rumsfeld summarized his philosophy two days after Saddam's statue was pulled down in a Baghdad square. "Freedom's untidy, and free people are free to make mistakes and commit crimes and do bad things," he said. "Stuff happens."

So it does – and too much bad stuff has happened on his watch. President Bush is known to be loyal to his team. Loyalty is fine, but success is better. Rumsfeld has been wrong too long. The Pentagon needs new leadership.

Obama: 2008

We Recommend Obama

An editorial in The Charlotte Observer May 4, 2008

Do the Democrats need a restoration of the past, or is it time for a change? We think it's time for a change. We recommend a vote for Barack Obama in Tuesday's primary.

The choice between Sen. Obama and Hillary Clinton is not easy. She is indeed ready to be president on day one. After two terms with her husband in the White House and almost eight years in the Senate, she knows how things work. Smart and tenacious, she offers a progressive agenda. There are many reasons to think she'd be a good president.

There are arguments against her as well. For example, many Democrats won't forgive her for voting to authorize President Bush to use force against Iraq. We don't fault her on that. She understood the need for firmness to force Saddam Hussein to admit U.N. inspectors to ensure Iraq wasn't building weapons of mass destruction. She received assurances that force would be used only as a last resort. She isn't responsible for the debacle in Iraq; President Bush is.

Yet we're troubled by, to cite a few examples, these aspects of her presidential campaign. Many of her supporters seem intent on depicting Sen. Obama as the Jesse Jackson of 2008, a leader who appeals to an ethnic minority but not to the broader electorate needed to win. She sometimes exaggerates her influence and experiences, as when she claimed she "helped to bring peace to Northern Ireland" and said she ducked under sniper fire in Bosnia. Florida and Michigan were stripped of national convention delegates after breaking party rules by scheduling their primaries too early. The candidates didn't campaign in them. Yet after Sen. Clinton did well in those states, she pushed to change the rules and count the votes. That's a cynical, self-serving effort to corrupt the selection process. Her tendency to tell voters what they want to hear is disturbing. Her proposal to suspend the federal tax on gasoline this summer is campaign gimmickry, not leadership. Her assertion that she was a critic of NAFTA from the beginning is simply unbelievable. The record shows she was an ardent advocate of the trade deal.

Some Democrats accept that as just the way the political game always has been played. Perhaps it is. But is that the best Americans can expect? We think not.

As to Sen. Obama, he's one of the most powerful, effective speakers to seek the presidency in years. He offers a different vision of politics. Is he ready to be president? His relative inexperience is reason for concern. He has been a U.S. senator for three years, an Illinois state senator for eight. He has no executive experience.

Experience is important, but it's no substitute for good judgment and the ability to assemble and wisely use capable advisers. George W. Bush had six years' experience as governor of a big, complex state, yet his administration has made some of the worst decisions in recent history.

Sen. Obama is a man of uncommon intelligence. He's a graduate of Columbia University with a law degree from Harvard, where he was editor of the law review. He bypassed lucrative job opportunities to become a community organizer with a church-based group seeking to improve living conditions in poor Chicago neighborhoods plagued with crime and joblessness.

In 2004, he became the third African American since Reconstruction to win a Senate seat. His record there is not extensive. It is impressive. His first law – cosponsored with Sen. Tom Coburn, R-Okla. – ensured greater citizen access to information by creating a searchable online database on federal spending. Early in his term he attracted the attention of Sen. Richard Lugar, R-Ind., who at the time chaired the Foreign Relations Committee. Sen. Lugar invited him on a trip through the former Soviet Union, inspecting projects to decommission Cold War-era weapons. The two worked together to pass legislation to control the spread of weapons. Sen. Lugar later observed that Sen. Obama has "a sense of idealism and principled leadership, a vision of the future. At certain points in history, certain people are the ones that are most likely to have the vision or imagination or be able to identify talent and to manage other people's ideas. And I think he does this well."

Sen. Obama's legislative achievements are few, but that's no surprise. He's near the bottom in seniority. Republicans ran the Senate his first two years there, so Democratic proposals rarely went anywhere. Nevertheless he has helped shape the national debate on immigration, energy and some other important issues. He sponsored or co-sponsored the bills that made up what the Washington Post called "the strongest ethics legislation to emerge from Congress yet."

He has made missteps in his first national campaign, such as failing to quickly and firmly reject radical statements by his former pastor. But in the campaign, as in the Senate, he has shown the ability to learn.

Nominating Sen. Obama would send a powerful message to the world. He's the son of a white mother from Kansas and an absent father from Kenya. His personal story would make it plain that America is changing for the better. His appreciation of the need for international cooperation is a welcome change from the Bush administration's know-it-all, go-it-alone tendencies.

Many N.C. Democratic leaders recognize his strengths. State Treasurer Richard Moore and Lt. Gov. Bev Perdue, the party's leading candidates for governor, have endorsed him. So have U.S. Reps. David Price, Mel Watt and G.K. Butterfield, as well as Harvey Gantt, a former Charlotte mayor; Jim Phillips Jr., a Greensboro lawyer who chairs the UNC Board of Governors; and state Senate majority leader Tony Rand of Fayetteville.

Early in the campaign, Sen. Obama said, "We want a politics that reflects our best values. We want a politics that reflects our core decency, a politics that is based on a simple premise that we stand and fall together."

Yes, we do.

Beyond Jeremiah Wright

An editorial in The Charlotte Observer March 19, 2008

When Barack Obama began to speak Tuesday, his presidential campaign was in crisis. Issues involving politics and race were arising, and his family's longtime pastor, the Rev. Jeremiah Wright, was under fire for such inflammatory statements as this one, from a sermon following the terrorist attacks of Sept. 11, 2001:

"We have supported state terrorism against the Palestinians and black South Africans and now we are indignant because the stuff we have done overseas is now brought right back into our own front yards. America's chickens are coming home to roost."

Sen. Obama emphatically denounced "incendiary language" Mr. Wright used to express views "that have the potential not only to widen the racial divide, but views that denigrate both the greatness and the goodness of our nation and that rightly offend white and black alike."

But Sen. Obama had a larger purpose in mind: not merely to handle a political problem, but to talk about race and the future of America. In a quiet, insightful, at times powerful speech he examined the reasons for both anger and hope. It was a message our nation sorely needs to hear, and one he is uncommonly qualified to deliver.

It's hardly surprising that there is anger about the racism that for so long has denied so many black citizens access to the American dream. Sen. Obama spoke in Philadelphia, not far from where rebels in 1776 signed the Declaration of Independence – a magnificent assertion of human liberty that did not mention American slavery.

From slavery to years of legally enforced segregation and second-class citizenship, our nation's treatment of African Americans mocked its self-image as the land of the free. Yet over time, thanks to the brave efforts of many citizens, our nation has moved forward. In the relatively few years since the civil rights revolution, black Americans have risen to prominence in every sector of the nation's life, from business to academia to the arts to politics. Now Barack Obama, born to a black father and a white mother, has a chance to be president.

Anger over race is not limited to black America. Many whites are angry when they see their children sent across the city to integrate schools, or lose out on jobs or admission to universities because of affirmative action programs designed to remedy years of discrimination against blacks.

Sen. Obama acknowledged that. "The anger is real; it is powerful; and to simply wish it away, to condemn it without understanding its roots, only serves to widen the chasm of misunderstanding that exists between the races," he said. To move beyond anger, Americans "must realize that your dreams do not have to come at the expense of my dreams, that investing in the health, welfare and education of black and brown and white children will ultimately help all of America prosper."

Sen. Obama faulted Mr. Wright for not realizing that America's ability to change "is the true genius of this nation." So it is. The vision described by Sen. Obama and shared by many Americans will keep our imperfect nation moving toward its goal: liberty and justice for all.

VII. Senator No

Jesse Helms ran for the U.S. Senate five times and won every election, defeating some of North Carolina's most prominent Democrats. His supporters liked his fiscal conservatism, his strict moral judgments and his outspoken distaste for much of modern life.

For the Senate: No Choice

An editorial in The Charlotte Observer Oct. 29, 1978

Many North Carolinians consider Jesse Helms a fine senator. We don't. Though on some occasions we have agreed with his stands on issues, and we have often admired his honesty and his attention to constituents, we think he is so far to the right of the country's mainstream that he would have to hike for miles to even dip his toe in it.

However, the issue Nov. 7 isn't whether Mr. Helms is a good senator. The issue is whether to replace him with John Ingram.

We never thought the Democrats could nominate anybody who'd seem less than a welcome alternative to Sen. Helms. If there were a third choice on the voting machine – something like "Leave the seat open until better candidates come along" – we'd pull that lever unhesitatingly.

But that's not an option. Mr. Helms or Mr. Ingram will be our senator, and the two men are different. There are some arguments for choosing one over the other. We're not for Sen. Helms, but we know too little about Mr. Ingram. That a man could campaign so long and say so little is astounding. We have no way, therefore, to confidently argue that the choice is any more than an option to be hit in the head with a bottle instead of a brick.

Let's examine the candidates, and the differences.

In his long involvement in public affairs, Jesse Helms has been on the small-minded, regressive side of too many important disagreements to list here. The attempt to limit freedom of speech at the University of North Carolina, the racist campaign to unseat Sen. Frank Porter Graham, the rear guard action against racial equality – pick almost any attempt to impose backwardness on North Carolina, and the odds are that Jesse Helms, as politician or TV editorialist, has been for it. It's no accident that in 1972, the grand dragon of the N.C. Ku Klux Klan could endorse Mr. Helms, saying, "Jesse is a Christian and a great American."

Mr. Helms will pick up much support because of what he is not – a big-spending Democrat. Many North Carolinians who are staunch fiscal conservatives are flocking to his side. But if you're considering voting for Sen. Helms, remember that he is not merely a champion of the fiscal restraint now so much – and so properly – in vogue. Jesse Helms has long represented and appealed to the most anti-progressive elements in North Carolina. A victory for him is a victory for that cause.

We say all that with no rancor toward Mr. Helms. We have found him a genial, cooperative senator, and have admired his personal commitment to openness and straightforwardness in government. It is his politics, not his personality, that we dislike. His politics lack the humanity, compassion and appreciation of complexity needed in a U.S. senator. His jingoist approach to foreign affairs is not a benign oddity. We do not underestimate his power, as a leading spokesman of the extreme right, to poison the national foreign policy debate.

Many North Carolinians think John Ingram would be a good senator. We wish we could be optimistic about that. Close observers of Mr. Ingram – people whose judgment we trust – say he is arrogant, bullheaded, erratic, disorganized, disdainful of good advice, unwilling – or unable – to say much about most issues except his opposition to the "special interests."

Even many Democrats who support him think his tendency to make wild statements and drive away good people would make him a Senate laughingstock. Some longtime Ingram-watchers consider his demagogic tendencies dangerous. The best thing many of his backers say about him is that he would support President Carter more often than Sen. Helms would.

That's the choice: Reelect Sen. Helms, aptly described by the KKK grand dragon in 1972 as a man who "started as an ultra-conservative and ... hasn't changed one bit." Or replace him with John Ingram, who in many ways may be as bad, or worse.

Sen. Helms is an articulate, informed advocate of a political viewpoint we don't share. Mr. Ingram is an incoherent, unpredictable politician who, we can hope, might sometimes vote the way we consider right, particularly on foreign policy and legislation to help the poor and elderly. But he won't answer direct questions about where he stands on many issues. There are too

KevinSiers / THE CHARLOTTE OBSERVER
©1993

AUSTRALOPITHECUS

HOMO HABILIS

HOMO ERECTUS

HOMO SAPIENS

I DON'T
WANT NOTHIN'
TO DO WITH ANY
HOMOS!

THE EVOLUTION of JESSE

many unanswered questions about his conduct of the N.C. Department of Insurance, his tendency to cut corners and his personal financial dealings.

If Mr. Ingram had run a more open, informative campaign, we might urge voters to take a chance on him rather than return Mr. Helms to the Senate. But his "aw, shucks" grin is not enough for us. We can't in good conscience endorse either man.

Dear Sen. Helms ...

A column in The Charlotte Observer Aug. 26, 2001, after Helms decided not to seek reelection

Jesse Helms went to the U.S. Senate in 1973, the same year I joined the Observer as an editorial writer. I cannot say that over the years we have become close.

He has run for the Senate five times. The Observer's editorial board has never endorsed him (though in 1978 we didn't endorse his opponent, John Ingram, either). In a 1978 editorial, we called Helms "an informed, articulate advocate of a political viewpoint we don't share." That remains true.

A few years ago he called me "poisonous." He recently described me in a letter as someone who "obviously despises" him. I assume that's part of his continuing political war with the press and don't take it personally. I hope his first statement isn't true. I know the second isn't.

Though he has consistently declined my invitations to meet with the Observer's editorial board, in our occasional conversations he has been unfailingly cordial. After I helped the Jesse Helms Center with its book of editorial cartoons featuring him, he autographed a copy for my son.

Most of our contact has come through the mail. He is a witty and combative man who delights in tweaking the press. To give you the flavor of the relationship, here's an exchange that followed my inviting him to meet with the editorial board before the 1990 election.

April 23, 1990
Dear Ed:

Anent your letter of April 13, there may be some mutually convenient time during the campaign when I can stop by, but we'll just have to see.

In any event, reflecting upon the tenor and the ferocity of your editorials and news coverage for the past 18 years, I know you will forgive me for concluding that your minds are made up about the Senate race.

It may be that both you and I can spend our time somewhat productively. But as time goes by, we can assess that again.
Sincerely,
Jesse

April 26, 1990
Dear Sen. Helms:

We'd welcome you for a visit whenever it fits in with your schedule.

As to whether our minds are made up about the Senate race, a lot of that depends on the circumstances. In fact, I have always held out the hope that as you grow in wisdom and stature, you will come to see the world more the way we do. I will admit, I'm not betting my son's college savings on the chance that'll happen, but as we Baptists know, history is full of miracles.

At any rate, I've never thought I had to agree with my U.S. senator to benefit from talking with him. I do hope you'll drop by.

Sincerely,

Ed Williams

May 4, 1990

Dear Ed:

If you ever become disenchanted with The Charlotte Observer, or vice versa, I'll be glad to recommend you for a job writing for Johnny Carson. You have a fine sense of humor.

My folks really enjoyed that line, "As to whether our minds are made up." In fact, it barely edged out your suggestions that in order to "grow in wisdom and stature" it will be essential for me to "come to see world more the way we do." As Lou Holtz once said about your Raleigh counterpart: "They have the comic page for people who can't read, and the editorial page for people who can't think."

As for "benefiting" from talking with your U.S. Senator, bear in mind that I have repeatedly suggested that all of you editors might want to give me a ring and get my views on issues before launching into tirades. You have never once done so. Rich Oppel did come by once – and brought his dad.

Any time you want me to write to Carson, let me know. But don't infer that I have any influence with him.

Sincerely,

Jesse

May 15, 1990

Dear Sen. Helms:

Senator, that [the assertion that I never called him] just isn't true. I've talked to you at least four or five times over the past half-dozen years, most recently when I was writing about you and the Robert Mapplethorpe photos. On that occasion you and I talked at least 10 minutes. You invited me to stop by for lunch next time I came to Washington, and you volunteered to send me some of the Mapplethorpe photos. I said I'd never thought of you as a distributor of such stuff. You sent 'em anyway, and urged me to print them. I didn't.

Observer Associate Editor Jerry Shinn (a former Observer

Washington correspondent) tells me you wrote to one of our readers that you'd never met Jerry, when in fact he has met you and talked with you numerous times.

If I were a suspicious fellow, I might suspect you were trying to score political points by poor-mouthin' about mean ol' editorial writers who won't even show you the courtesy of talking with you. But I know that editorialists – yourself excluded, of course – are not memorable folks, so I assume you have simply forgotten these conversations. I hope this note jogs your memory.

Sincerely,

Ed Williams

May 22, 1990

Dear Ed:

Now let me set the record straight. You have never "given me a ring" – each time we've talked, it was I who placed the call, not you. I didn't "urge you to print" the Mapplethorpe photos, I asked only that you make them available to responsible citizens who might want to come by and see what I was talking about. And of course you didn't print them – and insofar as I know you never made them available to interested citizens.

As for Jerry Shinn, he must be a forgettable man. I don't recall ever having talked with him.

As for "about poor-mouthin' about mean ol' editorial writers" (another line fit for Johnny Carson), I don't mind you folks being mean. It's when you get nasty in your bias that intrigues me.

Hang in there! You may get me yet. And the luncheon invitation still stands.

Sincerely,

Jesse

May 29, 1990

Dear Sen. Helms:

Senator, I know this could go on forever, given your proven hardiness in the fine art of filibuster, but I beg to differ with you again. When we talked about the Mapplethorpe photos, for example, I had called your office to get a copy of your amendment. Perhaps since I talked with someone else before I talked with you, you may not have known who initiated the conversation.

I remember Sen. Sam Ervin saying something to the effect that sometimes a good forgettery is more valuable than a good memory. Senator, it seems to me that when it comes to conversations with Observer folks, you've got a pretty good forgettery.

I do hope you'll stop by and see us before the election. And next time I'm in Washington, I'll be ready for lunch.

Sincerely,

Ed Williams

June 8, 1990

Dear Ed:

You're right – this could go on forever. So this will be my final note.

I did not and do not know anything about your calling some unidentified person in my office. ... My chief legislative assistant was sitting with me when I called the editors at Greensboro, Raleigh, and Charlotte.

Since you have quoted Sam Ervin, let me do likewise. He was quite disgusted with the Observer because, he said, you folks declined to publish his side of the argument about the Genocide Treaty. So he told me that The Charlotte Observer reminded him of something Lum Garrison, a town character in Morganton, once said: "Those folks don't know nothin' – and they got that all tangled up."

Hang in there, you may get me yet.

Sincerely,

Jesse

June 11, 1990

Dear Sen. Helms:

I'm beginning to worry about the memory problem in your office. You have forgotten Jerry Shinn. You have forgotten the other times I called you. Nobody in your office can remember my call on the NEA [National Endowment for the Arts] matter.

Could somebody be putting funny chemicals in your office water cooler? (Come to think of it, that might explain a lot of things that come out of your office.)

Speaking of Sen. Ervin, whatever wranglings he had with the Observer about the genocide treaty were before my time. But I did have a good bit of contact with him after he had retired from the Senate.

Three years before his death, he sent me a long article in which he argued that South Carolina's claim to be Andrew Jackson's birthplace was spurious and North Carolina's valid. Since the article just arrived out of the blue, I wrote Sen. Ervin and suggested we condense it a bit and use it on Andrew Jackson's birthday, about five months hence.

A couple of days later I received a call from Sen. Ervin. He urged me to publish the piece immediately. "Why?" I asked.

He replied with a chuckle, "Because I'm 85 years old, and I may not be around in five months." We published his article the next week.

I also remember Sen. Ervin's comment about a jury that he bombarded with fact, analysis, biblical quotation, homespun humor and legal history but was unable to convince of the merit of his client's case. He lamented, "I had to teach them more than they were able to learn."

Sen. Helms, I think we've taught each other about all we're able to learn in this correspondence. My invitation to you is still open.

Sincerely,

Ed Williams

Proud to be 'Sen. No'

An editorial in The Charlotte Observer July 5, 2008

Jesse Helms, who died Friday in Raleigh at the age of 86, was not simply a politician, he was a force of nature.

Steadfast in his views and politically skillful, he was a powerful figure in our nation's politics. He also became a conservative icon, a symbol as well as a senator. Todd Rundgren and Loudon Wainwright III wrote songs about him. A gay filmmaker made a documentary about him.

His political savvy and the fund-raising might of his National Congressional Club made him an influential player in conservative politics. In 1976, when Ronald Reagan's pursuit of the GOP presidential nomination had stalled, the Helms machine helped him beat President Gerald Ford

in the N.C. primary, reviving Mr. Reagan's career and bolstering the conservative movement that swept him into the White House in 1980.

Jesse Helms ran for the U.S. Senate five times and won every election, defeating some of the state's most prominent Democrats. He told voters what he wanted to do if elected, and he did his best to do it. His supporters liked his fiscal conservatism, his strict moral judgments and his outspoken distaste for much of modern life.

He opposed Medicare as "a step into the swampy field of socialized medicine." He called Social Security "nothing more than doles and handouts." He branded Martin Luther King Jr. a communist collaborator who preached "hatred for America." He called the University of North Carolina the "University of Negroes and Communists" and advocated fencing it in to prevent contamination of the rest of the state.

In an era when most conservative Southern politicians were moving away from racist campaigning, he continued to exploit racial issues to solidify his white support.

He opposed court-ordered integration, homosexuals, modern art and most foreign aid. He was a fierce anti-communist and a supporter of many right-wing dictators. He personified what many international observers disliked about U.S. politics. For example, his effort to penalize Canada for trading with Cuba prompted the Ottawa Citizen to call him "a ranting anti-communist, a jingoist, a southern conservative nincompoop."

Denunciations bothered Sen. Helms not at all. He believed that if such critics considered him an enemy, they were right.

About Jesse Helms the man there was much to like – his personal generosity, his courtliness, his devotion to his family.

His staff's dedication to meeting constituents' needs was legendary. He pushed for much-needed reform of the U.N. Near the end of his career, influenced by the singer Bono, he became an advocate of greater federal funding to fight AIDS overseas. He said he was ashamed for not "doing something really significant" to fight the spread of AIDS.

Early in his career we called him an effective advocate of a political philosophy we did not share. We considered the way he practiced politics to be divisive and harmful to the state. Over the years his views did not change. Neither did ours.

EDITOR'S NOTE: *In 2012, four years after Jesse Helms died, John Dodd, the president of the Jesse Helms Center in Wingate, denied that Sen. Helms called UNC "the University of Negroes and Communists." Dodd said he could find no evidence that Sen. Helms ever said or wrote it and called the quote "a fabrication." Is he right? Well, the quote was used in countless books, magazines and newspaper and TV reports for more than a decade while Sen. Helms was alive, and the senator – who, I can attest, had no reluctance to tell writers they were wrong – never objected. My conclusion: Either Sen. Helms said it, or he was content to have people think he did.*

VIII. Rights

DON STURKEY

Charlotte Police Chief Frank Littlejohn (left) confronts Klansmen led by James "Catfish" Cole (center) protesting the Visulite Theater's 1957 showing of the movie *Island in the Sun*, which features an interracial romance. Though the influence of racist groups has waned, race remains a factor in North Carolina life.

Race

Only Whites Think Racism is Dead
An editorial in The Charlotte Observer July 27, 1989

In white America, it has become fashionable to believe that racism is a distasteful relic of the nation's past, like child labor or not allowing women to vote. When blacks argue that racial prejudice and barriers still exist, many whites consider them whiners who are seeking excuses to cover their own inadequacy.

Too bad those whites weren't with the teenagers from a Methodist camp who went to swim at the Saluda, S.C., Jaycees' pool recently. The white teens in the group were invited to swim, but not the blacks. That's the club's policy: No blacks allowed. Nobody swam, thank God. The group left. And the nation's outrage focused on the Saluda swim club.

Why the surprise? Racism still lurks just beneath the surface of American society. When it suddenly is thrust into view, Americans are horrified, as though someone had stood up at the table and spit in the casserole. But when racism remains polite and out of public view, many white Americans forget about it.

For example, country clubs in Charlotte, like the swim club in Saluda, remain havens of racism. Unlike the Saluda Swim and Tennis Club, however, they probably are sophisticated enough not to let such blatant displays of prejudice occur. They practice their racism quietly, politely. And Charlotte's leading citizens go along with it.

White Americans, try this: Imagine that you are a black parent who has suffered the pain of racism all your life. For a time you hoped America would expel this evil, but then the national commitment waned. America entered a state of ignorant complacency about racism. The Reagan administration denied that it existed, the Bush administration seems only superficially in-

terested in it and the U.S. Supreme Court seems blind to it. So now you know your children will have to endure the same prejudice that you did – perhaps expressed in different ways, but sometimes just as raw and vicious as in the old days.

If you were a black parent, wouldn't you be anguished? Wouldn't you be angry? Wouldn't you feel that whites who aren't part of the solution are part of the problem?

Country Club Bigots

An editorial in The Charlotte Observer April 18, 1990

There is an odd idea in circulation among some members of Charlotte's social, civic and financial elite. It is that even though they support or belong to country clubs that discriminate on the basis of race, gender and religion, they are not themselves supporters of racism, sexism and religious bigotry.

They try to create a distinction where none exists. They support those policies with their presence and their money. If they support racist, sexist, anti-Semitic clubs, they are supporting racism, sexism and anti-Semitism. It's that simple.

They may argue in their own defense that they are not bigots, it's just that someone else makes club policies. It seems fair, then, to conclude that they are willing to tolerate a little racism, sexism and anti-Semitism rather than cause a fuss or lose access to private tennis courts, golf courses and dining rooms. Apparently, pleading that they are tolerant of bigotry, rather than practitioners of it, makes them feel better. It shouldn't.

There always will be people who see others through blinders of bigotry. Clubs whose policies reflect that view might serve some useful purpose if they were identifiable as havens for self- professed bigots. But when community leaders are members, they give those clubs a patina of respectability.

We would propose this policy for every person and every business, professional and civic organization that does not support racism, sexism and anti-Semitism: Do not support racist, sexist and anti-Semitic clubs with your presence and your money. Do not use their facilities.

It makes no sense to argue that you oppose bigotry while you are supporting organizations that practice it. You may be fooling yourself about where your priorities lie. You are not fooling anyone else.

Of Nigger and Such

A column in The Charlotte Observer June 7, 1994

For whites, it's a forbidden word. Eddie Murphy can use it. Rappers in L.A. can use it. But a white person can't say "nigger" without being assumed racist – or at least stupid.

Never underestimate the power of words. They can be provocative. The Supreme Court, even in defending the First Amendment freedom of speech, recognizes that some words used in some situations are "fighting words."

Not long ago, "nigger" wasn't such a word, at least in the South. Whites assumed the right to use it. Few blacks were in any position to object.

Now it is. That transformation, from commonplace to unacceptable, reflects an astonishing shift in American attitudes.

When I was a boy, my family ran a small grocery store in a tiny Southern town. Among the goods we sold were cans of Niggerhead brand oysters. The label showed a caricature of a black man about to inhale one.

I remember an old black man we called Nigger Rimpson. In a box in the closet of my boyhood room, there's a fourth-grade essay of mine in which I unselfconsciously refer to niggers.

I remember coming home from school one summer, with all the growing awareness and naivete of a college sophomore, and asking a neighbor why we thought we were better than colored people. "Why," he said, incredulously, "because God made us better."

I have a lot of unlearning to do. I'm working at it.

There are signs of progress. Now the word "nigger" is a social profanity, unwelcome in intelligent circles. Usually it's safe to assume any white person under age 80 who uses the word does so with some malice.

But not always. A few days ago Jaguar, the British luxury car maker, suspended its top U.S. public relations executive for using the word in front of a group of journalists. Discussing the federal luxury tax on expensive cars, PR man John Crawford referred to rival Mercedes-Benz as "the biggest nigger in the woodpile." Jaguar immediately suspended him "pending review" and announced it deeply regretted the "unfortunate incident."

Crawford, who is from Australia, apologized, too. He explained that the phrase "is unfortunately in such common usage Down Under that it slipped out due to my own thoughtlessness."

There was a black reporter in the group, Warren Brown of the Washington Post. He said he didn't like what Crawford said, but wasn't offended. "It was clear to me that no offense was meant. ... He wasn't trying to put down me or any other black person," Brown said.

Language is potent stuff. Words like "nigger," "kike" and "queer" have always been used to dehumanize people, to mark them as inferiors or outcasts. When you use them, you define yourself. You're foolish if you don't understand that some words have too much power, too much history, to play around with.

I remember a confrontation between a black demonstrator and a white onlooker at a civil rights march I covered in the '70s. The poorly dressed white man and the black college student exchanged hot words. Then the white man delivered what he obviously considered the last word: "At least I ain't a nigger!"

The word was meant to wound, to silence. I don't know where it would have led if policemen hadn't come between the two.

Later I asked the student about the exchange. He said he'd been called worse. Then he smiled, and putting on broad accent, he added, "I shoulda tol' him, 'Yo' momma is!' "

But he didn't. I think I know why. Saying that would have been a powerful retort. But he wasn't interested in debating points. He was interested in healing.

A Stain on N.C.'s History
An editorial in The Charlotte Observer Nov. 17, 2006

In today's Observer you'll find the dispiriting story of a crucial event in North Carolina's history. Inspired by the report of a state commission, it tells how some of our state's most prominent citizens in the 1890s led a violent, racist campaign to wrest political power from a biracial coalition of their fellow citizens and went on to establish a system of white supremacy that for most of the 20th century would deprive black North Carolinians of political rights and economic opportunity. That system would begin to crumble only with the civil rights revolution more than two generations later.

The damage done at the dawn of the 20th century lingers today, providing sad validation of William Faulkner's insight into history's enduring grip on our region. "The past isn't dead," he wrote. "It isn't even past."

Our journalistic forebears at The Charlotte Observer fiercely supported the white supremacy campaign. So did many Charlotte political and civic leaders – some of whom today are honored by plaques and statues and commemorated in history books for their contributions to our state.

In a special section in today's Observer and some other newspapers in the state, Duke University historian Timothy Tyson tells of the bloody coup d'etat in 1898 by which white supremacists seized power in Wilmington. That city at the time was the state's largest, with a black majority, a black-owned daily newspaper and several black officials, including four of the 10 aldermen. He tells how many of the black political leaders and their white allies were killed, banished or forced from public life and many prosperous black businessmen were ruined if not run out of town. On today's Viewpoint page, Associate Editor Jack Betts examines the Observer's role in the campaign to restore white rule.

Taken together, the two accounts offer a sobering illustration of what can happen when men who appear to be the best and brightest of their day pursue a course that is selfishly, tragically, murderously wrong.

As is often the case in such atrocities, this one arose from fear. Conservative white Democrats had regained political control of the state after the federal government lost interest in Reconstruction following the 1876 election. But in the 1890s, economic hard times aroused discontent with a government run by a self-serving elite that did not meet the people's needs. A new coalition formed, made up of white old-line Republicans, rural whites ground down by hard times and blacks seeking political rights. The so-called Fusion movement won every statewide office in the 1894 and 1896 elections, gained control of the legislature and elected one of its white leaders, Daniel Russell, as governor.

The conservative business elite, including many in Charlotte, was alarmed by Fusion politicians' commitment to making government more democratic. Though blacks made up only a third of the state's population, business leaders felt threatened by a political system in which blacks and poor whites held the balance of power at the polls. So they adopted an age-old strategy: divide and conquer. To drive a wedge between blacks and white farmers, they conducted a statewide propaganda campaign portraying blacks as sexual predators and corrupt incompetents and fomenting fear of black domination.

In 1897, a Fusion leader serving in the U.S. Senate said the only way moneyed interests could recapture the state legislature would be for the Raleigh and Charlotte newspapers to get "together in the same bed shouting 'nigger.' "

The Charlotte Daily Observer and the News & Observer did so – with a vengeance. On today's Viewpoint page Jack Betts explains how the Observer used news reports and editorials to fan the flames of racial fear.

The Observer's position was no surprise. A newspaper is a commercial enterprise, and its publisher is automatically a member of the community's business leadership. D.A. Tompkins was the Observer's publisher and arguably Charlotte's most influential and best-known citizen. He was a passionate advocate of laissez-faire economics and industrialization. His views, expressed in countless speeches and articles, were widely admired in business circles in the region and beyond. One historian noted, "He fashioned the Observer into a powerful vehicle to promote Charlotte and his gospel of the New South."

Mr. Tompkins shared the racial assumptions of his time, reflecting a form of Social Darwinism that lumped all blacks, regardless of their accomplishments, into one category of social and intellectual inferiority. He believed in rule by Anglo-Saxon men.

Under Editor J.P. Caldwell, the Observer covered black institutions, ran stories about notable black residents and published letters and columns by black correspondents. But an editorial defined the Observer's view of the proper relationship between the races: "Well-bred, intelligent and right-minded white people do not dislike black people because they are black, but they are opposed to their bearing authority because it is not well for either race that they should. Indeed, no greater unkindness can be done the colored race than to put members of it in authority over the white. It angers the white man, excites race antagonism and spoils the negro."

The primary concern of Mr. Tompkins, Mr. Caldwell and the Observer was to make our city and state safe for business. After the white supremacist triumph, an Observer editorial proclaimed, "The business men of the State are largely responsible for the victory." A sense of entitlement was evident in an editorial's assertion that "once again the white man's party will take possession of that which is its right by every law of birth, intelligence and principle."

When in 1900 the newly empowered Democrats sought to amend the state constitution to strip blacks of the right to vote, an Observer editorial called the move "a struggle of the white people to rid themselves of the dangers of rule by negroes and the lower class of whites." The success of this movement created what a later historian would call a "progressive plutocracy." It stood for education, economic development, pro-business policies – and white supremacy.

An apology is inadequate to atone for the Observer's role in promoting the white supremacist campaign. But an apology is due. As Mr. Faulkner observed, the past is not dead. For much of the 20th century black citizens were denied political rights, adequate education and economic opportunity because of their race. The legacy of that era helped shape North Carolina for decades. Only in recent years has our state begun to reap the benefits of talented blacks' full participation in its economic, cultural and political life.

We apologize to the black citizens and their descendants whose rights and interests we disregarded, and to all North Carolinians, whose trust we betrayed by our failure to fairly report the news and to stand firmly against injustice.

Why Name UNC Dorm for a Slave?

A column in The Charlotte Observer April 2, 2006

University buildings usually are named for generous benefactors or famous alums. Why did UNC-Chapel Hill recently name one for a slave? Read on.

George Moses Horton was born into slavery about 1798 on William Horton's farm in Northampton County, up near the Virginia border. When years of tobacco farming depleted the soil, the master moved his family and possessions to Chatham County, eight miles from the young university in Chapel Hill. George was among the possessions.

In about 1817, his master permitted George, a young man of wit and ambition, to walk to Chapel Hill on weekends to sell fruit. Students saw the slave's uncommon ability and invited him to make speeches, which they cheered in boisterous condescension.

George saw he was being played for a fool and turned to another talent – reciting poems he thought up while plowing behind a horse in his master's field. Soon he began to compose acrostics, poems and love letters for sale to students. His letters went to some of the most sought-after young women of the Carolinas and Virginia. By the 1830s, he was earning enough from his writing to pay his master to let him live in Chapel Hill.

UNC President Joseph Caldwell provided odd jobs to supplement his income. Friends helped him get poems published in New York and Massachusetts.

He would become a man of historic achievement: the first African American to publish a book in the South; the first American slave to protest his bondage in verse; the only slave to earn significant income from selling his poems. An admirer, Gov. John Owen, offered $100 to buy him, but his master wouldn't sell.

Horton described his intellectual development in a book of his poems published in 1845 in Hillsborough. He wrote that as a boy he was "fond of hearing people read," but "had but little or no thought of ever being able to read or spell one word or sentence in any book whatever."

His mother learned of his interest and encouraged him, but had no resources to help him. He resolved "to learn the alphabet at all events; and lighting by chance at times with some opportunities of being in the presence of school children, I learnt the letters by heart."

He got hold of some old parts of spelling books. "Playboys," as he called them, warned "I was a vain fool to attempt learning to read with as little chance as I had. But with defiance I accomplished the arduous task of spelling" with no assistance.

"From this I entered into reading lessons with triumph. I became very fond of reading parts of the New Testament, such as I could pick up as they lay about at random; but I soon became more fond of reading verses, Wesley's old hymns, and other peices (*sic*) of poetry."

In the first few decades of the 1800s in North Carolina, many citizens and newspapers favored emancipation. Several cities had organizations that supported resettling former slaves in such places as Liberia and Haiti.

In 1829, a Raleigh press published a collection of Horton's poems, *The Hope of Liberty*. The publisher said he hoped the booklet would earn enough to buy the author's freedom so he could settle in Liberia. One poem, "On Liberty and Slavery," was a cry of anguish:

Alas! and am I born for this,
To wear this slavish chain?
Deprived of all created bliss,
Through hardship, toil and pain!

But sales of the book were small, and Horton's dream didn't come true.

When the war came, the campus was deserted, and Horton returned to his master's farm. In 1865, he published his final book, *Naked Genius*. The book found no market. Horton went north and is thought to have died in Philadelphia. There is no record of his death and no marker to show his final resting place.

Why name a dorm for him? UNC was the scene of his triumphs. But for the color of his skin and condition of his birth, he might have been a star student there, a professor, who knows what more.

Naming a dorm for him recognizes his achievements, but that's not all. It also provides a reminder of the loss our society suffers when, through oppression or neglect, people are deprived of the opportunity to make full use of their talents. Horton dorm may help teach that lesson at the school he loved but could not attend.

Jim Mcmillan's Passion for Justice

An editorial in The Charlotte Observer March 3, 1995

Judge James B. McMillan, who died here Saturday at age 78, belonged to an extraordinary generation of North Carolina leaders. Now in their 70s or older, they grew up in the state's small cities, towns and rural areas, where they learned to value reverence, education and hard work. Many of them studied at Chapel Hill or another of the state's fine colleges and universities. Many served in World War II and came home with a compelling conviction: that it was their duty to make the world a better place.

In this era of diminished expectations, that post-war idealism sounds almost corny, like something from an old Jimmy Stewart movie on cable TV. But the war had showed them the power of evil, and united them in the belief that the most powerful weapon against it was the strong will of good people, working in their own ways in their own communities. So they plunged into public life, seeking political office, serving on boards and commissions, leading religious and civic groups, supporting progressive agendas. They weren't deterred by the conflict of public affairs; they knew that progress does not come without it.

The best of their generation – and Jim McMillan was among the best – had strong ideals, about justice and personal responsibility and compassion for the less fortunate, and they tried to live by them. Joined by others of different ages and backgrounds but similar motivation, they led this state and nation to decades of breathtaking progress in the pursuit of justice for all.

It is only natural to have a high regard for a community that rewards and honors you as generously as this community did Jim McMillan. But to him, life was not about achieving recognition. It was about seeking justice, and within him burned a quiet passion for the task. He served two masters, his religion and the law, and he saw no fundamental conflict between them. When, as a federal judge, he reluctantly realized that the way his beloved community provided public education for its black citizens was appallingly unjust, he faced a choice: He could do what was popular, or he could seek justice. For Jim McMillan, there was no choice at all. He had made it long ago.

There are men and women in North Carolina today as good as Jim McMillan was. But there are none better.

CMS Abandons Diversity

A column in The Charlotte Observer Aug. 27, 2006

It is an eye-catching contradiction. Employers here strive to build workforces that look more like the people they serve and to work effectively with all racial and ethnic groups.

Community leaders were appalled when a national survey found Charlotte ranked woefully low in a category called "racial trust." Many groups are working on remedies.

Yet this community has abandoned efforts to promote diversity in public schools. Once among the nation's most integrated, now they are divided along lines of race and wealth. How our community reached this point is a story of demographic shifts, legal actions and conflicting values.

Beginning in the 1970s, Charlotte-Mecklenburg Schools based pupil assignment plans on a federal court order to integrate schools across the county to eradicate the effects of decades of segregation. Many students were assigned to schools far from their homes and provided bus service to get there.

In 2000, several school critics sued to seek an end to the court's supervision, asserting that CMS had erased the vestiges of legally mandated segregation. U.S. District Judge Robert Potter agreed. So did the 4th Circuit Court of Appeals. CMS would stop considering race in assigning students.

The pressures that led to the lawsuit had been building for years. County population was booming. Many new residents of the fast-growing northern and southeastern towns and suburbs came from other states and felt no responsibility for racial injustices of the Southern past. Where many came from, schools served a town, not an entire county. They were dismayed to find that wasn't the case here.

Eric Smith, the superintendent at the time, believed CMS was at a crossroads. In 1999, he told me he thought either CMS would respond to parents' concerns in a way that would make them want to send their children to public schools, or the children would go elsewhere – to private schools or to other counties.

Public opinion no longer considered school diversity a priority. Nor did the law. And neither did school leaders. In 2001, the school board adopted a student assignment system called the "Family Choice Plan." As my colleague Fannie Flono pointed out, that was a misnomer: The only guaranteed choice for most students was their nearby "home" school.

The result was predictable: Schools reflected their areas. Some were filled mostly with students from white, prosperous families; others had mostly black, low-income enrollments.

The shift in policy created the quandary described in last Sunday's story about Pam Grundy, the mother who tried to persuade three other white, prosperous, well-educated families to join her by sending their children to Shamrock Gardens. At that elementary school last year, 90 percent of students were nonwhite; nearly all qualified for free or reduced price lunches, a measure of poverty.

She didn't succeed. All sent their children to public schools – but to magnet schools, not the mostly minority, mostly poor neighborhood school. That's the choice made by many similarly situated families – a magnet school, if not a private school.

This year the school board approved a new vision statement. No longer did it pledge to make CMS "the premier urban, integrated system in the nation." It focused instead on providing a good education for all – a priority everyone surely shares. The only mention of diversity is in the 10th of a dozen "core beliefs." CMS is committed to "embracing our community's diversity and using it to enhance the educational environment."

That shift in emphasis also showed up in the report of a blue-ribbon committee on CMS schools co-chaired by architect Harvey Gantt, Charlotte's first black mayor and Clemson's first black undergraduate. It treated diversity as an option.

The report recommended creating a few schools that parents who want diversity could choose for their children. Enrollment in those schools, it said, should be "balanced socio-economically at a target of 40 percent low-income students."

I don't think many parents oppose diversity. They just value neighborhood schools more. That's understandable. But a community that values diversity can't ignore its importance in public education. Coercion is unacceptable. So is neglect.

Crime and Punishment

N.C. to be No. 1 in Executions?
An editorial in The Charlotte Observer Jan. 3, 1974

The need for legislative reform or repeal of North Carolina's death penalty laws has been obvious since 1972, when the U.S. Supreme Court ruled unconstitutional the death penalty as it was applied in most states.

Today, 44 inmates await death in prisons throughout America. Twenty-three of them are in North Carolina. No other state has more than eight. This state thus may become the national leader in executions.

Because of legislative inaction, North Carolina's capital punishment laws now rank among the harshest in the nation. The Supreme Court did not rule the death penalty itself unconstitutional. The court found that it had been applied unevenly by most states. Some criminals were executed for crimes less serious than those for which others received lesser punishment. It was this uneven application that the Supreme Court forbade.

With that in mind, the N.C. Supreme court decided this state's capital punishment laws could stand if they were applied evenly. So the court ruled that judges and juries have no choice. Under present state law, they must impose the death penalty in cases where it is an option.

Any person in North Carolina convicted of a capital crime – rape, first-degree arson, first-degree murder or first-degree burglary – must be given the death penalty.

We oppose capital punishment. But even those who advocate it in some cases find the North Carolina laws too harsh. They would favor the execution of Henry Jarrette, who murdered three people and tried to kill another. But some supporters of capital punishment recoil at the thought of executing Samuel Poole, a Moore County laborer who broke into an occupied home but stole nothing and harmed no one. Both men now wait on Death

Row, in the same prison.

Gov. James Holshouser is using his clemency power to postpone executions and give the legislature a chance to act. Last session the legislators could not agree on proposed reforms. Simple justice demands that they do so during the session beginning in two weeks.

EDITOR'S NOTE: *In 1977, North Carolina revised its death penalty law, and in the next few years a series of court decisions and legislative actions made murder with aggravating circumstances the only crime punishable by death.*

A Fatal, Unjust Lottery
An editorial in The Charlotte Observer Sept. 12, 2000

Why do critics call the death penalty the only legal lottery in the Carolinas? Easy: Its application varies widely and unfairly from place to place across the two states, a six-month Observer investigation points out this week in the series "Uncertain Justice."

Defendants accused of similar crimes are far more likely to face the death penalty in some judicial districts than in others. Some prosecutors seem far more likely to engage in unethical practices, such as hiding evidence, than others.

The result is a flawed system in which those on trial for murder in one district can expect to risk being sent to Death Row, while defendants facing a similar charge in another district can expect no more than a long prison sentence. The uneven application of the death penalty is the key reason the Observer has recommended that North Carolina and South Carolina adopt a moratorium on executions until authorities examine the record and take whatever steps necessary to ensure that it is carried out fairly. This is not an argument to abolish the death penalty; that is a different debate.

The Observer's investigation found alarming variations in death sentence rates from county to county in the Carolinas. Generally, rural and suburban areas were much more likely than urban counties to impose death sentences in murder cases. For instance, in Northampton County, in North Carolina's northeast quadrant, there was one death sentence for every six adult murder arrests during the 1990s. In Mecklenburg County, the state's

most populous, there was only one death sentence for every 52 murder arrests. In Lexington County, S.C., where the prosecutor has sent 20 men to death row since 1977, the rate is one for every eight adult arrests. In Richland County, next door to Lexington, prosecutors don't pursue the death penalty for an unpremeditated murder, a charge for which the Lexington prosecutor won a death penalty conviction for one defendant. Such differences are in the system, not the crime. The system is a geographical crapshoot.

Sometimes, prosecutors hide evidence that would have helped a defendant. Sometimes they make improper arguments. Sometimes they break the law, such as when one prosecutor's staff illegally bugged a defendant while he was talking with his lawyer. Sometimes the court-appointed defense attorney is too inept to protect his client's rights. Sometimes the courts reverse these convictions. And sometimes they let a death sentence stand, concluding that the action did not affect the outcome of the trial.

That's why the death penalty seems like a game with changing rules. Everything depends on who's running the game and where it is played, making the death penalty an uncertain sanction that applies only to some people in some places under some circumstances. That's not what it was meant to be.

Advocates and opponents of the death penalty have this in common:

neither wants to see anyone railroaded into an execution. Both want to see justice done. Yet in both states, our system of justice treats people who have committed similar crimes so differently that there is no system at all, just an erratic procedure too greatly influenced by where the crime was committed, how eager the prosecutor is to seek the death penalty and how skilled and committed the court-appointed defense lawyers are to see that their poor client gets as strong a defense as a rich client would. Until policymakers in the Carolinas make sure the death penalty is carried out fairly and evenly, it will remain the most flawed and immoral practice in the Carolinas' courts.

Justices are Unpardonably Wrong
An editorial in The Charlotte Observer Jan. 27, 1993

For years, the U.S. Supreme Court has been trying to tidy up its work. Particularly annoying to some justices have been those last-minute appeals of death sentences, in which lawyers strain for any possible way to snag the high court's attention and delay the execution, however briefly. The justices prefer to deal at their own leisurely pace with clearly presented legal choices, not with the messy pleas of desperate prisoners facing death.

That was the background Monday when the court ruled 6-3 against a Texas death row inmate who sought a hearing on a claim of innocence based on new evidence.

The case involves Leonel Herrera, who was convicted and sentenced to death in 1982 for the murder of two police officers. He tried to reopen his case last year by presenting testimony that a brother who had since died had been the killer. But Texas law allows only 30 days after a conviction for filing a motion for new trial based on undiscovered evidence.

The Supreme Court majority didn't consider the validity of the new evidence. They ruled only that there was nothing unconstitutional about the 30-day deadline. They showed no interest in whether Mr. Herrera would get a hearing. Instead, they fretted about forcing the retrial of cases on the basis of old evidence. They worried about the need for "finality" in capital cases. Justice Antonin Scalia even derided the notion that situations "shocking to the conscience" should be of concern to the court. This clearly is a court majority devoted more to procedure than to justice.

Surely nobody believes courts and juries don't make mistakes. Last year Northeastern University Press published a book titled *In Spite of Innocence* in which the authors recounted the stories of 416 Americans wrongly convicted of crimes punishable by death. Twenty-three of them were executed; the others spent years in prison before their innocence was established.

The justices' distaste for dealing with death penalty appeals is understandable, but who said they'd get to deal only with cases they were comfortable with? The Constitution and years of precedent have made the Supreme Court the court of last resort in cases involving fundamental rights. No right is more fundamental than the right to live. Yes, the death penalty is difficult to carry out. It ought to be. It's the one penalty for which the state, if mistaken, can make no recompense. The justices are unpardonably wrong to wash their hands of these cases.

N.C.'s Blind Justices
An editorial in The Charlotte Observer July 11,1983

The N.C. Supreme Court's 4-3 decision condoning police use of faked evidence to pressure a suspect to confess is terribly wrong, written as though its authors were wholly ignorant of human nature and blind to Southern history.

Thursday's ruling came in a case involving the rape and murder of a white woman in Raleigh in 1981. The man who confessed is black. The circumstances that led to the confession were at issue in the appeal. Raleigh police used a detective's blood to make smeared fingerprints on a knife identical to the murder weapon. They told the suspect the fingerprints were his. They also told him they had a witness who had seen him running from the scene. In fact, they had no such witness.

A Wake County judge ruled that the police tactics made the confession inadmissible as evidence. In overruling him, Justice Harry Martin, writing for the majority, noted that the suspect wasn't in custody, wasn't deceived about the crime and its possible punishment, had served time in prison before and was aware of his rights. Justice Martin concluded that the confession was voluntary and "not a product of hope or induced by fear."

That's possible. There is, however, another equally plausible possibility: that a black ex-con, knowing the passions that surround trials of black men accused of the rape and murder of white women in the South, knowing that the police planned to use faked evidence and a phony witness against him, concluded that to go to trial was to risk death, and so confessed to a crime he didn't commit, to save his life. That is the possibility cited in a dissent by Justice James Exum, with Chief Justice Joseph Branch and Justice Henry Frye concurring.

Justice Martin and the three justices who shared his view assert that the accused man's confession was not "a product of hope or induced by fear." It may be easy for white Supreme Court justices to dismiss Southern racial history as though it were a dusty relic of the past, rather than an active force in the present; we doubt that a black ex-con accused of a horrible crime can dismiss it so easily.

We agree with Justice Exum's conclusion: "Absent torture or other physical abuse, it would be difficult to conceive of interrogation tactics more likely to produce an untruthful, unreliable confession than the ones utilized in this case."

Clemency for Zane Hill?

A column in The Charlotte Observer July 19, 1998

Friends and neighbors in the Beaverdam community near Asheville agree that Zane Hill is a pretty good man when he isn't drinking. But he's an alcoholic, and once or twice a year he'd go on a binge.

His wife, Bonnie, stuck with him through his binges, his troubles with the law while drunk, his stays in detox centers and hospitals.

Finally, at the beginning of what would become a long binge, she'd had enough. They separated. Twice during the binge he threatened her. She obtained a court order to keep him away.

One day Zane called Bonnie several times. He understood her to say he could go to a trailer on their property. He drank beer all afternoon, waiting for her to come home. When she arrived, he went to the house – expecting, he said, that he could move back in. He had his rifle with him.

When he entered the house, he found not only Bonnie but their grown son, Randy. They argued. Randy was armed, too, with a pistol. Zane said Randy pointed the pistol at him. When Randy left the room to call 911,

Zane followed. Zane later said he believed Randy pulled his pistol, and he shot his son in self-defense. He assaulted his wife as she fled.

When Zane Hill came to trial, prosecutors offered to let him plead guilty to second-degree murder. He refused, maintaining he'd fired in self-defense. So he was tried for first-degree murder, convicted and sentenced to death. On appeal, state courts found no reversible errors in Hill's trial. The U.S. Supreme Court refused to review the conviction.

I haven't personally investigated this case. What I know comes from written reports and from a man who's hardly impartial: Harold Bender, a renowned Charlotte lawyer who's working on Hill's appeal.

But from what I know, the Zane Hill case raises a fundamental question: Is this the kind of killing for which our state enacted the death penalty?

- Bender, who's been involved in many murder cases, thinks not.
- The prosecutors thought not – they offered Hill a second-degree charge if he'd plead guilty.
- Many people in Beaverdam think not. They visit him in prison.
- Bonnie Hill thinks not. They're still married. She visits him regularly in prison. She lost her son. She doesn't want her husband killed.

Working on Hill's appeal, Bender concluded that "everybody had treated this as a second-degree murder trial." Jury selection took only a couple of days, not the two to three weeks usually required for the thorough questioning of prospective jurors in capital cases. Pre-trial motions usually filed in a capital case weren't filed, Bender says. The trial took less than a week. The defense didn't call a lot of witnesses Bender says he'd have called, particularly during the sentencing phase. The jury didn't hear some evidence that Bender considers vital – such as that Randy Hill had showed his father the pistol.

Hill's lawyers have a few more legal cards to play, but the appeals process looks only at the conduct of the trial, not at the appropriateness of the result.

Hill is scheduled to die Aug. 14. His fate is likely to be up to Gov. Jim Hunt, who has the power to commute his sentence – to reduce it from death to life imprisonment.

Randy Hill died defending his mother. Zane Hill committed a horrible crime. He deserves severe punishment. But he's 62 years old. If he isn't executed, he'll die in prison. His community isn't demanding his death. His wife, the mother of the victim, wants his life spared. The prosecutors were willing to let him live. All this has not been the case with others North Carolina has executed.

Some argue that the judicial process worked, and Gov. Hunt shouldn't interfere with it. That's simply wrong. Our state constitution, ratified by vote of the people, explicitly includes the governor in the process by empowering him to commute sentences "upon such conditions as he may think proper." If Hunt commuted Hill's sentence, he wouldn't be interfering in the process, he'd be exercising his responsibility as part of it.

Jim Hunt is the only N.C. governor this century who has never commuted a death sentence. If the governor's inquiry finds the facts to be as I have stated them, he may agree this is a time for clemency.

EDITOR'S NOTE: *Gov. Hunt denied the clemency plea. Zane Hill was executed on Aug. 14, 1998.*

Gays

At Last, Court Decriminalizes Gay Sex

An editorial in The Charlotte Observer June 30, 2003

The U.S. Supreme Court did Thursday what it should have done 17 years ago. It ruled that while to many Americans gay sex may be morally offensive, they may not express their disapproval by making laws that put homosexuals in prison.

The court's sweeping 6-3 decision [in a Texas case] strikes down laws against anal and oral sex across the nation, including in North Carolina, where those acts are illegal for heterosexuals as well as homosexuals. In reaching that conclusion, the court explicitly overturned its ruling in a 1986 case that said just the opposite.

Few individual beliefs are more deeply held than those concerning sexual right and wrong. Yet over time society's attitudes change. Fifty years ago, every state had an anti-sodomy law. Since then, 37 states have either repealed those laws or had courts block their enforcement. Georgia, the state that gave rise to the 1986 case, later repealed the law the high court had upheld.

In states that still have the laws, including North Carolina, they are spottily and often selectively enforced. Even Justice Clarence Thomas, who dissented from the court's decision because he finds no "right of privacy" in the Constitution, called the statute "uncommonly silly" and said if he were a Texas legislator he'd vote to repeal it.

Justice Anthony Kennedy, writing for the court majority, invoked that right of privacy in overturning the law. Homosexuals, he wrote, "are entitled to respect for their private lives." Therefore, "The state cannot demean their existence or control their destiny by making their private sexual conduct a crime."

Justice Antonin Scalia, another dissenter (with Chief Justice William Rehnquist), complained that the court "has taken sides in the culture war." Tom Minnery, vice president of Focus on the Family, went further. "If the people have no right to regulate sexuality, then ultimately the institution of marriage is in peril, and with it, the welfare of the coming generations of children," he said.

That's almost comically farfetched. Ask yourself: Do men and women marry each other because they're forbidden to have sexual partners of the same gender? Hardly. Decriminalizing gay sex won't make it irresistible to heterosexuals. In fact, concerns about the future of the family would be better focused on heterosexuals. The greatest threat to the traditional family is not anything homosexuals do but the fact that more and more heterosexuals are choosing to live together and have children without marriage.

The court's decision will upset many Americans, but it will liberate many other Americans from fear that police will jail them for, as Justice Thomas put it, expressing their sexual preference through noncommercial, consensual conduct with another adult. The United States is distinguished by its bias in favor of individual liberty. The court's ruling is consistent with our nation's evolution toward increased personal freedom.

Mecklenburg's Gay 'Threat'
An editorial in The Charlotte Observer April 23, 1998

The upcoming election for Mecklenburg County commissioners has revived the debate over the present board's cutoff of funds for the Arts and Science Council, a decision made after a fierce argument about homosexuality on April Fool's Day last year.

By focusing primarily on ASC funding, the present debate misses a larger point. Even more important is how our county's elected leaders deal with homosexuality – among our citizens, in the arts and in the use of public facilities.

America's attitude about homosexuality is changing. Although the U.S. Supreme Court a few years ago upheld a Georgia law making homosexual acts a crime, public opinion is becoming more tolerant. Many corporations now provide health insurance for employees' homosexual partners. Major

We the STRAIGHT People

religious denominations are rethinking their policies on homosexuals. Many cities and some states now prohibit discrimination against them.

As the nation moved toward tolerance, five of our county commissioners, after a discussion memorable for ignorance and fear-mongering, lurched in the opposite direction.

The commissioners' official position on homosexuality may eventually affect far more than arts funding. The commissioners oversee such public facilities and services as Spirit Square, the public library and the health department. Will their attitude toward homosexuality lead to homophobic restrictions in these areas? Will it affect hiring and treatment of homosexuals?

Commissioner Hoyle Martin, whose crusade won the votes of commissioners Tom Bush, Bill James, Joel Carter and George Higgins, was the board's expert on the gay "threat." He asserted that "the traditional American family is the gay community's declared enemy." He claimed knowledge of a "homosexual agenda" that includes efforts to "undermine the values of the traditional American family" and a plan to "make Charlotte the Sodom and Gomorrah capital of the East Coast." He'd prefer, he said, to "shove them [homosexuals] off the face of the Earth."

He wasn't alone. Commissioner Joel Carter's dislike of homosexuality and what he called the "artsy-fartsy crowd" prompted him to propose selling

Spirit Square center for the arts. "The majority of people who do most of the performing in that place are homosexual-type people, plain and flat simple," he explained. Asked how he knew, Mr. Carter replied, "I don't know. It's just a perception that they are, or are sympathetic to, homosexuals."

Mr. Carter isn't worried that his hostility will generate a political backlash. Business and civic leaders "are going to be branded homosexual if they come after me too hard," he predicted.

The commissioners' attack on arts funding was unwise, but their descent into hysterical homophobia was worse. At present, these men and this hostile attitude represent our county. The upcoming elections give voters a chance to change that.

What if Your Child Were Gay?
A column in The Charlotte Observer July 3, 1991

Marcia Solomon of Charlotte called me some months ago to ask if I'd be on the program for the international conference of Parents and Friends of Lesbians and Gays here in October. She wanted me to do what I do for a lot of groups: explain how newspapers work, answer questions about how community groups can interest the media in telling their stories.

I said yes immediately.

The group, a letter from Mrs. Solomon informed me, is "firmly committed to the preservation of families in loving relationships, to the education of society regarding homosexuality, and the advocacy of full human and civil rights for our homosexual children."

I may not agree with everything they advocate, but from what I can tell they don't want their children beaten by homophobic thugs. I agree with that. They want their children to be able to work and earn their keep. I agree with that. They are trying to love their children despite difficult circumstances. I sympathize with that.

Still, I must admit that I felt a tiny edge of uneasiness. I grew up, as many of you did, in a small, rural town. I went to a fundamentalist Southern Baptist church; for 10 years, I never missed Sunday School. I shared the prejudices of my community – the unquestioning acceptance of the status of blacks, the wariness about Jews and Catholics, the feeling that homosexuals ("queers," we called them) were worthy only of ridicule and contempt. I was wrong about a lot of things, I know now.

I have never encountered any mincing queens who flaunt their sexual preference to shock the straitlaced. But over the years, I have known many homosexuals, and my most common feeling about them has been sympathy.

When a bright young editor here – a gentle, nonthreatening, slightly built young man – was beaten by a thug because he was homosexual, I couldn't understand why on God's earth any human being would do that to another.

When a local restaurant fired a good worker because – and only because – he admitted he was homosexual, it made me angry.

And as the "Concerned Charlotteans" now try to force the Omni Charlotte Hotel to bar the parents and friends of gays from holding a convention here, I wonder where these presumptuous guardians of Charlotte get the idea that they are serving God by tormenting the parents of gays.

After Mrs. Solomon asked me to be on the program, I tried to imagine how I'd feel if I learned my son was homosexual. I'd feel shock, I'm sure, and anger, pain, and embarrassment. I'd pray it wasn't true. I'd mourn the loss of grandchildren, the end of the family line. I know I'd blame myself: What did I do wrong? I'd probably try to find other parents who'd had the same experience, and seek solace and understanding from them.

And I think – I believe – I would continue to say to my son the last words I've said to him almost every night for the first eight years of his life: "I love you all the time."

Scouts vs. Gays

An editorial in The Charlotte Observer June 30, 2000

The U.S. Supreme Court has upheld the right of the Boy Scouts of America to bar gays from leadership positions and, presumably, from membership, but the victory may come at some cost. Many supporters of scouting see the anti-gay policy as a fundamental change in an organization they assumed was open to all.

And no wonder. Many gay men speak warmly of their youthful days in scouting. Many organizations that don't discriminate against gays sponsor troops that don't discriminate, either. In fact, the lawsuit that reached the Supreme Court involved the ousting of an assistant scoutmaster who had been an Eagle scout and as an adult leader was well-liked and widely admired – until scout officials learned he was gay.

The lack of a stated anti-gay policy caused the justices to split 5-4 on the case. The dissenters didn't argue that a group with an anti-gay policy had to accept gay leaders; they argued that the scouts never had the "clear, unequivocal statement" of policy necessary to satisfy the law. They were right on that point.

The Boy Scouts have had a valuable place in American society, teaching generations of boys the rudiments of outdooring and schooling them in important values. The scouts would have better served America's youth by welcoming all boys who want what scouting offers, and by seeking leaders who value those teachings. Now, however, the scouts have made their discriminatory policy plain. That clear statement must prompt many supporters to reevaluate their relationship with the organization.

For example, the Boy Scouts' Mecklenburg County Council and Central N.C. Council are among the agencies that receive money from United Way of Central Carolinas, which now is conducting its annual fund-raising campaign. Much of the campaigning is done by corporate volunteers who ask fellow employees for pledges to be collected by payroll deductions. Many of those companies have policies that bar discrimination against gays. Will companies that oppose such discrimination want to raise money for an organization that practices it? Will gays who are loyal United Way supporters want their money going to an organization that considers them unfit to participate?

Many churches and civic organizations sponsor scout troops. Will civic organizations and churches with gay members want to sponsor a youth group that says gays aren't welcome?

If discrimination against homosexuals is now the 13th Scout Law, local scout groups that have enjoyed broad public support must make clear where they stand: Are gays unwelcome?

Amendment One Confuses Supporters

An article in Creative Loafing April 24, 2012

Recent polls show that the people of North Carolina favor allowing same-sex unions. Yet the numbers also indicate that on May 8, voters are likely to approve a state constitutional amendment that would prohibit such unions.

What, exactly, is Amendment One? What would it do? Why is it coming before North Carolina voters now? And why, despite public opinion opposing its effect, does it seem likely to pass?

Backers of the amendment say it is needed for the "protection of marriage" and would align our state with 30 others whose constitutions define marriage as a legal union between a man and a woman.

In fact, the amendment would do much more. In addition to defining marriage, it would forbid the state's legislators and judges to recognize – in any way – any form of domestic legal union other than traditional marriage. That prohibition would apply not only to same-sex couples but also to unmarried male-female couples, who make up some 90 percent of the 222,000 unmarried households the 2010 Census found in our state.

The radical ban would go farther than the constitutional marriage provisions in all but three states. It even goes too far for some conservatives.

U.S. Rep. Renee Ellmers, a Republican from Dunn with libertarian leanings and strong Tea Party support, opposes it because she sees no reason to ban civil unions. John Hood, president of the conservative John Locke Foundation in Raleigh, wrote that amending the constitution "to forbid gay and lesbian couples from receiving any future legal recognition, including civil unions, is unwise and unfair." Robert Orr, a Republican former justice of the N.C. Supreme Court, said "it's probably not a provision that ought to be in" the constitution. And Richard Vinroot, the former Charlotte mayor who was the Republicans' candidate for governor in 2000, said it is "unnecessary and may have serious unintended consequences."

North Carolina law already defines marriage as a legal union between a man and a woman. If the amendment fails, same-sex marriage still won't be legal. But a legislative majority can change laws, and judges can overturn them. Advocates say amending the constitution is necessary to keep traditional marriage safe from so-called activist judges and reform-minded legislators. Changing the constitution isn't easy: It requires support by three-fifths of the state House and Senate and approval by voters.

But does North Carolina really need a stronger constitutional protection than Mississippi, for example, whose constitution defines marriage as being between a man and a woman and stops at that?

Yes, according to Republican Rep. Paul Stam, a Raleigh lawyer and co-author of the proposal. He said North Carolina has learned from "failures" in other states, like California, where in 1999 the state legislature authorized a same-sex union, called a domestic partnership, that granted the same rights as marriage.

Amendment One would prohibit cities and counties from granting employee benefits to same-sex and unmarried male-female partners. It would block any future legislature from giving such couples some or all the rights granted automatically to married couples in matters such as inheritance, child custody, property ownership and health-care decision-making.

Maxine Eichner, a specialist in family law at the UNC law school, worked with others there to publish a 27-page analysis of the amendment last year. "It is impossible to predict definitively how broadly courts would interpret the Amendment's prohibitions, given its vague and untested language," they wrote. "However, two things are clear: First, it will take courts years of litigation to settle the Amendment's meaning. Second, when the dust clears, unmarried couples will have fewer rights over their most important life decisions than they would have had otherwise."

Apprehension about the amendment's unintended impacts isn't unreasonable. In 2004, a marriage amendment in Ohio unexpectedly disrupted that state's handling of domestic-violence cases. Defense attorneys argued that domestic-violence laws in effect since 1979 no longer applied to people who were in relationships but not married. Legal turmoil ensued as judges in different parts of the state interpreted the law differently. The UNC researchers found that courts ruled in favor of challenges to domestic-violence charges at least 27 times before the Ohio Supreme Court ended the confusion by ruling that the amendment had not nullified domestic-violence laws.

Concerns over the way Amendment One could impact domestic-violence protections led the North Carolina Coalition Against Domestic Violence to oppose it, said Executive Director Beth Froehling, a lawyer.

Bill sponsor Stam said North Carolina's domestic-violence law is broad enough to be unaffected by the amendment and dismissed other "hypotheticals" raised by opponents. If problems do arise, he said, the legislature can resolve them. And he cheerfully feigns offense at critics who complain about the amendment's wording. "It sort of hurts my feelings that people say it is poorly worded," Stam said. "What they mean is it's so clearly worded that it will do exactly what it says it will do."

The amendment is coming to the voters now for two reasons, one political, the other cultural.

Since the state law defining marriage was enacted in 1996, there has been no legislative effort to overturn it and no significant court action to challenge it. But its backers see the political terrain shifting. They say they see judges in other states finding previously unnoticed support for same-sex unions in their constitutions. They want no such surprises here.

The amendment's backers also see scattered tremors in this state that threaten the status quo. Seven Tar Heel cities and counties – including Mecklenburg – have granted employee family benefits to same-sex couples. The Guilford County register of deeds and three ministers were among a group that sued the state in December, challenging the constitutionality of statutes that make the clergy act as involuntary agents of the government in performing weddings and deem it a crime for them to perform weddings for couples who don't have a state license. They called for "disentanglement of the state from the personal and religious institution of marriage." The state should be empowered, they said, only to prohibit marriage under certain circumstances, such as insanity, bigamy, polygamy and incest, and to prevent marriages as a result of "fraud, duress, joke or mistake." A Superior Court judge dismissed the complaint in April, but it's on appeal.

Eyeing such developments, Republican legislators tried for years to put a marriage amendment on the ballot, but Democrats, who controlled the legislature for more than a century, blocked those efforts. Sen. Jim Forrester, a Gaston County Republican, said in a Senate speech last year that he had offered the amendment eight times, but it had been sent to die in the Senate Ways and Means Committee, chaired by Sen. Charlie Dannelly, a Mecklenburg Democrat. "The committee never met," Forrester said, ruefully.

Then came the Republican landslide of 2010, giving the GOP control of the legislature for the first time since 1870. Republican priorities that had been bottled up for decades – including the marriage amendment – burst free. Gov. Beverly Perdue, a Democrat, vetoed many Republican measures, but a governor can't veto a proposed constitutional amendment.

Forrester, a Gaston County physician and former Air Force general who died in October, had a singular devotion to the marriage amendment and a colorful – and, to some, infuriating – way of deriding his adversaries. He called Asheville, which he considered a center of gay culture, a "cesspool of sin," a description that rankled city leaders but delighted Asheville's T-shirt makers. He told a Raleigh GOP group that "slick city lawyers and homosexual lobbies and African-American lobbies are running Raleigh." He later apologized.

Dan Soucek, a Senate Republican from Watauga County who co-sponsored legislation calling for the referendum, is a West Point graduate and former Army officer who worked with Samaritan's Purse, the Rev. Franklin Graham's international-relief and evangelical organization. Soucek speaks of marriage as a uniquely valuable social asset that deserves unique protection. The amendment "affirms the family," he told Creative Loafing, "which is the most critical building block in our society." Soucek believes state policy should support only traditional marriage, but he noted that the proposed amendment doesn't prohibit unmarried couples from entering into private contracts that could guarantee some of the rights that state law automatically gives to married couples.

In fact, Cheri C. Patrick, a Durham lawyer whose work includes family matters for same-sex couples, said if the amendment is adopted, the chief beneficiaries may be the lawyers who draw up those contracts.

The problem facing advocates of traditional marriage is that the outcome of the amendment will have little effect on the real threat to marriage: the inclination of more and more people to not get married or to not stay married.

The 21st-century American family doesn't look much like the *Leave It to Beaver* family portrait of a half-century ago. Today, some 26 percent of children under age 21 are being raised in single-parent households. Almost one child in 20 lives with a grandparent. In 1960, married couples accounted for 78 percent of U.S. households; they accounted for just 49.8 percent in 2005 – the first year they were in the minority.

Nor is marriage now the way most men and women begin their sexual lives. In the late 1960s, about 10 percent of U.S. couples lived together before marrying. Now, it's 60 percent. In 2010, 42 percent of births in North

Carolina were to unmarried mothers.

As Americans' opinion of marriage was changing, so were their attitudes about same-sex relationships. When Congress passed the Defense of Marriage Act in 1996, homosexual acts were illegal in many states. A Gallup poll found that 68 percent of Americans opposed gay marriage. No state allowed any sort of same-sex legal union.

Today, seven states allow same-sex marriage. Openly gay men and women serve in the military. A Pew Research Center poll released in November showed 46 percent of Americans were in favor of same-sex marriage and 44 percent opposed it, with 9 percent undecided. In a Pew survey five years earlier, just 35 percent approved of it.

The same trend is evident in North Carolina. In April, Elon University reported a statewide survey that found 67 percent of North Carolinians favored allowing either gay marriage (38 percent) or civil unions (29 percent).

The impetus for the change is obvious. As more gays and lesbians have emerged from the closet, the public has had more opportunity to form its opinion based on real people, not negative stereotypes. Those real people may be neighbors, co-workers, family members or the stars of hit TV shows, movies and bands.

This year, J.C. Penney, the quintessential merchandiser to Middle America, hired as its advertising spokeswoman the comedian Ellen DeGeneres, whose same-sex love life has been amply chronicled – and who, along with Michelle Obama, Oprah Winfrey and Sarah Palin, was named one of the nation's 10 Most Admired Women in 2011's USA Today/Gallup Poll.

A final reason the amendment is on the ballot now is evident in the polls: demographic change. Pew's November poll found a striking generational divide on same-sex unions. Baby Boomers opposed same-sex marriage 48 percent to 42 percent, and their elders rejected it by an even larger margin, 55 percent to 33 percent. But members of Generation X (ages 31-46) favored same-sex marriage 50 percent to 42 percent, and Millennials (born after 1980) approved of it even more emphatically, 59 percent to 35 percent. The same is true in this state. A January poll by Public Policy Polling of Raleigh found 63 percent of North Carolinians age 18-29 favor some form of gay union.

Thom Tillis, speaker of the N.C. House of Representatives, supports the amendment but thinks it would soon be swept away. Talking with students at N.C. State University in March, Tillis predicted voters will approve the amendment but predicted it would be repealed within 20 years. "It's a generational issue," he told them.

Paul Stam disagrees. He thinks as young people mature, their views on marriage and family will become more like his.

Mark Kleinschmidt graduated from UNC-Chapel Hill and then taught social studies at West Mecklenburg High School, where in 1997 he was named Teacher of the Year. He left teaching to attend UNC law school in 1997, worked as a defense attorney in death penalty cases and recently became the first lawyer in the Chapel Hill office of Tin Fulton Walker & Owen, a Charlotte firm.

Kleinschmidt is doubly motivated to oppose the amendment. He's mayor of Chapel Hill, whose benefits program for same-sex and unmarried male-female partners would be terminated by the amendment. And he's gay.

He told Creative Loafing that conservative legislators are using the amendment "as a mobilization tool to advance their own agenda and remain in power."

Despite the polls, he feels cautiously optimistic. He said voters are beginning to understand that most of those affected by the amendment would not be same-sex couples but male-female partners who aren't married – not only young couples but also elderly couples who live together but for family or financial reasons aren't married.

Results of an Elon University Poll released in April showed that 61 percent of North Carolinians say they oppose an amendment that would prevent all same-sex marriages, domestic partnerships or civil unions. But a March statewide poll by WRAL, a television station in Raleigh, showed this amendment, which would do that, winning with 58 percent of the vote. Who's wrong?

Maybe neither. The WRAL poll asked likely primary voters the question posed on the ballot. The Elon poll asked more general questions, and the people it polled weren't just likely primary voters. The proposal is on the primary ballot as a result of its Republican sponsors' compromise with Democrats, who didn't want it on the November ballot for fear it would attract more conservatives to the polls in the general election.

But most North Carolinians don't vote in primaries. In 2008, the year of the last big presidential primary, only 37 percent of registered voters went to the polls, compared to 70 percent in that year's general election.

A combination of lethargy and ignorance may produce an outcome on May 8 that most North Carolinians say they don't want. In an election, the only opinions that count are those of the people who vote.

Guns

Supreme Court Right on Guns
An editorial in The Charlotte Observer June 27, 2008

The U.S. Supreme Court got it right on the Washington, D.C., handgun ban. The Second Amendment, which guarantees the right of the people to keep and bear arms, is weirdly written and distinctly not a model of clear communication. But its obvious intent is simple: to guarantee the right of citizens to keep and bear arms. The Washington ban was doomed from the minute it went into federal courts. The only real question was why Washington local officials chose to defend the law rather than amend it.

It's important, however, to note what the court did not do. It did not bar regulation of the sale and use of firearms.

Justice Antonin Scalia, writing for the 5-4 majority, said it explicitly: "[N]othing in our opinion should be taken to cast doubt on longstanding prohibitions on the possession of firearms by felons and the mentally ill, or laws forbidding the carrying of firearms in sensitive places such as schools and government buildings, or laws imposing conditions and qualifications on the commercial sale of arms."

No right in the Bill of Rights is without limit. As a historical illustration, Justice Scalia cited an opinion by a Massachusetts chief justice: "The liberty of the press was to be unrestrained, but he who used it was to be responsible in cases of its abuse; like the right to keep fire arms, which does not protect him who uses them for annoyance or destruction."

Considerations of public safety and the public's welfare limit the rights of free speech and a free press – you can't falsely yell "Fire!" in a crowded theater and cause a panic, as Justice Oliver Wendell Holmes Jr. said in a 1919 opinion. Such considerations will allow sensible limits on the right to bear arms, too.

That means the significant battles in our nation's effort to limit the damage from firearms remain to be fought. As Justice Scalia noted, "The Constitution leaves the District of Columbia a variety of tools for combating that problem, including some measures regulating handguns. ... But the enshrinement of constitutional rights necessarily takes certain policy choices off the table. These include the absolute prohibition of handguns held and used for self-defense in the home."

That's a reasonable ruling, in keeping with the historical underpinnings of our Constitution. Certainly outlawing handguns would simplify efforts to limit the damage they do. But by clearly ruling out that option, the court's decision should bolster efforts to take practical steps to make guns safer, keep them out of the wrong hands and firmly punish those who use them to break the law.

Foes of firearms may wish our Founding Fathers had said something else, or said nothing at all, about citizens' right to bear arms. But Justice Scalia is right: They didn't.

Living with Guns
An editorial in The Charlotte Observer Dec. 21, 1993

Start with the obvious: Surely nobody believes that anything the federal government might do would stop all bad guys from getting guns. But a growing number of Americans – including a lot of National Rifle Association members – think further sensible regulation of guns must be part of the effort to combat violence.

The reason is obvious: fear. *Time* magazine researchers recently put together a sobering set of statistics on firearms:

- Private citizens in the United States own 67 million handguns.
- Some 640,000 violent crimes are committed with handguns annually.
- The annual cost of treating firearm injuries is $1 billion.
- Estimated total cost to the U.S. economy of firearms is $14 billion.
- A survey by the Harvard School of Public Health found that one parent in six knew a child who was found playing with a loaded gun, and one in seven knew a child who was wounded or killed by an adult

70% of americans favor gun control

with a gun.

- The rate of gunshot wounds in children under 16 doubled in just three years (1987-90).
- The number of murders by handgun in the United States has jumped by more than 50 percent in the past five years.

Charlotte lawyer William G. Robinson, writing on today's Viewpoint page, echoes a view held by a lot of Americans: It's time to control gun ownership. Numerous polls show that most Americans agree. They don't favor banning gun ownership, but do favor further controls on it. There is a strong feeling that something has changed – that gun crime is out of control. So a *Time*/CNN poll this month found that 70 percent of Americans favor gun control, and 78 percent favor mandatory registration of all guns.

What further regulation might be helpful? Here are some possibilities. Make it at least as tough to get a license to own a gun as to get a license to drive. Require registration of handgun transfers. Prohibit gun possession by those convicted of such violent misdemeanors as spouse abuse and child abuse. Prohibit gun ownership by minors, except under restricted circumstances requiring parental involvement. Require special licenses for possession of a large arsenal. Make punishment harsher for crimes involving

use of guns.

One step the federal government should take immediately involves regulation of licensed gun dealers. At present the federal license for gun dealers costs $10, and anyone who is at least 21 and has a fixed address and no criminal record can get one. As a result, there are more than 287,000 gun dealers and the federal Bureau of Alcohol, Tobacco and Firearms has only 225 inspectors to monitor them. You can imagine how thorough that monitoring is. Firearms dealers should be required to pay annual license fees that at least cover the costs of adequate monitoring.

Gun laws won't stop lawbreakers from getting guns. But laws can help keep guns away from children, can make it easier to trace the transfer of handguns, can ensure that gun owners have at least some training in gun use and safety, and can crack down on careless or lawless licensed gun dealers.

Beyond that, our society needs to combat violence in some ways that have nothing to do with gun ownership. The "Squash It'" campaign that Ellen Goodman writes about on today's Viewpoint page makes a lot of sense. Many schools, including some in Charlotte-Mecklenburg, are teaching dispute resolution skills that students may not have learned at home or in the neighborhood. Community policing is creating teams of neighbors and law officers that work to make areas inhospitable to violence.

The debate between those who advocate a gun in every pocket and those would ban gun ownership may be good for the TV talk shows, but it misses the point that some reasonable steps could be taken to make gun ownership safer and gun-running riskier. That's where the nation should focus its energies.

Preventing Mass Murder
From a column in The Charlotte Observer April 22, 2007

The political reaction to the Virginia Tech killings was familiar. Gun control advocates pointed to the need for tougher laws. Gun rights supporters disagreed. Some argued that if law-abiding Hokies had been allowed to carry guns on campus, they might have stopped the killer.

That may be true, but two thoughts occur to me. Murder is rare on college campuses. Suicide isn't. Does it make sense to put more guns around

US Worse in gun deaths

young people who may be abusing alcohol or drugs or suffering from depression that could make them suicidal? I don't think so.

In the nation that has the most guns and the most gun deaths in the world, does it make sense to think having guns in even more places would result in fewer gun deaths? Again, I don't think so. *BB Gun*

I'm not anti-gun. I got my first Daisy Red Ryder BB gun before I was 10 and my first shotgun (a .410 gauge single-shot) and a .22 rifle not many years later. I loved to shoot, though long ago I lost interest in hunting. I have a shotgun at home that hasn't been fired in years.

I wish thugs and drunks and gangsters would never get their hands on guns, but I'm not under any illusions about the effectiveness of gun control. Until someone can figure out how to get 260 million firearms (including 60 million or more handguns) away from mostly law-abiding citizens who don't want to give them up, firearms will be available. Laws can make it harder, but not impossible, for criminals to get and misuse them.

Prevent VT

So what can we do to prevent future Virginia Techs and Columbines? Start with the things we know need work. Learn to recognize mental health problems and deal with them. Do a better job of determining whether a potential gun buyer has a history of mental illness. Vigorously prosecute people who obtain guns illegally or use them in crimes.

Columbine

But the simple fact is this: If your country has a lot of dogs, it will have a lot of dog bites. And if your country has a lot of guns, it will have a lot of gun deaths. Sure, there are other means of killing, but it's hard to imagine killing 32 people with a knife.

No Guns on Campus

A column in The Charlotte Observer April 29, 2007

I've heard from readers who challenged my assertion a week ago that having more guns on the nation's college campuses wouldn't make them safer places. Their argument was this: If you'd been in one of those Virginia Tech classrooms, wouldn't you wish you had a gun?

My answer: Yes, of course. But that doesn't mean having more guns around would make campuses safer.

If you have been keeping up with news about the killings, you've no

Firearm deaths

doubt come across this statistic: America has the highest rate of firearms deaths in the industrialized world – an annual rate of 10.08 per 100,000 people. What you may not have noticed is this breakdown of those gun deaths. Most are not homicides. They're suicides. *Suicides*

In 2004, the most recent year for which complete national statistics are available, there were 29,645 firearms deaths – 16,869 suicides and 11,920 homicides. (The others were accidental or of undetermined cause.) Firearms were used in about 60 percent of suicides. Suicide is the nation's 11th leading cause of death. Homicide ranks 13th.

What does all this have to do with guns on campus? The U.S. Department of Education compiles an annual report of crimes on college campuses. Schools that receive federal student aid funding are required to report a variety of violent crimes, including homicides.

Now remember, each year there are 1,000 or more suicides on the nation's campuses. How many homicides do you think occurred in 2005, the latest year for which complete numbers are available? Would you say about 1,000? 500? 250?

If you said any of those, you'd be wrong. The answer is 11.

Seung-Hui Cho's murderous rampage at Virginia Tech was shocking, but it doesn't alter this reality: A college student is about as likely to win a prize in the lottery as to be killed on campus. So over time and across the country, having more guns on campus couldn't do much to lower the murder rate. But experts say more guns could dramatically raise the suicide rate.

Suicide is the second leading cause of death for college students, after traffic accidents. According to Dr. Lanny Berman, executive director of the American Association of Suicidology, more than 90 percent of people who commit suicide have a diagnosable mental disorder. Depression is the most common. When depression is combined with drug experimentation and/ or binge drinking, the results can be fatal. *Depression*

But consider this fact: Scientists know that women think about suicide more, and attempt it more often, than men. But death from suicide is more common among men. Why? One reason: firearms. Swallowing pills may not be fatal. Swallowing a gun barrel almost always is. Women are more likely than men to use poison rather than guns. *Poison vs. Guns*

Philip J. Cook, a professor at Duke's University's Terry Sanford Institute of Public Policy, has studied gun violence. He notes that for young people

impulsive act

suffering depression and high on drugs or alcohol, a suicide attempt is often an impulsive act. Having a gun close at hand can make that impulse deadly.

Young adults who aren't in college have higher suicide rates than their peers on campus. The reason? Again, guns. Because of college rules, there are far fewer guns on campus. *Guns available*

So I stand by my earlier assertion: Having more guns on college campuses wouldn't make them safer – just the opposite.

IX. Business and Labor

Lewis Hines shot this classic photograph of a 10-year-old mill worker in Lincolnton, N.C., in 1908. It brings to mind a 1916 poem by social reformer Sarah Norcliffe Cleghorn:

The golf links lie so near the mill
That almost every day
The laboring children can look out
And watch the men at play.

The Limits of Capitalism

A column in The Charlotte Observer Aug. 22, 2004

... I'm a fan and a beneficiary of capitalism. The only non-capitalist enterprise I've ever worked for is the U.S. Army. But economics isn't everything. Capitalism doesn't answer – in fact, doesn't deal with – some important questions involving values and morality. Society needs – and has – other ways of answering those questions.

This is hardly news. It doesn't take a degree in economics to see that a nation can have a capitalistic economy and still be unjust. A capitalist nation can deny fundamental rights to racial minorities, as the United States did for much of the 20th century. It can allow the poor to suffer from inadequate medical care, or from a legal system that favors those with enough money to hire lawyers. It can allow pollution of the air we breathe, the water we drink and the ground beneath our feet.

Every society defines a set of values that it considers important enough to enforce by law. In many cases the law forbids the capitalistic solution to a problem, reasonable as that solution may seem in purely economic terms.

For example, many couples who want children don't have them. Why not let them buy babies from parents who are willing to sell? Why not allow breeding franchises – call them Mom 'n' Pop stores – so people can order a tot, maybe with a six-month, no-questions-asked return policy? Because in this country the moral consensus against child selling has been written into law.

Many people with bad kidneys are seeking transplants. No doubt some people with two healthy kidneys would sell one for the right price. That may be a sensible market solution, but our nation forbids the sale of body parts.

Some people are looking for casual sex and would be happy to buy it from a willing seller, but that's against the law.

Another way capitalism may create problems is in its focus on individual transactions.

One lakeside home with no environmental controls may be a quaint retreat; a thousand such homes may threaten a region's water supply. A small hog farm makes a small impact; a giant farm may foul the air and water for miles.

That's where government comes in. Through the democratic process our society defines the public good and enacts laws to strike a balance between what individuals want and what the public good requires.

Such laws put restraints on capitalism. But the fact that capitalism operates under some restraints doesn't mean capitalists give up and embrace communism – or that the public interest would be better served if they did. That's the genius of capitalism: Whatever the rules under which it operates, capitalism is unrivaled in its ability to unleash ingenuity and promote risk-taking in return for possible reward. ...

Capitalism is an itchy, creative system, always seeking opportunity and profit. Our nation has benefited enormously from the wealth it has created. But many important choices involve moral and political values. Once society has made those choices, capitalism can work in support of them, but capitalism cannot make the choices. A sensible society both appreciates capitalism's marvelous strengths and recognizes its limits.

Jimmy Hoffa's Impact
A column in The Charlotte Observer May 7, 2011

In reports on political efforts in Wisconsin, Indiana and other states to restrict collective bargaining by public employees, North Carolina is frequently cited as a state that prohibits any collective bargaining by any public employees.

The N.C. ban was enacted in 1959. Some recent critics have called it a Jim Crow law, intended to prevent whites and blacks from forming alliances in the workplace. In fact, the impetus for the law came not from

Jim Crow but from Jimmy Hoffa.

Hoffa became the president of the powerful Teamsters union in 1957 and soon announced a nationwide effort to unionize 10 million public workers, including police and firefighters. That organizing crusade included Charlotte, where the Teamsters targeted the city's public transportation and police departments.

At first, city officials showed little concern. The city didn't sign contracts with unions or recognize unions as bargaining agents for employees, and state law prohibited strikes by municipal employees. But to many in North Carolina, Hoffa represented all that was dangerous about organized labor. His predecessor went to federal prison. Federal agents probed his reputed links to mob bosses, labor violence and racketeering.

Many business leaders wanted a more defiant stance. So did the Charlotte Observer's editorial board, which said so in a Dec. 17, 1958, editorial headlined "Jimmy Hoffa Has No Place in Charlotte's City Hall." The city's hands-off stance was "spineless, short-sighted and self-defeating," the editors asserted. The city should "do everything possible to keep Hoffa out of City Hall."

The Chamber of Commerce pushed the council to ban union membership by city employees. As anti-Hoffa sentiment grew, the council did adopt a resolution opposing "any organization of any employees" by the Teamsters union, but a companion resolution forbidding city workers to join unions died when its sponsor saw it wouldn't pass.

Hoffa's crusade encountered stiff resistance elsewhere. On Jan. 2, 1959, he announced the Teamsters would halt their efforts to organize New York City police because of opposition from the mayor, police chief and local nonunion police groups. In Charlotte, the local Teamsters representative told the Observer his group would try to organize transportation workers but not police.

But the issue of police unions was particularly sensitive for business leaders because of violence associated with attempts to organize textile workers. If law enforcement officers were unionized, could they be counted on if labor troubles arose?

State Rep. Frank Snepp of Charlotte, later a prominent judge, moved the action to Raleigh by proposing legislation to prohibit all public employees from engaging in collective bargaining or even belonging to a union. The bill swiftly became law.

A decade later a federal court struck down the part of the law forbidding public employees to join a union. But the court left intact the ban on collective bargaining by public employees, as did a state court.

It probably isn't coincidence that only 8 percent of North Carolina's state and local government workers belong to unions – the lowest rate in the nation – or that only 3.2 percent of this state's entire workforce is unionized – again, the lowest rate in the nation.

Union? Keep Out
An editorial in The Charlotte Observer July 31, 1977

It's not unheard of for a North Carolina community to turn away an industrial prospect because it has unionized workers. Raleigh business leaders, for example have done so twice in recent years.

Perhaps the most significant thing about Roxboro's recent "No, thank you" to an industry that wanted to build a plant there is that this time the governor and his economic development aides are openly perturbed by the rebuff. It's an encouraging sign that Gov. Jim Hunt knows how injurious that is to the state's economic welfare.

What the leading citizens of Roxboro, 30 miles north of Durham, did was turn away a Pennsylvania company that wanted to start a glass bottle factory there. The reasons: The factory would pay its workers from four to eight dollars an hour (well above the state's average industrial wage of $4.06 an hour) and the workers most likely would be unionized.

Michael Carden, a Roxboro lawyer who heads the town's industrial development committee, said there was concern that the new plant might attract workers from existing plants if it paid higher wages. And he said the town's business leaders just didn't like labor unions.

What's appalling is that the industrial development committee, which voted to accept the new plant only if it pledged not to pay wages higher than the average pay scale in town, is supported by tax money – including money from the pockets of the workers whom the committee deprived of higher-paying jobs. If there were such a crime as moral abuse of public funding, this would be a case of it.

Is there any reason for workers to feel that they and a community's "business leaders" have any interests in common when those business leaders brazenly repel good industry? It's difficult to imagine a strategy more likely to encourage the growth of labor unions.

Southern blue-collar workers are almost uniformly honest people, accustomed to giving a day's work for a day's pay. Many of them have an aversion to unions. That aversion stems in part from their individualism and their understanding that the benefits of unionization sometimes don't outweigh the burdens of it. And it stems in part from a prejudice against unions that has been drummed into their heads from birth by people and institutions with a financial interest in selling that idea.

The Greater Charlotte Chamber of Commerce, while hardly a hotbed of pro-union sentiment, is not so shortsighted as to think the Roxboro example is in the best interest of the business community. Charlotte's business leadership is far more enlightened than it was a decade or two ago. The work force of Charlotte is over 90 percent non-union, and business leaders certainly prefer it that way. But that has not kept the Chamber from actively pursuing industries that have unionized work forces. The Miller Brewing Co. plant, which Raleigh turned away for fear of its union, is one Charlotte wooed fervently.

If North Carolina industry is to avoid unionization over the next decade, it won't be because of a Right to Work law or an organization of business leaders that opposes the coming of any industry that isn't fiercely anti-union. It will be because business leaders learn from their mistakes and create a working climate that eliminates the need for workers to organize and slug it out with employers. Companies that believe otherwise will eventually move elsewhere or get unions. And they'll have earned them.

Who Protects Workers?
An editorial in The Charlotte Observer Sept. 15, 1991

Hardly any state official or business leader is saying about the disaster at Hamlet what virtually every North Carolinian knows. Why does the state do a dismal job of ensuring workplace safety? Why is there no public outcry when the state has so few safety inspectors and Labor Secretary John Brooks does not get the additional ones he seeks? Why are worker-protection laws so weak? Why are fines so low on employers who violate them? Why does it take 25 deaths in a chicken processing plant fire to tell North Carolinians that wildlife gets better protection than workers?

Here's why: Organized labor in North Carolina has little more political clout than those chickens that were plucked and packaged at the Imperial Food Products plant in Hamlet.

What happened in Hamlet is an unusual outrage, but behind it is a history of unprotected workers that reaches far into the region's past. University of Tennessee historian James C. Cobb described the attitudes surrounding industrialization of the region in his 1982 book, *The Selling of the South*. He wrote:

"Most incoming employers were concerned primarily with getting maximum productivity out of work forces consisting largely of ex-share-croppers, females and children, none of whom were likely to complain about wages and working conditions. ... Industrialists were less interested in schools or hospitals than in low taxes, and responsible political leadership was less important to them than freedom from regulation. The South's closed political system produced public officials disinclined to regulate but eager to protect the interests of industry, particularly in labor-management conflicts. In the name of progress, business leaders encouraged policy-makers to hold down taxes and starve education and services in order to create what they believed was the best possible climate for attracting industry."

In describing a region where the deck was stacked against organized labor, Dr. Cobb was writing of the South of 50 to 100 years ago. With little change in wording, he could be describing too much of the Carolinas today.

Heaven knows organized labor can cause problems. The corruption of many unions is a matter of record. In some industries union demands have ruined companies and deprived workers of jobs. Featherbedding, illegal strikes, criminal behavior – all these ills are evident in some unions in America.

But for every story of a bad union, there's an equally disturbing story of a bad employer. If the all-but-official policy of most state leaders is to be that workers don't need the protection of unions, then the state's employers and government must see to it that workers' safety and welfare are protected by other means. The alarming conditions brought to light after the Hamlet disaster show that adequate protections do not now exist. Labor unions have many faults, but they do not sit silently by while bosses deter pilfering by padlocking fire escape doors.

Tobacco Execs in Denial
An editorial in The Charlotte Observer April 18, 1994

The hearing was an anti-smoking zealot's dream. There were the heads of the big tobacco companies, men of substance, dressed in white shirts and conservative suits, arrayed along a table brightly illuminated by TV lights. Confronting them was a U.S. House subcommittee dominated by men who consider those executives killers.

The committee members told horror stories about the victims of smoking. They asked the executives questions and demanded one-word answers. They interrupted, bullied and ridiculed the executives. They had positioned the TV cameras to dwell on a large placard that mocked the tobacco men. It bore such messages as, "One American dies every 80 seconds from tobacco use," and charts showing rising nicotine levels in cigarettes and grisly photos of oral cancer. It was as if Fellini had returned to advise the subcommittee.

The behavior of the anti-smoking zealots was so contrived, so ill-mannered, so arrogant that it was easy to forget the essential fact: On the big questions, they are right.

The executives denied that cigarette smoking is addictive, though three out of four smokers say they are addicted, 80 percent say they wish they'd never started smoking, and of the 17 million adults who try to quit each year, only one in 10 succeeds. They denied that "smokeless tobacco" contributes to oral cancer, though research shows that users of snuff, for example, are 50 times as likely to develop oral cancer as non-users.

When pressed to acknowledge that cigarette smoking is harmful, a conclusion supported by virtually every authority not employed by the tobacco industry, the executives would admit only that cigarettes "may" pose risks. It's difficult not to suspect that profits cloud their judgment.

The public isn't confused. Public sentiment, not government action, led to recent restrictions on smoking at Charlotte Knights stadium and McDonald's restaurants. What role government should play isn't easy to determine. Cigarettes are not crack, but neither are they Twinkies; efforts to regulate them should recognize that. Prohibition wouldn't work. Higher taxes would help. Surely there's a way the Food and Drug Administration could monitor cigarette contents and advertising.

The hearings did show that whatever is done will have to be done to the tobacco executives, not with them. Their unanimous denial of reality suggests they'll rely on political clout, not compromise, to protect their interests. As the hearing droned on, a viewer might have wondered how the executives would react if confronted with X-rays showing that in the lungs, tobacco smoke releases zillions of microscopic terrorists who use stilettos to puncture lung tissue, then implant cancer cells in the holes. Would the executives say that was a natural occurrence, and one of the reasons people enjoy smoking?

The Tragedy of Brown Lung
An editorial in The Charlotte Observer Feb. 10, 1980

The tragedy of brown lung has little to do with the difficult questions that are causing legal and legislative battles, though settling those controversies is essential. The tragedy is that industry and government haven't done things that obviously should be done to reduce the suffering. Some examples:

- Workers' compensation systems in the Carolinas are so slow and so often inconclusive that workers may wait years, even die, with their claims not settled. Legislators should speed up the process.
- Mills that defiantly violate cotton dust standards should be given an ultimatum: Clean up or shut down. No mill in the Carolinas has ever been told that. Most North Carolina mills haven't even been inspected. The legislature should provide money for more in-

spectors.

- Smoking and brown lung seem to be deadly companions. Keeping smokers out of work areas where cotton dust levels are high is a sensible precaution. Yet nobody does it.

- Regular medical examinations could detect breathing problems early. Yet many mills don't provide regular checkups. When check-ups show brown lung, workers have a right to know it. Yet many mills don't tell them, and neither does the industrial commission in either of the Carolinas.

- Mills are required by law to report findings of brown lung, yet many don't, and the lack of concern by the industrial commissions encourages flouting of the law.

Leaders of the textile industry complain bitterly about the Carolina Brown Lung Association. It is, among other things, a political pressure group, and it sometimes exaggerates and makes questionable charges. The charges are particularly irritating to companies that have worked hard to make mills safe. But the harm done by the association's irresponsibility is minuscule compared to the harm done by mill owners who wail about federal interference instead of providing basic safeguards for their workers.

Brown Lung Should be a Political Issue
An editorial in The Charlotte Observer March 21, 1980

William Klopman, board chairman of the nation's largest textile company, lambasted gubernatorial candidate Bob Scott in a letter on this page yesterday for making byssinosis (brown lung) a political issue. Mr. Klopman, chairman of the Greensboro-based Burlington Industries, wrote,

"Byssinosis's place in the political arena is questionable at best, but when it is dragged there by the uninformed, nothing constructive can result."

Mr. Klopman is entitled to his point of view, but we don't share it.

When somebody mentions byssinosis, executives of the big textile firms cite their companies' efforts to eliminate it and suggest that it's no longer a problem. Their efforts are in many cases laudable, but that doesn't mean byssinosis isn't a problem.

Top textile executives acknowledge privately that many cotton mills are not doing what even industry leaders know should be done to make mills safer – and won't, unless forced to clean up or shut down. Textile executives we have talked to estimate that about 20 percent of the mills in the Carolinas fall into that outlaw category; other observers would double that figure.

The cotton textile industry's voluntary efforts won't make those outlaw mills safe. The industry is fiercely competitive, and some of the most dangerous mills are marginal businesses. Some won't, or can't, make the investment Burlington and others have made in modern equipment.

Those outlaw mills continue to operate much as they have for years. They violate health and safety regulations and get away with it, because government agencies charged with enforcement lack the resources and sometimes the will to stop them.

State government can – and should – force those mills to clean up or close down. State government can also speed up the process for granting workers' compensation, which was created to provide financial aid to workers disabled by on-the-job accidents or illnesses such as brown lung. But there has been little political support for either action. If candidates in this year's legislative and executive races can make it a campaign issue, more power to them.

The urgency of the need for political action was underscored by a story on the front page of the Observer the same day Mr. Klopman's letter appeared. It told of the death of Ephraim Lowder, 66, a former textile worker from Albemarle. Two doctors had diagnosed him as a brown lung victim and he had filed for workers' compensation two years ago, but he died without receiving a penny in benefits.

His plight is not unique. The workers' compensation system often is agonizingly slow. That is a political problem. So are the outlaw mills. Those problems exist because poor people lack the power to make the political process work, and powerful people lack the will to do so.

X. Religion

Myers Park Baptist in Charlotte was expelled from the N.C. Baptist State Convention in 2007 for welcoming gays into its congregation and church leadership.

Politics and the Ten Commandments

A column in The Charlotte Observer June 20, 1999

Washington is a city of clashing symbols. Rarely has that clash been more distracting than in last week's debate in the House over juvenile justice and gun control.

The parties played their traditional roles. Democrats pointed to the disasters at Columbine High and elsewhere and pushed for passage of new restrictions on gun sales and ownership. Some of the proposals were sensible, but with some 200 million firearms scattered around America, nothing on the House agenda would do much to make schools safer or disarm criminals. But Democrats know that most Americans worry about gun violence, and they know that Republicans toe the National Rifle Association line, so they take great delight in whacking Republicans in the face with gun legislation.

Republicans do not enter the culture war unarmed, however. The problem isn't guns, they say, it's morals. Rather than limit guns, they want to unleash the power of religion.

Thus the debate over guns miraculously evolved into a debate over posting the Ten Commandments in public school classrooms.

Republicans love debates about religion, for two reasons. First, standing in the well of the House and battling for the Lord puts a politician on the side of righteousness and invigorates the party's religious base. Second, Democrats who worry about improper state sponsorship of religion risk appearing to be anti-God. So the Republican political evangelists managed to seize the public's attention briefly by requiring a vote on authorizing states to decide whether to post the Ten Commandments in public schools.

Now think about that a minute. The fact that public schools aren't displaying the Ten Commandments has nothing to do with Congress. The problem is the U.S. Supreme Court.

The court ruled – logically, I'd say – that if you have a list of rules and the first four pertain to God and religious worship, then that list is a religious document. Since the Constitution says government can't endorse a particular religion, the Supreme Court rightly concluded that public schools can't post the Ten Commandments – or, by the same logic, the Charter of the Coven of Wicca, if there is such a thing.

If states want to defy the Supreme Court and post religious material in schoolrooms, they don't need Congress's permission. They can just do it, and see what happens. What is likely to happen is that they will be sued, go to court and be reminded of what the law is.

Members of Congress know, I presume, that a vote in favor of posting the Ten Commandments is about as meaningful as a vote in favor of teaching pigs to fly. But as I said, Washington is a city of symbols. What went on in the House last week is a symbol of why many Americans think that leaders in both parties consider us fools. Maybe they're right.

I am intrigued by our politicians' apparent belief in the power of religious documents. Maybe their attitude was shaped by watching *Raiders of the Lost Ark*, in which a vengeful spirit roasts Nazis who defile the sacred ark. In the movie, that scene had me cheering. Alas, in real life divine justice seems not to be meted out so directly.

In fact, Americans, though professing to be among the world's most religious people, tend not to believe religious objects have talismanic power. Most do not, so far as I can tell, believe that putting a "Jesus is my co-pilot" bumper sticker on your car will keep a drunk from rear-ending you. Or that wearing a cross on an ankle bracelet will keep chiggers away. Still, politicians seem to believe hanging the Ten Commandments on a schoolroom wall will turn students into paragons of morality. Hope springs eternal.

Here's what House members should do to show they're serious: Write the Ten Commandments into the House rules and kick out any member who breaks them. That would require keeping the Sabbath holy. It would mean no adultery, no stealing, no bearing false witness. If after a few years that has made the House a holier place, then we could expand it to the Senate.

As for putting the Ten Commandments on the schoolroom wall, I think that would make students moral to about the same degree that putting Einstein's Theory of Relativity on the wall would make them mathematicians.

Baptists vs. Homosexuals

A column in The Charlotte Observer Nov. 18, 2007

Well, we've done it again.

The "we," in this case, is Myers Park Baptist Church, where I've been a member for a couple of decades. What we've done this time is get kicked out of the N.C. Baptist State Convention.

This is not the first time the church has been at odds with a Baptist organization. Back in 1967, the Mecklenburg Baptist Association decided to exclude churches that accepted members who had not been baptized by immersion. Among them was Myers Park Baptist.

Our first senior minister, George Heaton, considered baptism a revered tradition but not at all essential. He told of having a dream in which Dr. Albert Schweitzer, the theologian and medical missionary, wanted to join our church. He said he had to tell him, "I'm sorry, Dr. Schweitzer, you can't belong to this church because your baptism was by the spoonful and ours is by the gallon."

When the county Baptist association voted in 1967 to bar churches that didn't baptize by immersion, our congregation adopted a policy statement that began, "There is no rite or ceremony the inclusion of which can make

a confessor eligible or ineligible for membership in the Church of Christ."

So here we are again.

Our conflict with the Baptist state convention involved two points. One was the authority of the local church to set its own policies. The convention had no quarrel with that fundamental principle of Baptist governance.

The other was homosexuals and the church. Our policy on homosexuals is simple. We welcome them to full fellowship of the church – membership, eligibility for leadership positions, everything.

It's easy to get into an argument about what the Bible says about homosexuals, if you want to. I don't. If they come to our church to worship and to serve, our door is open to them.

The N.C. Baptist State Convention, however, sees homosexuality not only as a sin but as a special sort of sin. In 2006 the group adopted a policy saying, "Among churches not in friendly cooperation with the Convention are churches which knowingly act to affirm, approve, endorse, promote, support or bless homosexual behavior."

The policy was framed by a seven-member committee chaired by Mark Harris, pastor of First Baptist Church in Charlotte. The convention has a right to take that position. It can make any membership rules it wants, based on its values and beliefs.

Though a few other churches have left quietly over the policy, the convention supports it emphatically. When the delegates in Greensboro kicked us out Tuesday, they did it by a big margin. I wonder if the delegates at some point will want to adopt a similar policy on other matters.

For instance, Jesus said a good bit about greed and covetousness. Have you ever heard of a church being barred from the convention because it accepts members who are "greedy of filthy lucre," to quote 1 Timothy, and are unrepentant? I haven't.

Jesus didn't say anything, so far as I can tell, about sex, except in his teaching about how we are to treat one another. He did say something about divorce: Unless one of the partners committed adultery, it's a sin. That goes for remarriage after such a divorce, too.

The state convention doesn't bar churches that welcome divorced people who've remarried and are unrepentant about it. Maybe the convention believes greedy people and divorced people need the support of a loving church community. I do. We welcome them, too.

I have no idea how many homosexuals are in our 1,900-member congregation – maybe a few dozen. Of the members I know are homosexuals, most are couples in loving, committed relationships. Some have children. I certainly affirm, support and welcome them.

The fact is, we all have sinned – homosexuals and heterosexuals, members of Myers Park Baptist Church and members of the N.C. Baptist State Convention. And we're all going to sin again.

The conflict, as I see it, boils down to this: Should a church open its doors to sinners and, if they earn the congregation's respect, even put them in positions of responsibility? At Myers Park Baptist, our answer is yes. If sinners are barred, who's left?

Doug Marlette and Religion
A column in The Charlotte Observer July 2, 1978

Doug Marlette's troubles don't come when he attacks government or lampoons the oppressors of the downtrodden, though he may nurture that conceit when he yearns for the persecution his professional forebears suffered.

Marlette's troubles come when his cartoons touch a subject near the hearts of many Observer readers: religion.

Religious faith should not be joked about, I agree. But I consider Marlette's cartoons about religion to be as serious as most sermons.

Permit me, as one grown to manhood in the bosom of the Southern Baptist Church, one who has thumbed through sword drills at Vacation Bible School many a sweltering afternoon, to say why I think Marlette's cartoons on religion have a place in the Observer.

I can speak only from a background of fundamentalist Christianity, a background I share with many of you.

Religion has two facets: people's relationship to God and people's relationship to each other.

A person's relationship to God is nobody else's business. A person's relationship to others necessarily affects others, particularly when that person is a well-known religious figure – a Jim Bakker, a Billy Graham, a Rev. Ike. Their lives, their actions symbolize religion to many people. Because of that, some of their followers unconsciously consider them almost divine. That, I think, is dangerous. Jim Bakker, Billy Graham and the others are not God, or even God-like. They don't claim to be. They are sinners, like you and me – not just subject to errors, but sure to commit some.

If my reading of the Bible is correct, God doesn't put much store in celebrity or great works, even in the service of religion. When the roll is called, God won't be pulling names out of *People* magazine. The man who runs the corner service station, the woman who works at the dry cleaners, may rank just as high in God's eyes – and be just as valuable in His service – as any well-known evangelist.

Yet we tend to think of preachers as being somehow more godly. Therein lies the danger: If people expect a religious leader to be perfect, then discover he isn't, they might conclude that religion has failed.

If we are thus misled, we miss what I consider the essential meaning of religion: Man is not perfect, and faith in God will not make him so. What God requires of man is faith and effort, not perfection. The miracle of religion is not that God loves mankind because it is perfect, but that God loves mankind despite its imperfections.

Living a Christian life is no easy matter. Everybody who tries fails in some way, for the standard is simple yet impossible: "What would Jesus do in this situation?"

That's where Marlette, and his cartoons, come in. By their fruits you shall know them, the Bible says, and Marlette sometimes provokes outrage when he suggests that there are flaws in the fruits some religious leaders bear. A few examples:

- In the recent cartoon depicting Jim Bakker firing some PTL employees, Marlette's question was clear: Is that the way Jesus would have handled it?
- In a cartoon about Billy Graham's $22.9 million fund, Marlette repeated what a Savior who was a poor carpenter had instructed his followers to do: Give what you have to the poor and come follow me.
- In a cartoon about capital punishment – one Editor David Lawrence decided not to publish – Marlette reminded us that Jesus, too, was a victim of a state execution.

Some readers have complained about Marlette's depicting Jesus in cartoons. I understand their feelings, but I see it another way. While Marlette's

depictions of Jesus are hardly as heroic as Rembrandt's, they are as serious and reverent as any in a Sunday School book.

Don't conclude from this that I consider Marlette (or myself) a great religious teacher. I don't. I am an editorial writer, commenting on the world about me as I see it. He is a cartoonist, and his work is sometimes noticeably short on Christian charity. His view isn't the only view, and may not be the right view, but his cartoons do not scoff at religion. Rather, they suggest, "Here's one way to look at a situation." If you look at it his way, then look at it your way, you may decide that he is wrong – and you may be right.

But he may be right, too. Religious people, like other human beings, can learn from criticism, if they will honestly consider it. Too often they won't; religious leaders, like the rest of us, prefer not to admit they might be wrong. That's why I consider them fit subjects for Marlette's cartoons.

The Bakkers' Bubble
An editorial in The Charlotte Observer June 17, 1987

The PTL board`s decision to seek Chapter 11 bankruptcy may be the most fiscally prudent step ever taken by the TV ministry/recreation center, though in the history of the enterprise there is not a lot of competition for that honor. Still, the news does prompt a feeling of sadness.

Jim Bakker's "I have a dream" ministry was always one step away from collision with economic reality. But while it lasted there was, as Mr. Bakker might put it, a miraculous air about the Heritage Village boom. Mr. Bakker was getting money in the simplest way imaginable: by asking for it. He would dream and ask, dream and ask, and he could always dream up projects larger than he could pay for. So there was an air of impending disaster about his appeals – a desperate breathlessness, as though he were tied to the railroad track with the freight train coming, and he needed your donation, and yours and yours and yours, to avert tragedy. That went on day after day.

Over the years his pleas and the public's response made Mr. Bakker's improbable dream rise from the South Carolina countryside. And while the more traditional Christians and the Internal Revenue Service may find it difficult to discern a religious purpose in a giant water slide and a restaurant resembling a fairy-tale castle, Mr. Bakker – and presumably his supporters – apparently have no trouble seeing them as part of God's development plan for York County.

Now the accountants are poring over the books and bemoaning the mishandling of millions of dollars. A glum realization has taken hold: There

was never money on hand to pay for everything. Projects were begun with the faith that donations would come in to pay for them. Now there's talk of tax penalties, lawsuits, perhaps even criminal indictments.

So the robust growth at Heritage Village appears to be over. We hope the new PTL management can protect innocent investors and developers from financial harm. But the Bakker phenomenon was never really a business enterprise. Like a child's giant soap bubble, it was fascinating but insubstantial, and at some point it had to burst.

Bakker Promised Too Much
An editorial in The Charlotte Observer Oct. 6, 1989

The verdict in the Jim Bakker trial reflects a fundamental distinction in American law. In soliciting donations from his flock, a preacher may promise eternal life in a celestial city whose streets are paved with gold, and that's none of the law's business. But if he promises an annual free stay in a luxury hotel on Earth, he'd better have the rooms available.

Jim and Tammy Faye Bakker often depict themselves as victims of persecutions by rivals and nonbelievers. The trial of Jim Bakker, however, had nothing to do with religion. The question before the jury was whether he had repeatedly offered viewers a real estate deal that he knew he couldn't deliver on, and had profited enormously from the scam. The jury listened to the prosecutors' charges and to Mr. Bakker's defense and found him guilty – 24 times.

Given the nature of the people involved, the trial might have become a quasi-religious circus. Judge Robert Potter, however, tolerated no clowning. He kept the trial sharply focused on the legal issues, and moved it along briskly despite a fainting witness, a defendant seized by a panic attack and a devastating hurricane.

The verdict is the culmination of a long effort. For years, the government showed little interest in Mr. Bakker's activities, despite ample evidence that he was raising millions through the mail by making false promises over television. But when federal investigators finally developed an interest, they turned up evidence strong enough to convince even a Bible Belt jury of Mr. Bakker's guilt. The prosecutors skillfully presented the facts; the jury fairly applied the law.

Evangelists who are motivated as much by profits as by prophets are nothing new. But television gives them a far greater audience than a canvas tent could hold.

Government should have no interest in the religious content of their preaching. But Jim Bakker's example should make law enforcement agencies alert to future possibilities of massive mail fraud via television.

Some televangelists' efforts at honest disclosure are welcome, but self-policing alone isn't the answer. The possibility of using the power of religious faith to raise millions of dollars from people you'll never see presents a powerful temptation for televangelists. The strongest incentive for TV preachers to deliver what they promise is their knowledge that somebody with subpoena power is watching.

For viewers of television religious shows, the Bakker conviction sends a message: People who make their living praising God may have some deviltry in them. You viewers may want to ponder Jim Bakker's example and ask yourselves whether you do more good by giving your religious donations to a TV preacher or to the local church that christens, marries, ministers to and eventually buries you, your friends and neighbors.

Jim Bakker will proclaim his innocence till Heritage USA's water slide freezes over. Twelve ordinary citizens heard all the facts and decided otherwise. His lawyers will no doubt appeal, but the jury was right.

Franklin Graham's Assault on Islam
An editorial in The Charlotte Observer Nov. 20, 2001

Suppose you encountered a religion whose sacred book taught that everyone who didn't profess that faith would fry for eternity in a fiery pit, a religion whose teachings were cited as the justification for burning unbelievers at the stake, keeping blacks in slavery, restricting women's freedom, banning books and executing scientists whose findings contradicted the religion's tenets. Hardly a religion based in love and tolerance, you might say.

That religion would be Christianity.

Given the intolerant, aggressive, bloody history of people acting in Christ's name, you'd hope Christians would think twice before calling somebody else's religion "wicked." There's no evidence, however, that Christian evangelist Franklin Graham thought even once before putting that brand on Islam.

Mr. Graham, who directs the praiseworthy efforts of Samaritan's Purse ministry in Boone, said in statements aired Friday on *NBC Nightly News* that "we're not attacking Islam, but Islam has attacked us. The God of Islam is not the same God. He's not the son of God of the Christian or Judeo-Christian faith. It's a different God and I believe it is a very evil and wicked religion."

Offered a chance to reconsider his statement, Mr. Graham declined to do so. He did acknowledge in a statement Sunday that "it is not my calling to analyze Islam or any other religions though I recognize that all religions have differences." He should have thought of that earlier.

Laying aside Mr. Graham's certainty about which faith God belongs to, his assertion about the Sept. 11 attacks raises these questions. If it was Islam that attacked us, and not suicidal terrorists who had swallowed a poisoned interpretation of the faith, why have Islamic scholars worldwide condemned the act as contrary to Islamic teachings? Why have nations such as Pakistan, where Islam is the dominant religion, supported our efforts to

BIBLICAL INERRANCY TEST ➡

DO YOU BELIEVE THIS CHURCH DOCTRINE IS **LITERALLY TRUE?**

IF SO, YOU MAY QUALIFY AS A BIBLE-BELIEVIN', BORN-AGAIN, FUNDAMENTALIST **SOUTHERN BAPTIST!**

punish those responsible for the attack?

In fact, both Christianity and Islam have had their demented extremists. Osama bin Laden says his Islamic beliefs support the slaughter of thousands of innocents in New York and Washington Sept. 11. Adolf Hitler in numerous speeches referred to himself as a Christian and his Third Reich as an instrument of Christ. The list of murderers and terrorists who claimed God was on their side is long and depressing. The question of whether a religion should be judged by its best or its worst adherents is open to debate, but it's plainly unfair to use one standard for somebody else's religion and another for your own.

Mr. Graham is right to be concerned about human rights abuses in some Muslim nations. The diversity within the Muslim world suggests, however, that national traditions and leaders have as much to do with the abuses as the Quran.

The greatest advance in religious freedom has come with the separation of church and state. When church and state are one, it's tempting to use state power to impose religious teachings. Religious freedom removes that danger of coercion. Thus Islam as practiced in the United States is different from Islam as practiced in the Taliban's Afghanistan. And Mr. Graham's statements reflect his views, not national policy. Thank heavens.

A Christmas Story

A column in The Charlotte Observer Dec. 21, 1997

I want to tell you a story of the Christmas season, but it needs a preface. So first, a few words about religion and me.

I don't see angels in the clouds or hear God speaking in the ocean's roar or the gurgle of the Mr. Coffee machine. I claim no special religious understanding or theological insight. Some see themselves as instruments of God's indignation about modern life, and devote a good deal of time to separating sheep from goats. I see myself simply as a beneficiary of God's grace.

I grew up with the certainties of the fundamentalist Baptist faith. As my list of questions grew to rival my list of answers, I experienced my share of internal tensions between belief and doubt. I am comforted by the knowledge that others also engage in that struggle.

In my younger days I focused on the uncertainties. As I age, I find myself more comfortable with the mystery, and I find in myself an inclination simply to trust.

I bring this up, as I said, because I want to tell you a Christmas story.

Last year before Christmas I was attending an editors' meeting in Miami. I had forgotten how warm Miami can be in December, and had packed only long-sleeved shirts. The downtown hotel where we met is connected to a shopping mall, so I strolled over the first evening to buy cooler clothing.

I went into J.C. Penney. The menswear area opened directly onto the large hallway near the escalators. As I looked at shirts I could feel the throng of shoppers bustling nearby.

I looked up to see a young man emerge from the crowd and zero in on me. I sensed he intended to ask for something. I braced myself for his pitch. But his question took me by surprise: "Do you believe in Jesus?"

I looked him over. He was a thin, pleasant-looking man in his mid-30s, but his hair was tousled and he needed a shave. He had on a rumpled shirt, worn jeans and loafers with no socks. And he had large sores, visible on his arms and neck, the telltale lesions – Kaposi's sarcoma, I'm told they are called – associated with AIDS.

"Why do you ask?" I said. He told me this story.

He had come to Miami years ago from a nearby town. When he was diagnosed with HIV, his family told him not to come home. Over time his condition had developed into AIDS.

A few days earlier, he said, his family called. For some reason they had a change of heart. They invited him home for Christmas. He couldn't tell them, he said, that he was broke. He needed money for bus fare. Ten dollars would get him home for Christmas.

I'm in a Wednesday morning Bible study class at Myers Park Baptist Church. Not long before my Miami trip we had discussed the passage in Matthew where Jesus speaks to those who are to inherit the kingdom and reminds them of how they had helped him when he was down and out.

They ask, when did we do this? He responds, in the compelling language of the King James Version, "Inasmuch as ye have done it unto one of the least of these my brethren, ye have done it unto me."

There's a problem with knowing these Bible stories: They keep calling you to account. This one is particularly troubling for prosperous people who usually manage to ignore the poverty around us. People like me.

In my pocket I had a $20 bill that I intended to spend on a shirt. I didn't know whether to believe him. It didn't matter. He obviously needed the money more than I did.

I handed him the twenty. "Here," I said. "Merry Christmas."

He was surprised. Apparently he hadn't expected it to be so easy. He took the money and looked straight into my eyes. "Thank you," he said, and it was as heartfelt a thanks as I have ever received. Then he put the money in his pocket and walked away.

Just before he melded into the crowd, he turned and raised his hand in a farewell salute. And he said, "I think you are Jesus."

I was stunned. Before I could respond, he vanished into the crowd of shoppers. What I would have said to him was, "I thought you were Jesus."

Merry Christmas.

XI. Family

Vina and Carl Williams with their son Eddie, age two

The Edmonstons' Reunion

A column in The Charlotte Observer Oct. 5, 1982

Friday I flew to Memphis, rented a car and drove 90 miles to southeast Missouri, where I was born and my forebears – the Williamses, Wilkinses and Edmonstons – have lived and worked for nearly a century.

It is farm country, made bountifully fertile by eons of floods from the Mississippi River and its tributaries. The dark land's flatness is broken only by single files of trees planted as windbreaks, an occasional Indian mound and the levees built to restrain the tendency toward local violation of the global separation of water and land that Jehovah ordered on the Second Day.

My wife, Marylyn, had duties in Charlotte on Saturday, but she would join me in time for the Edmonston family reunion Sunday.

Hornersville is a town of some 600 people, a Missouri replica of the Texas outpost examined in the movie *The Last Picture Show*. It has the bare essentials – an oil and gas supplier, a couple of service stations, a bank, a clinic, a small post office, three or four churches (all Protestant), a video game parlor (is no place safe?) and an elementary school. Hornersville High School, where my graduating class of 1960 had 25 members, long ago consolidated with others nearby and left town.

My uncle, Clyde Ray, who has an insurance agency, tells me there is one remaining grocery store. Williams Gro. and Mkt. ("We deliver," Telephone No. 55), where my family once sold groceries, minnows, ice and coal – too much of it on credit, alas – is closed and locked. It now appears to be a graveyard for deceased appliances, their hulks gleaming in a porcelain heap.

When cotton was picked by hand, Hornersville on a fall Saturday was a boom town, filled with farm families in to socialize and buy provisions. But now giant machines do the picking, and those families have gone elsewhere, many to St. Louis, Detroit and Flint to work in factories.

Young people there today have never seen cotton sacks, those long tubes of heavy canvas that men, women and children strapped over their shoulders each fall and stuffed with cotton plucked by hand from spiny dry bolls. My mother says the last cotton sack she saw was in an exhibit of agricultural memorabilia.

Our people have scattered, too, farther with each generation. Perhaps four dozen, from toddlers to folks long retired, made it back for Sunday dinner. Nobody made a speech, but there was lots of hugging, and enough flash bulbs popped to give me a slight sunburn.

What I regard as the town's most interesting tourist attraction wasn't on display: a giant fish – a 6-foot, 200-pound (if memory serves) alligator gar – pulled from the sluggish brown river where I spent much of my Huck Finn boyhood.

But we did get to see the huge, hollow cypress stump that a man had hauled in from the Little River bottomland and transformed into a marvelous child's playhouse. And Sonny Lomax, the mayor, gave us a tour of Edmonston Gin Co., a state of the art cotton gin owned by some cousins that left me wide-eyed. I had worked in that gin 20 years ago when men strained to do jobs that machines and women now do easily.

I don't go to Hornersville much, the constraints of time and money being what they are. Marylyn and I are only children; our mothers, both widows, live half a continent apart, so they tend to fly here for Christmas and other visits. But when I do go there, and resume the old friendships and familiar rhythms of life, I do not feel a stranger very long.

It's funny. When we lose little things – a car key, a credit card – we know it. But as we move about, seeking adventure or opportunity, we may lose some other, profoundly more important things – a familiar place, filled with memories; the uncritical love and support of family; friendships that span generations – and never quite know what is missing.

We feel their absence, though, from time to time. The feeling takes the form of a vague loneliness, a subconscious longing for certainty and security that was but never will be again.

Marriage, the Best Investment

From a column in The Charlotte Observer Nov. 8, 1998

I am hitting the quarter-century mark with a couple of long-term investments. One is professional. I came to The Charlotte Observer in October of 1973. The other is personal. Shortly after I began work here, I took a month off and married Marylyn Lentine.

Both relationships have had their ups and downs, as long-standing relationships inevitably do, but all in all for me it has been a terrific 25 years.

I wrote a couple of weeks ago about the joy of saying "I quit." My topic was a job that rewarded me handsomely but made me miserable. Don't interpret that as an endorsement of being quick to quit. Some things aren't worth the cost of sticking with them; others are. Knowing the difference is called wisdom.

All of you who have been married as long as Marylyn and I have probably have experienced days when you want to say the hell with it.

If you're essentially a loner, as I am, you may grow weary of the compromises and tiny sacrifices that are essential to maintaining a relationship. You may suffer a disappointment or a loss. As you grow older, you may just tire of your life and yearn for a new start, a new opportunity. Or you may conclude that men and women are so fundamentally different that a permanent alliance is impossible. That's not disloyalty. That's life.

Being married a long time is not an easy thing. Married life involves a good number of frustrations and temptations, endurable only so long as mutual commitment endures. What has made it last for Marylyn and me, I think, is that we are a couple of fairly decent people who tend to get into things for the long haul. People don't stay married a long time because it's easy. They stay married because they don't quit when it's hard.

I have a friend who was married for years and years, raised some fine children, then suddenly divorced. People commiserated with her about her failed marriage. It wasn't a failure, she replied. It was a great success. It just ended.

That happens. People lose whatever held them together. But some people I know seem to me to have given up too quickly, almost out of spite. I hate to see that, especially when children are involved. I know this is an unpopular philosophy these days when personal fulfillment is the ultimate goal, but it seems to me that if grown-ups see fit to bring children into the world, they have an obligation to make some sacrifices to provide a stable upbringing for those children.

Once when Marylyn and I were having a particularly rocky time, she said something that went straight to the heart of the matter, and to my heart as well. "We've got a lot invested in this," she said. "Let's work it out."

So we have, my love, and so we did. It's the best investment I ever made.

Question to me from a reader in The Charlotte Observer *Nov. 15, 1988*

Q. You wrote about your marriage in your column last week. Did your wife let you get away with that?

A. In the 25 years we've been married, my wife, Marylyn, has quit smoking, quit drinking and given birth to a son who came out feet first. She has run a 10K race and a few weeks ago she rode her bicycle 150 miles as part of a charity fund-raiser. I doubt she'd be fazed by anything I'd write. But just to be sure, I had her read it first. I'm smarter than I look.

Coach Bubba's Progress

A column in The Charlotte Observer March 25, 1983

Newsweek magazine, the one with the cover story on superkids, arrived at our house Wednesday. The cover story describes the efforts of parents to make sure their toddlers don't waste a moment in idle play when they should be developing the skills they'll need to get into Harvard.

It's a competitive world out there. As parents of an 11-week-old boy, should Marylyn and I hire a tutor to make sure Jonathan doesn't fall forever behind these well-drilled early achievers? Or should we be content to enjoy his happy kicking and waving when I tickle his tummy or Marylyn blows gently on his face?

We care very much about Jonathan's future. In fact, I wanted to give him a head start by naming him Coach Bubba Williams. Coach, after all, is the most respected title in the South, and a boy named Bubba will be a likable fellow who can get away with anything.

Marylyn dealt with my proposal by refusing to take it seriously. Her mother, in New England, needed periodic reassurance. Regional humor sometimes doesn't travel well.

No doubt the parents in the *Newsweek* article are well-meaning, but something about them reminded me of parents of some of the boys on a basketball team I used to coach. It wasn't enough for these parents that their boys tried hard and improved their skills. The boys had to play well.

But playing well was simply beyond the capability of some of them. Some of the parents were not only disappointed by that, they disapproved of their kids' exuberant gracelessness. Almost maliciously, it seemed to me, they let their children see their disapproval.

That didn't bother some of my players. Kids are, after all, among God's more resilient creations. But others got their parents' message: You let me down. You made me look bad. You owe it to me to do better.

I'm not qualified to give any lectures on parenthood. All I can tell you is what Marylyn and I hope for our son. We hope we'll be able to give Jonathan the opportunity to swim before he can walk and read as soon as he's ready and play a midget Stradivarius if he's interested. We will do what we can to help him build his physical and mental skills.

But most of all, we want him to think of learning as an interesting challenge, not as a chore. We hope he'll approach that challenge eagerly. We want him to understand that it isn't necessary to do everything well; it's OK to do things just for fun.

We hope he'll be able to tell the trivial from the important, and that on the important things he will not necessarily be the best but will always do his best.

We hope we will have the strength to avoid imposing our fantasies on our son, and that we will never push him to succeed at anything just because his success would make us look good.

And we hope we can help him understand that the most valuable lessons have nothing to do with playing the violin or translating Sanskrit or doing triple backflips. They have to do with love and honesty and courage and loyalty and tolerance and perseverance – qualities no more abundant among graduates of Harvard than among people who couldn't find Cambridge on a map.

Jonathan Lentine Williams, born a week before my 41st birthday, has brought exciting unpredictability into our lives. Marylyn worked until two hours before his birth. He arrived 31 minutes after we checked into Memorial Hospital. He entered the world feet first, his impatience to get on with life foiling the doctor's plan to deliver him by Cesarean section to avoid the perils of breech birth.

No doubt more surprises await us, not all of them so joyful.

Friday morning we all were in our living room. The *Newsweek* with the superkids article was on a table. Jonathan was in his bassinet, newly fed and diapered. Marylyn and I had that morning grogginess inflicted by an infant who keeps odd hours and places no value on personal hygiene.

Marylyn peeked into the bassinet and beckoned to me. Our son had made an important discovery: his thumb. For the first time, he was hungrily sucking it. We couldn't have been happier if he'd recited a passage from Shakespeare.

The Power of Fireflies
An editorial in The Charlotte Observer June 13, 1989

It was dusk Sunday evening, close to bath- and bedtime for the neighborhood's 6-year-olds, when the boy spotted the first one. "Look there, Dad," he shouted, voice filled with excitement and wonder. "A firefly!"

Soon Dad saw it, too – a half-inch-long beetle moving haphazardly through the air, intermittently flashing a greenish light.

The boy rushed after his butterfly net, eager to capture a jarful of the bugs and watch them glow. Soon the boys across the street saw the action and came running to join in. Their dads followed, and soon the moms came out, too.

At first the boys darted after the sluggish bugs, then they learned that they had better luck when they moved slowly. The parents sat on the porch, talking quietly and watching the beautiful sight.

Fireflies, or lightning bugs, have a remarkable ability. These dull-colored, soft-bodied beetles can produce virtually heatless light by oxidizing a chemical called luciferin. On humid summer evenings, masses of them can turn a lawn into a silent light show.

The ability to chemically produce soft, cool light is not the only miracle fireflies perform. They work an even greater miracle on people. As kids pursue them and we parents watch, they gently pry us loose from the concerns of the present and transport us back to the carefree days of long ago, when we were the gleeful kids chasing fireflies and our parents watched us from porch chairs.

How miraculous that a tiny insect can do what the greatest scientists cannot: It can launch us on a languid journey back through time, reinforcing the link between generations forged by love and preserved in memory.

Whoever said "the best things in life are free" could have had in mind an evening watching kids chase fireflies.

Fathers Playing Catch with Sons
An editorial in The Charlotte Observer April 13, 1990

It is a warm sunny Saturday, the perfect day for the big event: a trip to the toy store to buy the boy's first baseball.

The balls, all encased in plastic bubbles, come in varying degrees of firmness, from squeezable rubber models to real hardballs. The boy and his dad settle on the Dwight Gooden model, almost as hard as they come. Dad, envisioning his 7-year-old with a smashed nose, argues gently for a softer ball. No, this is it, says the boy, a veteran of one year of T-ball. So it is.

At home, the boy unwraps the ball and gets his glove. Dad goes to the closet and digs out his glove, so old it was made in America. The leather thongs that held the fingers together are broken, but no matter. Three decades of use have shaped the glove to his hand. They go out to play catch.

The boy is a lefty, with a strong arm but erratic aim – bystanders, be alert. They toss and catch, toss and catch. Often the boy bobbles. Occasionally he misses and runs after the ball. The boy is noticeably better than last spring, when he had as much success catching butterflies as baseballs.

As they practice, Dad gives advice. Point your glove up when the ball comes at you high. Step in the direction you're throwing and your aim will be better. When the ball hits your glove, use your throwing hand to trap it. Don't jump around when you're catching the ball; the more you move, the harder it is to catch.

The father needs to say these things, as his father had said them years ago. The boy doesn't need to do them, of course. He's only 7, and his goal is enjoying the moment, not mastering the game. The father understands that.

They catch and toss, catch and toss, in the familiar rhythm, as dusk settles in. Mom comes to the window and signals that dinner is on the table.

Throw me a pop-up, Dad says. The boy responds by throwing the ball hard about 10 feet above his dad's head. It hits the faraway fence and tunnels into the ivy. They poke around a while, laughing, then find it and go in.

There are many demands on fathers' time – making money, community service, church, outings with friends. But it just may be, in the long journey of life, that none of those is as important as fathers playing catch with sons.

Mother's Day

A column in The Charlotte Observer May 14, 2006

My mother was born in the cotton lands of rural northeast Arkansas and lived almost all her life within 50 miles of her birthplace. She and Dad ran our small grocery in a town of 700 where I spent most of my childhood. She ran it by herself when Dad could find other local jobs – hauling melons or gravel in our dump truck, buying local produce for shipment to big stores in Memphis. We had our town's only ice house, so early in the morning she might be the one who'd chip and sell the 12½- and 25-pound blocks that people picked up for home iceboxes or to provide cool water for field hands. When I was big enough I took that job.

There were two kinds of kids in town. Some of us could never imagine living anywhere else. Others couldn't wait to leave. I was one of the latter.

After I left for college at the University of Mississippi, 150 miles away, I came home only for Thanksgiving and Christmas. In summers I worked harvesting peas and corn for Del Monte in the vast farmlands of Illinois. Because it was harvest work, there was no limit on our hours. The 100-hour weeks enabled even low-wage workers to make what was, by my standards, a lot of money in a hurry.

Dad died during my second year in college. I took most of a year off to help at home.

We sold the store. Mom, an avid reader, became the only staffer in the local branch of the county library. I worked in a cotton gin until I could earn and borrow enough money to return to school.

After college I went into the Army and then got a series of jobs far from her home. We kept in touch with occasional phone calls and letters, but each of us always knew the other was there, and we had that unbreakable bond of love and kinship.

After Marylyn and I settled in Charlotte, we always flew our mothers in for the holidays. But one year Mom stumbled getting off the plane and hurt her leg. She didn't want to fly after that.

In her small town Mom lived by herself but surrounded by family and friends. She was a warm, friendly woman with quiet good humor and uncommon resilience. We talked often on the phone. She seemed fine.

She wasn't. A neighbor called one day to tell me Mom had stopped answering the door. A friend went in and found the house a mess and Mom spending most of her time in a soiled bed.

I tried to create a better situation for her. I hired a woman to clean her house once a week and arranged for a meals-on-wheels group to bring lunch every day. She soon came to regard this as intrusive and sent them away. Her fierce independence, which had carried her through a hard but happy life, had become a danger to her. She needed a little help but would not accept it.

There was no place in her town where she could live and get the support she needed. So we brought her here – 700 miles from home. She lived with us for a year, but she needed more attention than our two-worker family could provide. Or, at least, was willing to provide.

We found her a place in a nursing home in Matthews. It was a clean, well-run institution, but she never considered herself more than a visitor there.

I had a demanding job, with a young son. I didn't visit her as much as I should have. Often when I did, she'd forget I'd been there. Her knees were bad, her eyesight and memory faded. She had always lived around people she had known from birth. Now she felt she had been thrust into a society of uncaring strangers.

Sometimes I tried to get her to go places with me – to church, a movie, shopping. She rarely wanted to. Though she was happy to see us when we visited, she eventually didn't want to come to our house for holidays. When I offered to take her to her hometown to visit, she didn't feel like making the trip. One day she said to me, "I think I've just lived too long." Soon afterward, she died in her sleep.

If I had it to do again, what would I do differently? For one thing, I would try to devise a way to let her live in her hometown, near old friends and relatives. Bringing her here made her safer. It didn't make her happier.

Mom loved me and I loved her. She lived with courage and independence until her body failed her. I know in some ways I failed her, too. But if she blamed me, she never told me so. She was, to the end, my mother.

The Best Gift for Fathers
A column in The Charlotte Observer June 17, 2001

Father's Day is a bittersweet occasion for me this year. In a couple of months our son will leave home for college. Friends are already kidding (or consoling) Marylyn and me about living with the empty nest.

I smile and say no problem, he's going off to Princeton and taking most of our money with him, so we'll fill our idle hours working part-time jobs at the neighborhood Harris-Teeter.

I may be eating these words in a few months, but I doubt that our lives will descend into emptiness when Jonathan departs for college. Marylyn and I were married for 10 enjoyable years before we thought about having a child. Our 18 years with our son have been an enriching experience, but he's clearly ready – let's face it, he's eager – to go.

The sadness of his departure will be at least partly soothed by the new freedom Marylyn and I will have, and the smaller piles of dirty clothes we'll need to wash.

To every thing there is a season, says the narrator in Ecclesiastes, and a time to every purpose under heaven. For Jonathan it is time to go off on the adventure that will be the rest of his life.

For Marylyn and me it is time to be grateful for the years the three of us have lived together, to be content in knowing that we have taught him what we knew to teach, to appreciate the opportunities presented by this new phase in our lives together, and to enjoy the evolving relationship we will have with the young man who was once our child.

I have learned a lot in 18 years of fatherhood. No undertaking on Earth requires you to make more decisions, and nothing adequately prepares you to make them.

I learned, over time, to appreciate both the pleasure of saying "yes" and the duty of saying "no." I am his father, not his buddy, and at times

"NO, I DON'T WANT TO KNOW WHAT BILL COSBY WOULD DO IN A CASE LIKE THIS!"

my judgment has had to overrule his preferences. His mother and I owed him loving guidance, not easy acquiescence in whatever somebody else's kids might be doing.

But he seemed from his early years to have an internal compass that kept him headed pretty much in the right direction. We learned we could trust his judgment, so more and more often we did.

I can't say how it happened, but somehow the three of us accomplished the goal that parents both aim for and dread: We have seen a child grow into a young man who is prepared to go out on his own.

Father's Day presents are nice, but our son already has given me the most precious gift: more love and trust and joy than I ever expected, or anyone could deserve.

XII. Education

A Cry for Help

A column in The Charlotte Observer Sept. 18, 1990

There's a hot debate in this community, reflected in letters to the editor, about school people's complaint that it's tough to teach some of the impoverished students they get. Baloney, some readers respond; a lot of kids from poor families have done well in school.

Virginia McLaughlin's letter in today's Forum is a good and thoughtful example. She's right, of course. When she was teaching in Harlan County, I was going to school in a tiny farm town where nobody had much money. Poor kids went to school, studied, and learned.

But I must say, I never knew children hobbled by the problems I see kids bringing to my son's school today.

Every child I knew growing up had a family – a two-parent family, as a rule. There were a few ne'er-do-wells and charity cases in town, but neighbors helped make sure their kids had what they needed. The superintendent knew every student by name and family. There were guns in almost every home (I had my first shotgun before I was 12) but nobody brought them to school. There was little crime. No drugs. No TV.

I see two great problems in our schools today. One involves teachers. A lot of the bright women who were teachers in my day are lawyers and bankers and real estate agents today. And many of those who do teach today can't scratch their backs unless (a) somebody upstairs approves it and (b) they fill out a form.

The other problem is that too many kids don't get the family support they need. My son goes to Dilworth Elementary School. My wife and I are active in the school. I chair the school committee. I know what a strong, smart principal and splendid, highly motivated teachers can do. But I also know that at least one child in five comes to school with so little nurturing and support from home that he or she is behind from day one.

I'm not at all satisfied with our schools. I get angry when I see widespread tolerance of failure. There's only one test of a good school: Are children learning what they need to know? If significant numbers of them consistently aren't, then the schools are failing – and something must change.

What? Pay good teachers well and treat them as professionals. Help weak teachers get better or get out. No job guarantees for principals – if they're not doing the job, get somebody else. Take an ax to the top-down bureaucracy that hobbles talented people. And if what's being done isn't working, try something else.

But something also must be done to reach some children outside the schoolhouse. Before school and throughout school, children need support at home.

America has a terrible family problem. School people can't solve it. They aren't whining. They're crying for help.

Business as Usual is Failing
A column in The Charlotte Observer May 27, 2001

Some North Carolina parents and educators think a year-end test to determine whether public school students will be promoted is a fundamentally bad idea. They favor scrapping North Carolina's end-of-grade tests in grades 3, 5 and 8 and coming up with a variety of ways, including classwork and teacher evaluations, to assess student progress.

Many of their concerns and suggestions make sense. But if the question is whether to stick with or abandon periodic mandatory testing of all students, I say stick with it.

If tests are flawed, fix the flaws. If high-stakes tests are the wrong instrument, devise a better one. But do not, under any circumstances, go back to the days when schools measured their success or failure by some standard other than whether their students learn what they need to know.

Our son will graduate, God willing, from Myers Park High School in a couple of weeks. I have been involved with his schools since his kindergarten days.

A dozen years ago I was one of two or three parents invited to serve on an advisory council at his elementary school. One evening we parents worked for hours with teachers and administrators to put together the school's goals for the coming year.

They were good goals, involving teacher education and training, parental participation, team teaching and mentoring, etc. The teachers and administrators who worked on them were among the smartest and most committed educators I've known.

But as the session neared its end, something was missing. These are good goals, I told the group, but as a parent, I have one essential measure of the school's success or failure: Is my son learning what he needs to know? I recommended adding a goal: Ensure each child makes one year's academic progress during the year.

Nobody disagreed with my intent, but the principal and teachers explained to me the problem with such a goal. They had no systematic way of measuring the yearly progress of each student, they said, and no reliable way of linking what teachers do to how much students learn.

I was amazed. The school system didn't have a reliable way to determine whether it was accomplishing its primary goal: to ensure, year by year, that each child reached a certain level of basic academic skill.

In fact, some students simply slipped through, promoted year after year though they had made little academic progress.

I would soon learn that good teachers and principals were quite dissatisfied with the system. They knew that in many schools perhaps a third of their students – and at some schools even more – were doomed to failure.

It was predictable and disheartening. The students would drop out. Or, hobbled by inadequate preparation and lack of support at home, they would fall behind in reading and never catch up. This went on at school after school, year after year, and nobody made much of a fuss. Why? Because the children who were failing were the children of the poor. They weren't failing because teachers were inept or didn't care. They were failing because the system wasn't designed to meet their needs. The system didn't require the schools to teach them – in fact, didn't realistically expect it.

That's what's behind the accountability movement that is changing the way public schools operate in North Carolina and many other states. The idea is simple: If we set standards for what students should know at a certain grade level, and test to determine whether they know it, then we'll have some basis for judging whether our schools are doing the job we need them to do.

Real life isn't so simple, of course. Kids progress at different rates. High-stakes tests are an imperfect instrument even when administered effectively. Teachers may be tempted (or told) to teach only for the tests, making education a rote, joyless enterprise.

But one thing is sure: The tests provide a better measure of how our schools are doing than any we've had before.

How are they doing? Quite well with students like our son, who come well prepared and live in homes where success in school is expected. Not so well with students who are ill-prepared and lack support at home.

Now that all North Carolina students must take periodic tests of proficiency in reading, writing and math, there's no escaping the fact that we're running a two-tiered school system, with the bottom tier headed toward failure.

This disconcerting fact presents a challenge for citizens who understand that a democratic republic with a free-enterprise economy must have educated citizens. The challenge is this: Will we continue to run public schools the way we have in the past, and hope for different results? Or will we acknowledge that for a substantial minority of students, the system has failed, and create a new system that serves them, too?

Eric Smith, the Charlotte-Mecklenburg superintendent of schools, thinks massive changes are needed. In his annual budget request he has asked county commissioners to fund many of them.

The county manager's proposed budget, however, falls short – embarrassingly short – of doing so. As an editorial on the preceding page points out, it wouldn't even fund expansion of the justly praised Bright Beginnings program for needy preschoolers.

Is Smith asking for too much? Your answer may depend on whether you think "Leave no child behind" is a catchy political slogan or a moral imperative.

Charlotte-Mecklenburg and North Carolina haven't yet awakened to the new economy's new demands on public education. Business as usual in education won't do the job, even with a little more money thrown in. The nation's economy has changed. The demands are unprecedented.

Not many years ago teenagers could drop out or do poorly in school and still find work that would support a family. No more. The gap between the prosperous and the poor is more than ever before a gap between the educated and the uneducated. Somewhere, sometime, somebody must recognize and meet this new challenge. Let's do it here and now.

My Advice to Graduates
A column in The Charlotte Observer May 28, 2006

Being a graduation speaker is no easy task. That's why I've never accepted an invitation to do it.

What's so tough about it? For one thing, you'll labor over a speech that hardly anyone will listen to. The stars of the day, after all, are the students, not you, and their minds will be everywhere but on your words.

A few dedicated souls, however, will listen. They'll expect you to have something to say. If your speech is a bomb, they'll remember it forever. That happened a couple of years ago at my son's college graduation. Comedian Chevy Chase was a speaker and he wasn't funny – wasn't, in fact, even coherent. He was a memorable speaker, but not in a good way.

For those reasons I don't do graduation speeches. I do, from time to time, consider what I might say if I did. If you're interested, read on.

Students, parents, faculty and friends: I graduated from high school 46 years ago. Since then I've learned some things, mostly by trial and error. Perhaps you'll find value in these thoughts, inspired by things I've experienced, read, listened to and thought about over the years.

1. Understand that in any job, and in all of life, some undertakings allow for creativity and variety, but others require you to do the same things everyone else does. Boring? Maybe. But happiness does not lie ahead for the NASCAR driver who decides to turn right instead of left.

2. In thinking about life and work, remember what you learn in squeezing a tube of toothpaste. You'll get a little out of it if you insist on starting at the top, but you'll get a lot more if you're willing to start at the bottom.

3. A vastly under-appreciated virtue is enthusiasm. Potential employers, friends and lovers are more likely to be drawn to people whose attitude brings energy into a room, rather than sucks energy out of it.

4. This probably is not an old Chinese saying, but it is nevertheless

true: A person who stands by the side of the road with his mouth open, in hope that the bird of paradise will fly in, is likely to wind up with a mouthful of flies.

5. Do not think of graduation day as the end of something. The ceremony, after all, is called commencement – the act or time of beginning. Graduation day is when you embark on education, not when you complete it. The ceremony celebrating the completion of your education is called a funeral.

6. Graduates, do not worry if you didn't get into the college of your choice or you weren't hired for the job you've always dreamed of. Opportunity doesn't make something of you; you make something of it.

7. In serious conversations, listen critically to what people say. Much of conversation consists of cliches that sound authoritative but whose primary function is to allow the speaker to avoid thinking. This is almost always the case when someone uses a term like "political correctness." Don't mistake glibness for insight.

8. Don't be reluctant to do something because you fear you won't do it as well as others. Differences enrich life. If only the most beautiful plants grew, there'd be roses but no potatoes. Yet no matter how much ketchup you dip it in, a rose will never taste as good as a french fry.

9. The feeling that the best is yet to come isn't limited to the young, but it's harder to maintain when your future is much shorter than your past. So when older people tell you how much more virtuous, more competent and more dedicated everybody was in the good old days, understand that years from now you'll probably think so, too.

10. Many people have said this, and it is true: Smart people learn from experience; wise people learn from the experience of others. If you practice putting this to use, you'll develop a skill that will help you succeed in the game of life.

Once at an editors' meeting a labor lawyer gave us several rules that if followed, he said, would ensure we'd never be sued over workplace problems. After his speech, I asked why he'd told us this. If we followed his rules, we'd never need his services, would we?

He smiled and replied, "I've worked with editors for many years, and I know this: They never follow all the rules, even those that are good for them."

Neither will you, graduates. But have a good life anyway.

XIII. Arts and Letters

APRYL CHAPMAN THOMAS

Rowan Oak, the William Faulkner home in Oxford, Miss., was
guarded by a vigilant cow.

Mr. Faulkner's Watchcow

A column in The Charlotte Observer April 24, 2005

I received an invitation to the May 1 dedication of Rowan Oak, the recently restored William Faulkner home in Oxford, Miss. Though I can't attend, I'd like to contribute to the occasion by offering this personal footnote to the history of the place. It involves my 1965 encounter with the Faulkner family cow.

Rowan Oak, built in the 1840s, is a white clapboard house in a primitive Greek Revival style. It's a 10-minute walk from Courthouse Square and Oxford's Confederate monument. When Faulkner bought it in 1930, the two-story house was run down — no plumbing, lights or running water. Strapped for money, Faulkner did much of the renovation himself. He, his wife and her two children from a previous marriage moved in. A few years later daughter Jill was born. Rowan Oak was the family home until 1962, when Faulkner died.

The place seemed a fitting home for Faulkner — proud but a bit shabby, famous but private. Visitors approached the front of the house on a broad brick walkway flanked by giant cedars. Behind the house were some outbuildings, a pasture and Bailey's woods, named for an earlier owner. My adventure began in those woods.

In April 1965, Ole Miss hosted the Southern Literary Festival, a three-day gathering of the region's literary scholars and student writers. Guests Robert Penn Warren, Eudora Welty, Malcolm Cowley and others were on hand to pay tribute to Faulkner.

For the first time since the festival began in 1937, blacks would be attending. The decision to invite a delegation from Tougaloo, a black college near Jackson, was difficult because of the recent history of Ole Miss. In the fall of 1962, two men died in a night of rioting on campus following the school's court-ordered integration. Federal troops put down the insurrection and occupied the campus.

The Tougaloo students arrived Thursday. By evening hundreds of students had gathered outside the dorm where they were staying, chanting "8-6-4-2, send them back to Tougaloo." Ole Miss students – angry or drunk or both – battered and set fire to the Tougaloo delegation's rental car, parked near the dorm. I was editor of the student newspaper, the Daily Mississippian. When the action ended I rushed to the office to write an editorial denouncing the riot.

During the festival Faulkner's house was supposed to be open to visitors, but it wasn't. No explanation was offered, but Dorothy Oldham, Faulkner's sister-in-law, controlled access to the house, and she was notoriously unwelcoming to visitors.

Undeterred, two of my fellow aspiring writers and I decided we'd pay an uninvited visit. We tromped through Bailey's woods and made our way into the pasture behind the house. We didn't know what to expect. Vicious dogs? Armed guards? Hidden bear traps?

We didn't expect a cow. Yet there she was, attached by a long chain to a post near the house. She looked harmless, but eyed us warily. We set out to creep quietly around her.

No deal. She moved quickly to block our progress – head lowered, gaze fixed on us. We moved to our left. She followed. We moved to our right. So did she. Clearly this was Faulkner's watchcow, a bovine agent of the writer's wish to be "the last private person in the world."

One of my companions was Henry Hurt, a gifted writer who had received a top prize at the festival. He had enrolled at Ole Miss after involuntarily departing from Randolph-Macon in Virginia, where some escapades had made him unwelcome. He was keeping a low profile by writing in the Mississippian under a pen name, Hank Paine.

In Hank's account, our third co-sneaker reasoned with the cow by means of a hard left hook to her nose. Maybe so. Somehow we did evade the cow and creep up to the house. We peered into the window but couldn't see much in the dark, deserted rooms. No matter. It was the principle that was important.

At a reunion of student newspaper editors several years later I was invited inside the house. When I mentioned my last visit to our guide, I discovered that the Hank Paine report had become part of Rowan Oak lore.

The literati had concluded the cow was a clever symbol for Dorothy Oldham. No, no, I told him. The cow was really a cow.

To Chancellor Robert Khayat, thanks for the invitation. And watch out for that cow.

The Day I Made Eudora Disappear

A column in The Charlotte Observer July 29, 2001

On page 7F of today's Observer you'll find a collection of quotes about and from Eudora Welty, the great writer who died Monday at her home in Jackson, Miss.

I was struck by the quote from Shelby Foote, the Mississippi-born novelist and Civil War historian: "I never knew anyone who spent five minutes in her presence who did not love her."

Amen.

Regular readers may remember my story about how William Faulkner's belligerent cow deterred me from peeking into Faulkner's unoccupied house. That's not my only misadventure with great writers. Someday I'll tell you about the time I declined an offer from then-unknown Alice Walker to write for a journal I was editing. But now, let me recall for you my near-disaster with Ms. Welty.

In the late 1960s and early '70s I was a journalist in Jackson, working for a group of tiny daily newspapers. I lived in a series of cheap unfurnished apartments in old houses that were scheduled for demolition.

It seemed like paradise. I was in my 20s with no ambition except to do work I enjoyed and keep company with people I liked.

I worked a variety of part-time jobs to supplement my meager salary. Some of them I did just for the paycheck – clerking at the S&H Green Stamps redemption center, for example – but mostly I found journalistic odd jobs.

A particularly lucrative job – $100, which was more than I made most weeks – was sent my way by my friend Bill Minor, the longtime New Orleans Times-Picayune correspondent in Jackson who also wrote for the New York

Times, *Newsweek* and numerous other publications.

Bill called one morning to say *Newsweek* wanted a photograph of Eudora Welty to run with a review of her forthcoming novel, *Losing Battles*. Could I shoot it?

Can kudzu climb?

I was acquainted with Ms. Welty through friends. I knew her to be uncommonly hospitable for someone so famous. I called her house. She answered the phone. We set a time for me to come over.

We spent an hour or more in the garden beside her comfortable but unimposing old family home near the state Capitol. I suggested settings and poses; she politely followed my directions. I thanked her and went off to develop the film.

I didn't have a darkroom, but the United Press International bureau chief allowed me to use theirs. All the chemicals were ready when I arrived. I wound the film on the reel, plunged it into the developing solution and started the timer. When the process was done, I looked at the negatives.

The sight was horrifying. The negatives were all black. I could see nothing in them – no flowers, no trees and worst of all no Eudora Welty.

What had happened? There had been a big fire in Jackson the night before. Apparently the photographer who had used the darkroom had strengthened the developer to increase the contrast in the film shot at night. I, expecting the normal developing time, had overdeveloped my film.

Or maybe I just did something wrong. Who knows? What I did know was that one of America's finest writers had graciously spent a lot of time with me, and I had nothing to show for it.

I called Bill Minor for advice. Buy a dozen roses, he said. Go to her house, knock on the door, give her the flowers and tell her what happened. Throw yourself on her mercy.

That's what I did. "Oh," she said, "I know how you feel. I've done things like that a hundred times." I could have hugged her. She invited me back into the garden where we did it all again. This time, no darkroom disaster.

Later I learned she had been a photographer for the Works Progress Administration during the Depression, touring Mississippi with a cheap camera and doing the lab work in her kitchen at night. In 1971, Random House published a collection of her photos, *One Time, One Place: Mississippi in the Depression*.

Her own experience was the explanation she gave for her understanding response to my blunder. It wasn't, I think, the real reason. The empathy evident in her writing also shaped her relationships with others. She was a great lady as well as a great writer.

Joe Martin's Journey

A column in The Charlotte Observer Nov. 18, 2001

How does one prepare to be a novelist? That question was on my mind last week as I prepared to introduce my old friend Joe Martin at Myers Park Baptist Church before a discussion of his new novel, *Fire in the Rock*, a coming-of-age novel inspired by his own youth in South Carolina.

Joe and Joan Martin would be there, along with son David, who would read excerpts from the book. Our minister, Steve Shoemaker, would then lead a discussion.

So how did Joe Martin get to be a novelist? Here is his orderly path. He was a cheerleader at Davidson College. He earned a master's degree in American studies at the University of Minnesota and a doctorate in medieval English at Duke University. Which prepared him, of course, to work for a bank.

In 1973, he joined a modest regional bank known as NCNB and became one of the platoon of visionaries who eventually made it Bank of America, the nation's largest.

In 1978, he walked away from a successful career to become a college administrator. He went to raise money and head the college relations department at Queens College. He returned to the bank in 1983 when Hugh McColl Jr. was named CEO.

While Joe worked for the bank, no one mistook him for a banker. You'd have had more luck getting a loan from your brother-in-law than from Joe. Instead, he was one of the bank's premier idea men. Some also saw him as the bank's conscience, a sort of Jiminy Cricket in pinstripes whom the money managers counted on for ideas about how to use the bank to build a better community.

Joe also was an active supporter of public education. The Martin children went to public schools here. In the late 1980s, his concern about schools led him to seek and win a seat on the Charlotte-Mecklenburg school board. It's hard to imagine an unlikelier elected official than Joe – not because he lacked knowledge or commitment, but because he has notoriously small tolerance for idiots, a substantial number of whom focused their attention on (or even served on) the school board.

In October of 1994, Joe entered a new phase of his life. He was diagnosed with amyotrophic lateral sclerosis – Lou Gehrig's disease. ALS has sapped his physical powers but hasn't weakened his mind. He can move his eyes and raise his eyebrows. It's amazing how much communication those small movements allow. He writes now with the aid of an Eyegaze computer system, which enables him to type by focusing his eyes on a letter of the alphabet. He told my colleague David Perlmutt in an e-mail exchange earlier this year, "My mother was able to make the whole world do whatever she wanted with a look. As far as I know, this is the same system."

In recent years he has become a spokesman for social justice and racial unity, and has rightly received the community's gratitude for those efforts.

He's also a 60-year-old guy in a wheelchair. Here's what he told reporter Perlmutt about his condition: "I want you to understand, the paralyzed man you see is not who I am. 'Paralyzed' is something I have now been given to do, but it is not who I am.

"I am who I was. And the discovery of that enabled me to get on with my life, despite the diagnosis of inevitable total paralysis."

He added, "I don't think I am courageous; I suppose people may think I am dying, and that may even be fair – I thought so for a while, too. But I think I am still living, and the evidence suggests that I am! And so I am just doing what I think living people should do."

So he is. Encased in a body that has pretty much retired from action, the essential Joe Martin carries on, with humor and resoluteness. He does so with a conviction that what he's doing isn't courageous, it's just getting on with a life that now must be lived under unusual circumstances.

How do you prepare to be a novelist? In Joe's case, you develop the ability to observe the human condition clearly and sympathetically, to separate what's important from what isn't and to comment on it in an insightful, meaningful way.

Joe Martin is traveling that path. The wisdom he has gained along the way is on display in his work, and in his life.

Hail, Fiona!

A column in The Charlotte Observer May 26, 1993

Who's that Scottish girl playing the garlic music? And how do I get one of her beer mugs?
— one of Fiona Ritchie's early fans

When Fiona Ritchie first ventured onto the airwaves at Charlotte radio station WFAE, many listeners probably figured Celtic music was what the Boston Garden band played when Larry Bird hit a long jump shot. Ms. Ritchie had come to UNC-Charlotte from her native Scotland in 1981 to be a teaching assistant in the psychology department. There she fell in with Jennifer Roth and the small, hard-working band of dreamers who were building a radio station from scratch.

It was a time when everything was new, and therefore anything seemed possible. So using albums she had brought from home, Fiona filled the air with lilting pipes and Celtic harps playing the lively reels and lovely ballads of the British Isles. Uncertain at first that anyone was out there listening, Ms. Ritchie would offer listeners fund-raising incentives such as beer mats (coasters) she'd picked up in Scottish pubs, prompting the listener's query noted above.

Ten years ago WFAE launched her radio show, "The Thistle and Shamrock," and now hundreds of thousands of listeners hear it weekly on more than 260 National Public Radio member stations across the country. Ms. Ritchie has been the Billy Graham of the Celtic music revival in the United States, and the eerie thumping of the bodhran is heard throughout the land.

The music is wonderful, to be sure, but many listeners would tune in weekly to hear Ms. Ritchie read the instructions for filling out IRS Form 1040A. Her lilting voice trills cheerily in a half-brogue that brings to mind pure stream water rushing over rocks. In her case, the voice reveals the soul: Though she has traveled the world and accumulated honors and fame, she remains essentially the enthusiastic, optimistic, intelligent young woman who began playing the music she loved on WFAE in June 1983 and hoped somebody would listen.

Happy anniversary, Fiona. You're always welcome at our place.

Dorothy Masterson, theater pioneer

An editorial in The Charlotte Observer April 8, 1991

As an actress and director, Dorothy Masterson made an evening at the theater magic time. In a career spanning three decades, she oversaw the creation of serious theater here. She died March 22 in Gaithersburg, Md.

Mrs. Masterson knew her craft. She played a movie role in Denver at age 12. She studied in New York with Antoinette Perry, for whom Broadway's Tony awards are named. She acted in community theaters as she and her husband, a salesman, moved around the country. She won her first stage role here 12 days after they came to Charlotte in 1948. In 1949, she honed her directorial skills with the TownPark Players, sponsored by the city parks and recreation department. She insisted that actors strive to be worthy of the plays she directed. One of her young actors, Charles Kuralt, recalled her as a tough taskmaster with "a bit of a temper. She was professional; we were decidedly not."

In 1954, she founded her theater, the Mint Theatre Guild, and made it Charlotte's center for serious drama. Gladys Lavitan, who acted under her at the Mint, said of her methods: "One actor said it was like someone opening a watch case with a hammer. We took it because we knew it was never personal – when she found fault with you it was because she wanted to improve you." When she retired from directing in 1977, Mrs. Masterson was Charlotte's First Lady of the theater.

It is said that when Ludwig van Beethoven composed, he considered himself in tune with the music of God. When a violinist complained to him that one passage was so awkwardly written as to be virtually unplayable, the maestro replied, "When I composed that, I was conscious of being inspired by God Almighty. Do you think I can consider your puny little fiddle when He speaks to me?"

It is impossible to say whether Dorothy Masterson felt similarly attuned to the divine intent, but to her actors nothing about her suggested otherwise.

Today, when a curtain opens here, Dorothy Masterson's spirit is there, for she more than anyone else created the artistic community that made serious theater possible.

The Novelist for Our Time

A column in The Charlotte Observer May 13, 1990

Walker Percy, who died Thursday, was not a writer who offered easy answers, but his questions were superb.

The fundamental question in his novels (*The Moviegoer*, *Lancelot*) is the most compelling one for American society today: Why, in this land of plenty, do so many people find life so empty?

To Percy, that was a religious question. In the cosmology of modern America, science has displaced God, profoundly disorienting us humans. If we're not God's children, are we mere cousins of baboons? Without God, is life meaningless? If such questions make us uncomfortable, would we be better off – better "adjusted" – if we didn't ask them?

To Percy, the questions had to be asked. To not do so would suggest that we consider the questions unimportant or fear the answers.

In Percy's novels, the sanest people appear slightly insane – genial drunks and failed businessmen at odds with the lunacy of modern life. They are gentle, intelligent people, seeking both the meaning of life and some way to get their balance in a world that is slightly askew.

In his 1983 work of nonfiction, *Lost in the Cosmos: The Last Self-Help Book*, Percy's recommendation for living sanely is to challenge the insane world's assumptions. To readers who feel depressed, he urges, "Assume that you are quite right. You are depressed because you have every reason to be depressed. ... You live in a deranged age – more deranged than usual, because despite great scientific and technological advances, man has not the faintest idea of who he is or what he is doing. ... Consider the only adults who are never depressed: chuckleheads, California surfers, and fundamentalists who believe they have had a personal encounter with Jesus and are saved for once and all. Would you trade your depression to become any of these?"

Rafael Sabatini, author of several adventure novels that would become Erroll Flynn movies, opened his *Scaramouche* with a wonderful sentence: "He was born with the gift of laughter and the sense that the world was mad. ... "

Walker Percy had those qualities, too. Combined with his wry insight into our materially rich, spiritually poor society, they made him the novelist for our time.

Is That What You Call 'Art'?

An editorial in The Charlotte Observer Dec. 9, 1980

If one purpose of a museum is to make its exhibitions the talk of the town, the Mint Museum deserves a bravo for displaying Arthur Weyhe's pole sculpture in Thompson Park, near the intersection of Third Street and Kings Drive.

Some traditionalists are outraged, but so what? New ventures in art, good or bad, always outrage traditionalists. Keeping the dust off the old masters isn't a museum's only function. It should be just as interested in exposing audiences to the varieties of modern artistic expression. When people have the opportunity to compare the old and the new, to see styles in the making, they can decide for themselves what's worthwhile and what's a waste of time. Time will weed out the trash.

What about Mr. Weyhe's teepee-frame arrangement of 26-foot cedar poles? Is that "art"? That's like asking if a baby is cute. To somebody, somewhere, it is, for reasons probably too subjective to argue about. We wouldn't buy the pole sculpture, but neither did the Mint. Not a penny of taxpayers' money was spent to put it there.

Our conclusion, arrived at after maybe six minutes of study of the leaning poles, is a feeling of admiration for Mr. Weyhe's ability to make a living doing what summer campers do for fun. We say give him a merit badge in woodcraft and, after a decent interval, move his creation closer to the Boy Scout office on East 7th Street.

Nobody should be awed by the fact that Mr. Weyhe is a fellow with a beard whose work brings big money in New York. As the inexplicable popularity of Andy Warhol indicates, New York is a place where anything outrageous is likely to be praised and purchased, at least until something more outrageous comes along.

There is a herd instinct among art enthusiasts – or maybe it's a fear of being branded a Philistine – that discourages giggling at obvious put-ons. Mr. Weyhe no doubt has a lot of fun with what he's doing. Charlotte should, too. His series of teepee frames may not be as impressive as Thomasville's big chair, but then every city can't be that lucky.

Policing Arts Grants

An editorial in The Charlotte Observer July 3, 1989

When you read the restrictions Sen. Jesse Helms wants to put on grants given by the National Endowment for the Arts, you see why the system has to rely on human judgment, not just written rules. Here's what the Helms amendment says:

> None of the funds authorized to be appropriated pursuant to this Act may be used to promote, disseminate, or produce –
>
> (1) obscene or indecent materials, including but not limited to depictions of sadomasochism, homoeroticism, the exploitation of children, or individuals engaged in sex acts; or
>
> (2) material which denigrates, debases, or reviles a person, group, or class of citizens on the basis of race, creed, sex, handicap, age, or national origin.

Sen. Helms may know what he means, but how would his rules be applied?

Is a marble sculpture of a naked man, penis dangling, "indecent"? If so, no federal money could promote Michelangelo's splendid "David."

What about a painting that includes a naked figure with flowers protruding from his (or her) rectum? That's "The Garden of Earthly Delights," the 15th-century masterpiece by Hieronymus Bosch, one of history's most imaginative painters.

Does "engage in sex acts" mean no grant to exhibit a sculpture of a nude man and woman passionately embracing and fondling? That's Auguste Rodin's classic "The Kiss."

What Sen. Helms wants, surely, is not to ban federal grants to "promote, disseminate or produce" great art, but to remind people who award NEA grants that some discretion is necessary when spending public money. Such a reminder makes sense. Some advocates of the avant garde seem to think the public should finance whatever bizarre creation some expert ooohs and aaahs over. When non-experts have the audacity to object, the arrogant response of some members of the arts elite can be a little hard to take.

However, no system will ensure that everybody will be happy with every piece of art that gets NEA support. The best way to ensure that good judgment will be used is not to adopt Sen. Helms's rules but to continue the present system: Give the responsibility to men and women of judgment and experience who are chosen by the president and confirmed by the Congress – and hold them accountable.

Over the years, that system has worked well. Congressman Sidney Yates, D-Ill., points out that less than 20 of the approximately 85,000 grants the NEA has made during the last 24 years have aroused controversy involving obscenity, pornography, racial degradation or frivolity. That, he notes, "is less than one-quarter of one-tenth of one percent of all grants."

By and large, the relationship between artists and the public has been good. The public has shown tolerance, if not always enthusiasm, for a wide array of artistic styles and subjects. A controversy from time to time is a messy but effective way of reminding the people who make NEA grants that the money they're spending isn't their own.

The point has been made, The NEA has been reminded. The Helms amendment is unnecessary and unworkable. It should be rejected.

The Dirty Book Man

An editorial in The Charlotte Observer March 14, 2001

Like many reformed sinners, Martin Davis is obsessed with the notion that everyone should embrace his version of morality. He is on a one-man crusade to purge from Charlotte-Mecklenburg Library shelves some books that contain graphic sexual passages, especially homosexual passages. The county library board, correctly, has refused to give him veto power over what others may read. So have county commissioners, who fund the library system.

But Mr. Davis, a former New York actor who acknowledges he has had his wilder days, dramatically marches on. When the commissioners offer open-mike nights to hear constituents' views, he is likely to show up and read the most lurid passages from books he dislikes.

When Mr. Davis last appeared, commissioners' chairman Parks Helms ordered him not to read and threatened to have him ejected from the meeting chamber if he persisted. A security guard grasped Mr. Davis's arm, prompting an additional conflict over whether the county will pay for his visit to the doctor.

The issue isn't simple. Certainly there are books suitable for reading in private that are inappropriate for reading aloud at a commissioners' meeting, just as there are personal acts that are fine in private but shouldn't be done in the middle of Tryon Street. Mr. Davis's insistence on inflicting lurid passages on a captive audience at the televised meeting says a lot about his taste and lack of consideration for others.

Bad taste and inconsiderateness aren't illegal, however. Mr. Davis is exercising a right guaranteed by the U.S. Constitution – the right to petition the government for redress of grievances. His grievance is the content of some books in the library, and he is expressing it by displaying for the commissioners precisely what he finds objectionable.

We asked several constitutional experts about the situation. All gave essentially the same response: If the commissioners offer citizens a forum to speak about general public concerns, Mr. Davis has the same right to use it as anyone else, provided the material he's presenting isn't obscene or otherwise illegal. Unless the commissioners find some solution that we didn't, they may be stuck with Mr. Davis's raunchiness.

An ideal resolution would be for Mr. Davis and the commissioners to work out a less offensive way for him to present his complaint. But that depends on him. Some ex-actors can't give up the spotlight, even when the audience is weary of their performance.

The Storm Over *Angels*
A column in The Charlotte Observer, March 24, 1996

The storm over *Angels in America* didn't reveal anything unique about Charlotte, except that if you have a silly law it can be used to do silly things. The furor did raise some provocative questions. Here's how I'd answer them.

1. *Must good art be "decent"?*
No. "Polite" society defines what's decent. Artists in pursuit of their own vision often strain against the conventions of polite society.

That tendency has landed artists in trouble, and sometimes in jail, at least since authorities in ancient Athens prosecuted the dramatist Euripides for blasphemy. It's why Walt Whitman was fired from his clerk's job in the U.S. Interior Department; a government official considered *Leaves of Grass* indecent.

Like his artistic predecessors, *Angels* playwright Tony Kushner defies convention in the quest for revelation. He examines situations that polite society knows exist but prefers not to mention. He uses language polite society deems offensive and homosexual situations it considers indecent. That is both the power of and the problem with his work: It reveals what polite society prefers to leave unseen.

2. Is nudity in Angels *necessary?*

Mayor Pat McCrory and other critics say reasonably that slightly modifying seven seconds of the seven-hour play would hardly constitute artistic butchery. (One might make the same argument about a movie the mayor had a bit part in, *Nell*, which showed Jodie Foster in the altogether.) But the author of *Angels* put the glimpse of nudity there for a purpose: as a shocking revelation of how AIDS strips away our cover, our invulnerability, our dignity.

The questions raised here are fundamental. Does the artist decide, or do censors? Do those who don't like a play have the right to prevent others from seeing it, or merely the right to avoid it themselves? In our free society, I'd say the artist and the public should make their own decisions.

3. Should tax money support such stuff?

The public absolutely may decide its tax dollars won't support art it finds offensive. *Angels* may provoke a debate, since the Performing Arts Center receives city money and the Charlotte Repertory Theatre is partly funded by the Arts and Science Council, which receives city and county funding.

But in this case, what is the public's view? There were far more ticket-buyers than protesters. An Observer poll of 400 adults in Mecklenburg County last week found that 81 percent said adults should be able to see *Angels* with no restriction on content.

4. When public money is involved, what standards should apply?

Don't expect universal approval. Even if Charlotte had nothing but a steady diet of *The Sound of Music*, members of SPSA (the Society for the Prevention of Saccharin Art) might object.

Don't expect unlimited tolerance. If the *Crazy Horse Revue (Nude Dancers Fresh From Gay Paree)* tours the South, don't look for it at the Performing Arts Center.

I'd say *Angels in America* is at the outer edge of public acceptability, but there's ample theatrical territory to explore between *Angels* and "Doe, a deer, a female deer. ... "

Sure, *Angels* drew some protests. But if you're interested in numbers, the protesters are vastly outnumbered by people who this week in Charlotte will rent videos that contain far more foul language and frontal nudity than *Angels.*

I favor a simpler standard: Producers should offer works of obvious artistic merit, and as long as they do local officials should stay out of the programming business.

5. *What next?*

The philosopher Plato thought the state should ban poets because, he argued, they lie about gods and heroes and thus impede the formation of public virtue. Plato's definition of "to lie" seems to be "to go against the prejudices of the powerful."

If you want Charlotte to welcome serious works of art, tell your city and county officials so, because they'll surely hear from those who want only sanitized art. If you want politicians to defend free expression in a free society, give them your support. Otherwise they may yield to the natural tendency of politicians and play it safe.

The Venue Makes a Difference

A column in The Charlotte Observer Oct. 26, 1997

Not long ago I received a letter from a man urging me to run, verbatim, the "controversial" sections of the play *Angels in America* to show why it offends some people. He also wanted me to publish essays he would write describing homosexual sex. Doing so would help our readers make a "more informed judgment" about such matters, he asserted.

The man, a Duke graduate, said I could refuse to do so for only two reasons: The Observer either "wants to keep readers uninformed," or "knows that a candid discussion of these subjects would repel your readers," which to his mind would be an admission by me that "opponents of funding of homosexual art are correct."

Here is how I replied:

"No doubt the varieties of homosexual encounter are astonishing, as are the varieties of heterosexual encounter (I'm sure the Marquis de Sade was required reading at Duke), but there are limits to how far the Observer is interested in going into homosexual, heterosexual or monosexual mechanics.

"The Observer is a mass circulation newspaper with a family audience, and hopes to stay that way. A description or illustration that might be perfectly at home in the *Journal of the American College of Gynecology* might not be in the Observer. Similarly, many fine works of drama and fiction contain language that is suitable for a self-selected audience of interested people but not for this newspaper. ...

"I'm sure you're not suggesting that anything that's not suitable for the Observer is therefore not suitable anywhere. I wouldn't ban *Playboy*; neither would I publish its photos and jokes in the Observer. And what's appropriate in your bedroom (with, one assumes, willing participants) may not be appropriate on stage in the Performing Arts Center, just as what's appropriate there may not be appropriate in the pages of the Observer.

"I'm not suggesting, heaven forbid, that what goes on in your bedroom is in any way indecent, only that as venue and audience vary, so do standards of appropriateness."

I'd say the same about Martin Davis's performance at the county commissioners meeting. Place and audience make a difference. An audience that welcomes the challenge of seeing *Angels in America* in a theater, or readers who silently read literature with unseemly language and grotesque descriptions, are one thing; a television audience that tunes into a local government meeting is quite another. I'm sorry our would-be censors don't see the difference.

Behind *Little Tree*

An editorial in The Charlotte Observer Oct. 14, 1991

It would be no less shocking to learn that Santa Claus was a child molester.

There are reports that Forrest Carter, author of the gentle, heartwarming *The Education of Little Tree*, was in fact Asa Earl "Ace" Carter, an Alabama-born Ku Klux Klansman who wrote some of former Alabama Gov. George Wallace's most virulently segregationist speeches. "It was common knowledge among the Wallace people" that Ace Carter the racist was also Forrest Carter the writer, according to Gerald Wallace, the former governor's brother.

Forrest Carter's agent, New Yorker Julie Friede, doesn't believe it. "Come on – that kind of honesty and truth? Could that come from a bigot?" she asks. Nor do others who met the author in the last few years before his death in 1979. Mr. Carter's widow won't comment. Still, there is ample evidence that the two men are in fact one.

Why the fuss? Because the phenomenally successful *Little Tree* is the tender reminiscence of a Cherokee boyhood in the 1930s, full of mountain tales, love, respect, and gentle humor from Little Tree and the poor but wise grandparents who reared him. It is not *War and Peace*, but in simple stories told in a juvenile voice, it says a lot about pride and prejudice – hardly what you'd expect from an author who was a bigot.

Little Tree is a publishing success story almost beyond belief. It had gone out of print when the University of New Mexico Press revived it in 1984. Now it has soared to the top of the New York Times paperback best-seller list, mostly by word-of-mouth recommendation from reader to reader. The American Booksellers Association in April voted it the book merchants' favorite title to sell.

Newsweek magazine asked if the press planned to drop the book. No, said the UNM marketing director, "We certainly are not going to burn them. It would seem an incredible waste of trees."

Newsweek sneered, "In the light of the evidence, the book's folksy homilies, like the publisher's New Age fastidiousness, seem a tasteless joke."

Really? *Newsweek* seems to confuse the life of the author with the content of the book. Those qualities of truth and love that make Sunday School classes discuss the book, ministers quote from it and readers adore it are in *The Story of Little Tree*, not in the biography of Asa/Forrest Carter.

If near the end of a life filled with bitterness and bigotry Forrest Carter produced one book that contains all the humor, compassion and wisdom he had to offer, it seems to us that does not make the book a fraud. It makes the book a miracle.

The Aumans' Legacy

An editorial in The Charlotte Observer Oct. 24, 1991

Dorothy Cole Auman of Seagrove, near Asheboro, was an eighth-generation potter. Her husband, Walter Shoten Auman, was the grandson of a potter. For nearly four decades, they operated Seagrove Pottery, creating and selling utilitarian and decorative ware to buyers drawn by the area's tradition of craftsmanship.

The Aumans died last Thursday when a load of lumber slipped from a passing truck on U.S. 220 near Asheboro and crushed their van. She was 66. He was 65.

Anyone who spent time with them at Seagrove Pottery will mourn these fine people. The Aumans were good-humored, kind and patient, ever ready to welcome the browser and share their love of pottery and its lore.

North Carolina pottery heritage dates at least to 1750, when Peter Craven operated a shop in Jugtown, near Seagrove. He and other potters came to North Carolina before the Revolution to escape royal attempts to make colonists dependent on English wares by forbidding them to produce their own. The fine gray and red clays of the Seagrove area gave early 18th-century potters a home beyond the grasp of royal authorities.

Dot Auman in particular was an inheritor and conservator of that rich legacy. She could tell of the flush times when jugs were in demand for corn whiskey, and of the steady market among rich people vacationing in nearby Pinehurst. When the origin of a piece was in doubt, she was the expert people went to. Milton Bloch, former director of Charlotte's Mint Museum, recalls seeing her "look at a piece, turn it in her hands, and then say so and so did this, he was an itinerant potter who stayed with such and such a family back in the 1930s while he was passing through town."

In the 1950s, the Aumans began collecting the work of early potters of the area, some of it dating from the early 1800s. In 1968, they moved the abandoned Seagrove depot to their property and founded the Seagrove Pottery Museum. Later, concerned about their health and the security of the valuable collection, they decided to look for a buyer. The Smithsonian Institution in Washington was interested, but the Aumans wanted the collection to stay in North Carolina. Their long association with Charlotte's Mint Museum eventually led to an agreement that put the collection – nearly

2,000 pieces – here.

Dorothy and Walter Auman understood their place in a long line of dedicated, independent artisans who helped build this state. Their vision and generosity will enable future generations to share their love of craft and place.

Harry Dalton's Joyous Life
A column in The Charlotte Observer July 30, 1990

It would be difficult to live a fuller, happier, more successful life than Harry Dalton did. Some people have been more places, done more things, made more money, but it's hard to imagine anyone who enjoyed life more. When he died here Thursday at age 95, he left a legion of friends and admirers and a legacy that will share his delights with future generations.

Mr. Dalton was a born salesman and a great one, from his childhood job hawking the Winston-Salem Sentinel to his fabulous career selling artificial fibers. He had the salesman's essential attribute: He understood people and enjoyed them. He liked a good story, a good joke, a good nugget of – well, gossip.

He became rich not because he was money-hungry but because he was splendid at what he did – and, he would acknowledge, because he was fortunate.

After serving in World War I, he went to work for Hunter Manufacturing Co.'s Pomona Mill in Greensboro (picking up bobbins off the floor, as he recalled it). Soon the company put him in sales; before long he was outselling his competitors. Then he joined Gastonia Cotton Yarn Co., a Pennsylvania-based representative for 20 mills.

In 1925 American Viscose Co. was seeking a top salesman and found Harry Dalton. He opened a Southern office and hit the rails, urging mill men throughout the South to try the new "artificial silk" – rayon. He was smart, energetic and enormously successful.

Harry Dalton had brass and good humor, and he could mimic anyone – including his company's chairman. There's a story that one day he called his boss and, imitating the chairman's voice, said, "This young fellow Dalton, he's pretty good. I think we ought to give him a raise."

"You do? When?" his boss replied.

"Right now," the "chairman" said.

As the story goes, Mr. Dalton got the raise, and the chairman later heard about it and thought it was hilarious.

That may not have happened, but it certainly sounds like Harry Dalton – sly, bold and worth every penny anybody ever paid him.

During World War II, he was a "dollar a year" man, chief of the silk and nylon section of the War Production Board. Rayon was the miracle fiber – better than silk for parachutes, better than cotton for tires. American Viscose boomed, and so did Mr. Dalton's fortunes. He became a director and vice chairman of the company.

Mr. Dalton and his wife, Mary, used their money joyously. They became amateur art collectors in the original sense of the word: "We buy these things because we like them," he said. "We never bought them for the value." They acquired many splendid paintings, from Old Masters to the Ash Can school, but they also enjoyed buying works of young artists who showed promise and needed a boost.

Mr. Dalton was adventurous. He once made the proprietor of a Washington, D.C., book store a proposition: "I don't know what is in that old dusty trunk down in the basement and neither do you," Mr. Dalton began, and then made a moderately substantial offer. The owner accepted. In the trunk were letters from George Washington and Thomas Jefferson.

Many people trudge resolutely through their days, thinking they'll seek happiness when they have a little more time. Harry Dalton, however, knew the secret: Life is nothing but a series of days, and happiness consists of making the most of each of them. That' what he did, and in doing so he made this a better place.

XIV. Sports

University of North Carolina Coach Roy Williams and his team celebrate winning the NCAA men's basketball tournament. College sports have evolved from a campus activity into a major entertainment business in North Carolina and elsewhere, and top coaches' paychecks rival those of corporate CEOs.

Graham's Quaint View of Sports

An editorial in The Charlotte Observer Feb. 8, 1982

The argument over whether big-college sports should be amateur or professional is pretty much over. Professionalism is a fact, and it has its merits. On the days of big games, not just students and alumni but well-wishers throughout the nation pin their hopes on their favorite teams.

The result is a community of interest that can bring fame and fortune to winning campuses. Success in sports keeps a school's name in the public eye, encouraging friends and legislators to support academic as well as athletic programs.

It's difficult to imagine how things would be if UNC President Frank Porter Graham hadn't been thwarted in the mid-1930s. As a story in Sunday's Observer recalled, he pushed for regulations that would have kept college athletics truly a student pastime, not quite like the debate club but certainly not the multi-billion-dollar entertainment enterprise it is today.

One thing intercollegiate athletics probably would not be, if Dr. Graham had succeeded, is proof that if the payoff is big enough, many colleges will tolerate corruption, exploitation of students and violation of the ethical principles taught in their classrooms.

Dr. Graham thought intercollegiate athletics should be run for the students by the university, not for the fans by the alumni association. You can see how old-fashioned he was.

Dr. Graham's problem was a certain narrowness of perspective. He thought the business of a university was education, not mass entertainment. And he believed every activity of a university ought to be in keeping with the principles that were valued there. If it wasn't, the fault, he believed, was not the coach's or the fans', but the university leaders'.

As one of his admirers observed, Dr. Graham, who died in 1972, was guilty of being an idealist. How in the world did he get to run a big business like a university, anyway?

All Hail, Bahskeet-Baal

A March 13, 1992 editorial in The Charlotte Observer welcoming the Atlantic Coast Conference men's basketball tournament to Charlotte

The faithful have gathered, as many as have the money and energy to make the pilgrimage, for their annual festival in honor of Bahskeet-Baal. While we welcome the worshipers, we recognize that some of their practices may seem strange to nonbelievers, and some may even frighten children or cause panic in the streets.

Part of the problem may be ignorance of Bahskeet-Baalite practices. The unexpected can be alarming. Therefore we offer this introduction to the origin and practices of the faith.

Bahskeet-Baal was founded in Massachusetts a century ago. Because it is based on a revelation to one James Naismith, who worked at the Young Men's Christian Association, some consider it an offshoot of Christianity. Its attraction, however, transcends traditional religious divisions.

The faith is organized into somewhat regional tribes. The devotees gathered here now belong to a tribe called the Hey-See-See.

Here are some of the practices of Bahskeet-Baal worship that you may see among the faithful:

1. At the slightest mention of the religion, its devotees become agitated. Frequently they proclaim their devotion in enthusiastic terms. They demonstrate intimate familiarity with the dogma and history of the faith, attainable only by years of resolute study.

2. They usually belong to cults. Often these cults involve identification with animals, such as tigers, rams, wolves, yellow jackets, even terrapins. One of the cults follows a yin-yang figure, the Demon Deacon. One worships a diabolical creature, the Blue Devil. Devotees of some cults display symbols upon their faces – the Tar Heel, the Tiger Paw.

3. Bahskeet-Baal is a winter religion, practiced at temples throughout

the nation and through extensive television ministries. These electronic ministries are funded by the sale of holy items: (1) elixirs that, when ingested, make one young, energetic, happy and attractive to the opposite sex; and (2) shoes that empower their wearers to fly and make money. Devotees of Bahskeet-Baal may spend several hours a week in TV worship, shunning thought and conversation while swallowing alarming quantities of drinks and junk food.

4. The cults seem to regard some forms of mental illness as holy. One television ministry, for example, features regular appearances by a creature called Dik-Vi-Towell. He is an agitated man who speaks gibberish in a squeaky voice – an example, perhaps, of speaking in tongues. (A Bahskeet-Baal joke: What is the difference between God and Dik-Vi-Towell? God doesn't think He's Dik-Vi-Towell.)

5. During the annual holy days, cult members gather in large temples to conduct frenzied orgies called Turn-Ah-Mints. These involve a few priests and many onlookers. The priests (or at some temples, priestesses) are young and scantily clad. They speed haphazardly on a wooden floor, tossing and bouncing a round symbol of Bahskeet-Baal, made from an inflated animal skin. Their object is to insert the inflated skin into an elevated metal circle, an act with obvious sexual connotations. Often the insertion is forceful; that produces roars from the onlookers. During the rite, the faithful wave their arms and shout, often to the accompaniment of raucous music. Nubile maidens and muscular lads urge worshippers to heights of frenzy.

6. Super-human powers are attributed to some of these priests. One mythic figure, called Mi-Kell Jor-Dan, is said to have the power of flight. One elder, called Deen, is said to be able to make the sky blue. A large temple has been built in his honor at a sacred mount called Chapel Hill. Most seats in it are reserved for aged followers, who conduct themselves reverently therein. Another elder, Sha-Shef-Ski, is said to be able to withstand the most skillful tickling without smiling. His elite young acolytes chide other cults with chants such as "Someday you'll work for us."

While devotees of Bahskeet-Baal may exhibit unusual behavior, they are seldom dangerous unless their faith is criticized. Some celebrants may consume large vials of mind-altering potions, however, so late at night it is wise to treat them warily. As a whole they are considerate, if boisterous, visitors. In the spirit of religious tolerance, we welcome them to Charlotte.

Don't Keep Athletes Poor

An editorial in The Charlotte Observer June 25, 1989

There's no reason to lament the resignation of Oklahoma football coach Barry Switzer. The football program he ran was scandalous. But one parting comment by Mr. Switzer should not be dismissed as sour grapes.

"We have created a system that does not permit me or the program to buy a pair of shoes or a decent coat for a player whose family can't afford these basic necessities," he said. "How can any coach stick to these rules when a young man's father dies many miles away and the son has no money for a plane ticket home to the funeral?"

On that point – if hardly any others – Mr. Switzer was right. The NCAA's limits on aid to scholarship athletes have created some outrageous situations: a player from an impoverished family in the South goes to a Northern school but has no money to buy winter clothes; players are stranded on campus during Christmas holidays because they have no money for travel home.

Sure, money is tight for a lot of students. But scholarship athletes have a unique problem because the NCAA won't let them accept gifts or even take part-time jobs.

The NCAA's caution is understandable. A lot of well-off fans are eager to shower wealth on players, before and after they enroll. But keeping poor players broke is scandalous, too. Why add to the problems of students from impoverished families by denying them enough money to pay for a winter coat, a trip home or even an occasional pizza? That is not merely insensitive, it's insane. Many players remain poor while making their athletic programs rich. What's amazing is not that so many take money under the table, but that so few do.

UNC Coach Dean Smith is among the coaches pushing for creation of a need-based monthly stipend for student-athletes whose families can provide them little or no financial help. The NCAA should allow it – soon.

Why Aren't Shoe Deals a Scandal?
An editorial in The Charlotte Observer April 25, 1993

Duke's Mike Krzyzewski is taking a bit of buffeting these days for the big-bucks deal he recently signed with a big-time shoe company. But whatever chill wind the critics are blowing his way, he has his contract to keep him warm. And it's reported to be a BIG contract: a million dollars just to switch his allegiance from Adidas to Nike, plus more than $5 million in salary long-term, plus stock options.

What does Nike get in return for the deal? Nike vice president Harry Carsh said Coach K will be expected to provide the company with feedback. Feedback, sure. And, oh, yes, the company will provide free shoes for the Blue Devils. Team members won't be required to wear the shoes, of course. Gee, think they will?

The official position of The Charlotte Observer's editorial board is this: We love college basketball. But even at the schools that run honest, above-board programs, big-time college basketball is not simply an intercollegiate

sport. Like its more violent brother, football, basketball can be a highly organized, well-financed, immensely profitable business. Not all the profits go
to the sponsoring schools, of course. A lot of them go to the companies such
as Nike, and to coaches such as Mike Krzyzewski, Dean Smith, John
Thompson – good guys, who run good programs. Some of them even share
the booty with their schools. None of it, however, goes to the players. They
get scholarships. Just like tuba players.

The NCAA rulemakers, in their wisdom, see nothing wrong with keeping an athlete in penury while others profit off his skills. A coach takes
millions from a shoe company and everybody considers it one of the perks
of the job. If a player took a free ride on the shoe company plane to see his
mom at Christmas, the NCAA would boot him out of the sport.

In this atmosphere of glitz and riches, it's no wonder that some players
succumb to the temptation to take a little cash under the table. The wonder,
with all the cash changing hands around them, is that most of them don't.

Guts and Glory at UNC
An editorial in The Charlotte Observer Nov. 20, 1987

Well-heeled Tar Heel fans are rumored to be raising $1 million to give UNC-
Chapel Hill football coach Dick Crum if he will resign. That sort of flagrant
meddling leads to corruption in university athletic programs. Everyone who
values the integrity of the University of North Carolina – including UNC
Board Chairman Philip Carson, UNC system President Dick Spangler,
Chapel Hill Chancellor Christopher Fordham and Athletic Director John
Swofford – has a duty to tell those overzealous fans, "Hands off!"

Coach Crum has four years remaining on a 10-year contract. He has re-
cruited excellent student-athletes while running a scandal-free program. He
has done nothing, personally or professionally, to detract from the integrity of
the university. In addition, he has the best won-lost record in UNC history.

If, despite all that, university officials believe they have valid reasons to
fire Coach Crum, let them state those reasons and fire him. But they should
not let well-to-do alumni run the athletic program.

If Coach Crum has not failed in any important aspect – and so far no
university official has suggested that he has – he should not be fired, forced
out or bought out simply because some maniacal fans feel that in recent sea-

sons he has lost a few games too many, and because his teams play a brand of football that those fans consider timid.

At some schools, those might be firing offenses. At those schools, athletic programs are not so much part of the university's mission as they are big-budget entertainment enterprises run for – and virtually by – fans, who in gratitude contribute large sums of money to the university, not just for sports but for other programs as well.

At UNC, that is not what athletics has been, or should be. UNC is trying to run a sports program that fields winning teams while reflecting the university's values and integrity. However, success in big-time sports can bring enormous financial rewards to a university, and the love of money can be as corrupting to a university as to an individual.

This pressure from fans to get rid of Coach Crum comes at a difficult time. President Spangler is relatively new on the job. Chancellor Fordham is nearing retirement. And UNC is about to embark on a huge fund-raising campaign to increase its endowment and move it to an even higher academic stature – a campaign that no doubt will approach some of the very fans who want Coach Crum out. Under those circumstances, nobody wants a confrontation with some of UNC's most fervid and affluent supporters.

It isn't difficult, however, to see where UNC's true interests lie. The glory of a university does not come from its football record, or from how fans feel about any coach. A university's glory comes from its dedication to such values as integrity, justice and truth. A great university does not sacrifice its values to satisfy a public whim – not in its study of history, not in its pursuit of scientific truth, and not in its conduct of athletic programs.

There's an old maxim taped to a lot of locker-room walls: "No guts, no glory." If the glory of UNC is to be preserved, the university's leaders and supporters must have the guts to speak out now.

EDITOR'S NOTE: *Coach Crum resigned Nov. 30, 1987. The Educational Foundation, an athletic booster organization known as the Rams Club, donated $800,000 to UNC to buy out his contract. The Rams Club was formed in 1938 to provide athletic scholarships. In 1987, it gave UNC $2.25 million for that purpose. Earlier, the Rams Club had raised $36 million to build the Dean Smith Center, the 21,500-seat coliseum for UNC basketball, which opened in 1985.*

HA! REPORT SEZ YOU COLLEGE PRESIDENTS GOTTA GET MORE INVOLVED...! IMAGINE!

BIG TIME COLLEGE $PORT$

WHUMPITA WHUMPITA

Lust for TV Money Reshapes ACC
A column in The Charlotte Observer June 26, 2003

My preference is not to expand the Atlantic Coast Conference at all. But that's not the preference of almost all the schools in the conference. At least the expansion proposal now on the table looks better than the made-for-TV monstrosity ACC officials first came up with.

Duke University President Nan Keohane and UNC-Chapel Hill Chancellor James Moeser may not like the present proposal – as I write, they haven't said anything publicly – but they deserve thanks for helping block the push for a 12-team conference ranging almost from Cuba to Canada.

That proposal would have added Boston College, Syracuse and Miami. The new one would add only Virginia Tech and Miami, two schools from the ACC 's home region. Their presence would create strong in-state rivalries in Virginia and Florida to join the traditional rivalries in the Carolinas.

In expressing her reservations about a 12-team conference, Keohane raised concerns that might be more easily resolved under the present proposal. One involved preserving traditional rivalries. Another involved the additional burden placed on athletes and schools by longer road trips. A third – and so far as I know, this is still up in the air – involved how a larger league might be split in divisions. ACC officials at first envisioned splitting the league into the same two divisions for all sports. Keohane argued for divisions that suited the sports, rather than a one-size-fits-all division.

The effort to lure schools from the Big East conference has bruised the ACC 's reputation. The way the league pursued expansion reminded some observers of a sneak attack by a military power bent on conquest. The Cuba-to-Canada proposal made no sense except as a way to add rich TV markets in the Northeast and create a lucrative conference football championship playoff.

It was hard to see the move as anything other than a power-driven enterprise, aimed at increasing revenue and status in big-time sports, not at preserving valuable traditions and promoting the welfare of student athletes. Every time some ACC official or booster of expansion denied it was about money and power, that reinforced my conviction that it was about nothing else.

It may be too late to do anything about many universities' unhealthy embrace of the entertainment business, with students as low-cost stars. But it's not too late to remind athletic enthusiasts that while college sports must pay attention to the bottom line, they also must be more than a business.

As more and more schools sell pieces of their reputation to TV networks and shoe companies, Keohane and Moeser were right to stand up for values not set by the marketplace. Among them are treating other schools with respect, dealing with concerns before rather than after decisions are made, preserving college traditions and not imposing unnecessary burdens on student athletes.

Duke basketball coach Mike Krzyzewski spoke of some of those concerns in a press conference earlier this week. "There's a business part of everything that we do, there's no question about it," he said. "But also, we're still a university. We have to be sensitive to our brethren in other conferences. This isn't about big business swooping in and getting another company. If that's what it's about, the hidden cost there is the destruction of in essence what intercollegiate sports should be about."

He added, "I think there is a lot to be said about your geographic area.

You don't go in and just say, 'We're going to take you and you and you' and not have sensitivity." On all counts, he's right.

Important concerns remain, but a more geographically compact expansion should make dealing with them easier.

Still, the real challenge for the ACC doesn't change with the number and location of members. It involves a fundamental choice: Should college sports be about money and power or about the welfare of students and the values of the university? The struggle over that choice gets harder as the money involved increases.

EDITOR'S NOTE: *In 2013 the ACC expanded to 15 schools, spanning nearly from Cuba to Canada, with a TV contract expected to be worth $20 million for each school.*

XV. Coda

Ed Williams confesses, "It is said that many people grow crankier as they grow older. About me that is not true. I've always been cranky. I've just stopped concealing it."

Rescued by a Junior Leaguer

A column in The Charlotte Observer Jan. 4, 1998

In 1997 I was honored by an invitation to read a column I'd written, "10 Rules for Living," at the annual luncheon of the Junior League's sustaining members. Running a little late, I snatched what I thought was a copy of the column off my desk, stuck it in my folder and sped to the luncheon. When I got there, I discovered to my dismay that instead of my text I'd picked up a copy of Conservative Views, Joe Miller's fax newsletter.

I pondered my choices. When the time came to speak, I could read Joe's comments, hoping the Junior League members would not notice that they didn't sound like 10 rules for living (or at least like my 10 rules for living). Or I could admit my error and throw myself on the mercy of the Junior Leaguers and hope an excerpt I had brought along as a bonus, "Six Rules for Doing Laundry," would suffice.

I threw myself on their mercy. As soon as I did so, a Junior League member said, "Oh, that's no problem, I have a copy of the column with me." I read it to a receptive audience. Apparently believing all's well that ends well, nobody called me an idiot – to my face, at least.

I shouldn't have worried. The Junior League has an awesome reputation for overcoming difficulties. If I'd said, "I won't be able to speak because I've been bitten by a rare South American spider and will be struck mute in two minutes," someone there probably would have said, "Oh, don't worry, I have the antidote in my car. Let me run get it."

10 Rules for Living

A column in The Charlotte Observer June 8, 1997

With graduation ceremonies and various other rites of passage occurring throughout the land, spring is the season of advice-giving. It is not necessarily the season of advice-taking, of course. Sometimes wisdom has to seep in, as a gentle rain provides the moisture that eventually helps seeds sprout.

The tradition and formality of these ceremonial occasions provide the conditions necessary for the dispensing of advice. Young people are required to be there and sit more or less quietly. Adults are expected to speak to them about important matters.

Whether the young people listen is beside the point. The desire of adults to hand down what they've learned (whether or not they've lived by it) is inherent in our species. It is so strong that the younger generation's tendency to pay little or no attention is no deterrent. With lessons in virtue, as with sit-ups, repetition is presumed to build strength.

Permit me, please, to join the chorus. Here are 10 of my own rules for living. Use them if they seem useful.

1. Finish what you start, usually.

If you open it, close it. If you drop it, pick it up. If you mess it up, clean it up. Otherwise somebody else will have to. Seldom will that person be grateful for the opportunity.

1a. Sometimes perseverance is invaluable; sometimes it is foolish. Learn to tell the difference.

In his inauguration as president of the University of North Carolina a decade ago, Dick Spangler cited a memorable dictum: "No matter how far you've gone down a wrong road, turn back."

2. Associate with the kind of people you want to be.

Find people you admire, and learn from them. Usually they are glad to pass on what they've learned. After all, that's how they learned it. Give them the opportunity to teach, and be grateful for it.

3. Don't dismiss what you don't understand.

However things are, they probably are that way for what somebody considered a good reason. Before making a judgment, find that reason. Such knowledge may not change your mind, but may inform your thinking, and certainly will help you understand people who disagree with you.

4. Be reliable.

The world is full of smart people, quick people, good-looking people, smooth-talking people. There is a persistent shortage, however, of reliable people. Be one, and you'll be a scarce item in a hungry market.

Addendum: Being responsible doesn't always mean doing what you said you'd do. It does always mean making sure that the people expecting you to do it know you won't, and why.

5. Value something more than you value yourself.

There are timeless values that people have lived for and died for. Learn about them. If they make sense to you, embrace them. It's important to be a part of something that is larger than you are. People who are wrapped up in themselves make very small packages.

6. When you know what you want to do, take at least one step toward that goal each day.

At that rate your progress may be slow, but it gets you farther faster than any amount of sitting and wishing.

7. Understand that you are a work in progress.

You have more power to determine who you will be than most people ever imagine. Use it.

8. Treat people the way you'd like to be treated.

If they don't reciprocate, the problem is with them, not you. Don't let others determine how you act.

9. Learn to laugh at the world, and especially to laugh at yourself.

Life is so full of ridiculous things that sometimes laughter is the best, and the healthiest, response.

10. Expect things to go wrong.

Sometimes things don't work out as you wished, and your plans crumble. That's life. The only time there is no possibility of conflict with others is when you're alone. The only way to avoid errors entirely is to do nothing. Unless you want to spend your time by yourself doing nothing, expect setbacks. Deal with them using rules 1-9.

A Cranky Man's Credo
A column in The Charlotte Observer Jan. 25, 1998

It is said that many people grow crankier as they grow older. About me that is not true. I've always been cranky. I've just stopped concealing it.

A cranky man's credo (abridged version):

1. A customer on the line is rarely more important than one in front of you.

I went to my neighborhood video store Thursday to pick up a movie. The place was not busy, and there was only one cashier. He entered my card and the movie into the cash register, but before he collected my money, the phone rang. He answered it, then launched a conversation with someone who apparently had an overdue movie. Then he began chatting about movies. I stood there waiting.

But not for long. After a couple of minutes, I said in a loud voice, "I need to go now. Either let me pay or you keep the movies."

He didn't react, but another clerk rushed up and saved the day. "Let me take care of you," he said politely, and he did.

My family ran a grocery store. One lesson drummed into me from toddlerhood was that when people came into the store, we paid attention. Greet them. Ask if you can help. If they say no, don't hover over them, but tell them to let you know when you can help, and stay aware of them. Serve them promptly and politely. And when you complete the transaction, say thank you.

Only in the rarest cases is someone on the phone more important than someone standing in front of you waiting to give you money.

2. Familiarity breeds contempt.

Often I answer the phone at home to hear someone ask for Edwin Williams. I am Edwin Williams – Edwin Neel Williams, to be precise – but only my mother ever called me that, and only when she was especially put out with me. But I digress.

After I say, "This is he," the caller says, "Hello, Edwin ... ," and launches a sales pitch.

I'm tolerant of telephone marketers, but I'm seldom in the market for anything sold by phone, so I say politely, "Thanks for calling, but I'm not interested,'" and hang up.

But one evening when a call interrupted our dinner and the caller referred to me as "Edwin," I stopped him. "Do you know me?" I asked. No, he replied. "Then don't you think it's a bit presumptuous of you to call me by my first name?" He said something huffy and hung up.

It seems to me that if you call a stranger at home, you should have the courtesy not to assume a familiarity you're not entitled to. It's Mr. Williams, bub.

3. Th- th- th- th- th... . Come on, come on. You can do it.

Growing up in a family business, I had no trouble remembering to say thank you to our customers. I knew they were the ones who'd determine whether I had the money to buy a new baseball glove.

Over the years it became automatic with me. Now, even to readers who call to complain, I always say "Thanks for calling." I mean it. They value what we do enough to call and tell us how they think we could do it better.

Many people today apparently consider expressing gratitude to be quaint and outdated – the commercial equivalent of knowing how to use a finger bowl.

Count the times you go through checkout or drive-in lines where the clerk acknowledges your presence only by saying how much you owe. Often I'm served by someone who the entire time carries on a conversation with someone else. Gee, sorry to inconvenience you, but I'm trying to pay your salary.

4. If you throw it down, somebody has to pick it up.

A few years ago I was at a stop light and the passenger in the car beside me threw a drink can out the window. I got out of my car, picked up the can and handed it to him. "You dropped your can," I said.

"It's empty," he said.

"I'm sure you didn't mean to drop it on the street," I said.

He took it. No doubt he threw it out as soon as the crazy man was out of sight.

What breed of person thoughtlessly tosses trash out the car window? A common breed these days, alas. I wouldn't advocate spaying or neutering them, but I do wish they'd stop reproducing.

Why, you may ask, do I devote all this paper and ink to such trivial concerns? If you think these are trivial concerns, that's the reason.

Acknowledgments

The liberation of Dixie from the burdens of its past is a work in progress, of course, but I am amazed at the changes I've seen during my half-century of analyzing, praising and prodding the South. In social justice, economic and educational opportunity and intellectual and artistic freedom, the region has come far beyond what I would have imagined possible.

As to my own progress, I owe more than I could ever repay to a few men and women who shared – and shaped – my values and vision. My parents, Carl Edwin Williams and Vina Edmonston Williams, were independent and fair-minded people, hard workers, active citizens and avid readers. Early on they gave me an uncommon degree of independence and expected me to use it responsibly. In the book I mention Professor James Silver. Also at Ole Miss, Dr. Samuel Talbert, who chaired the journalism department when I worked on the student newspaper, believed my future was in journalism long before I did. Though I was a history major, he encouraged me, cajoled me and nudged me into my first newspaper jobs.

After two years in the Army, I planned to go to graduate school in history, but Hodding Carter III lured me into a reporting job at the Delta Democrat-Times, promising long hours, low pay and an opportunity to write about history in the making. Over the years no one has been more generous to my family and me than Hodding. Patricia Derian, a leader in the crusade for justice in Mississippi (and later President Jimmy Carter's Assistant Secretary of State for Human Rights and Humanitarian Affairs), provided many years of warm friendship and a challenging example of courage and clarity of thought. And Reese Cleghorn hired me as an editorial writer in Charlotte and by editing and example schooled me in the art of writing with power and grace.

To have a strong editorial voice a newspaper must have a strong publisher. I couldn't imagine a better one than my first publisher, Rolfe

Neill, a skilled journalist and wise counselor. His successor, Peter Ridder, was an amiable and fair man, though at times our relationship was (how shall I say it?) a bit rocky. My final publisher, Ann Caulkins, was a godsend – smart, energetic, and tough, with a bone-deep commitment to the value of journalism to the community.

For my final four years at the Observer I reported to the publisher, but before that the editorial page editor reported to the editor. I had excellent relationships with my editors: the talented David Lawrence, who gave me the job when both of us were too young to know better; Rich Oppel, whose quiet demeanor never concealed his passion for excellence; and the thoughtful Jennie Buckner, who rescued me during a dispute with a publisher (and never ceased to hope I'd become better organized). The current editor, Rick Thames, generously made available to me material from the newspaper's archives, and the Observer's Maria David expertly searched those archives and provided most of the photographs that enliven these pages. I'm honored that my friend Don Sturkey, who for decades captured the essence of this region with his camera, provided a photograph for this book.

From the outset of my career I benefited enormously from the friendship of some splendid journalists, particularly Wilson F. Minor, Roy Reed and Curtis Wilkie. At the Observer, the excellence of my colleagues in the editorial department made coming to work a joy. Two hold a special place in my heart: Lew Powell, my best friend and co-conspirator in many delightful enterprises for nearly 50 years; and the late Doug Marlette, whose cartoonist's id sometimes collided with my editor's ego, providing invaluable lessons in patience and understanding for both of us. I'm grateful to Melinda Hartley Marlette for allowing me to use Doug's work in this book. Thanks, too, to Doug's successor, Kevin Siers, who made available some of his fine cartoons. In addition, two Charlotte friends, Dannye Romine Powell and Elizabeth Kamarck Minnich, deserve credit for relentlessly encouraging me to do this book.

Finally, thanks to my wonderful wife, the elegant and resilient Marylyn Lentine Williams, who tolerated my odd hours and frequent obsessions and didn't appear at all unsettled when I came home one evening to tell her I would probably lose my job in a dispute with the publisher; and to our son, Jonathan, who is the kind of man we hoped he would be.

 For 25 years Ed Williams was editor of the editorial pages at The Charlotte Observer, where his columns and editorials were part of projects that won the Pulitzer Prize for Public Service in 1981 and 1988. He earned a B.A. in history from the University of Mississippi, where he edited the Daily Mississippian. He served two years in the U.S. Army and in 1967 joined Hodding Carter's Delta Democrat-Times in Greenville, Mississippi, as a reporter. He was a Nieman Fellow at Harvard University and a writer for the Ford Foundation before coming to the Observer as an editorial writer in 1973. He retired in 2008 and was inducted into the North Carolina Journalism Hall of Fame. He lives in Charlotte, North Carolina, with his wife, Marylyn.

abortion 79, 84
Abu Ghraib 117
ACC 252, 258-260
Adams, John 73-75
Adidas 255
Afghanistan 202
Afro-American Cultural Center 5
AIDS 134, 203, 242
Alcoholic Beverage Control Divison (ABC) 30, 31, 32
Alexander, Fred 60
Alexander, Kelly Sr. 60
Alexander, Zechariah Sr. 60
Allende, Salvador 28
al-Qaida 112
ALS 234
Amendment One 163-169
American Anti-Slavery Society 22
American Association of Suicidology 175
American Bar Association (ABA) 38, 39
American Viscose Co. 247-248
Angels in America 241-244
anti-Catholicism 35
anti-communist 27
anti-Semitism 138-139
Arabs 12, 88-92
Arbenz, Jacobo 27
Armor Holdings 116
Arts and Science Council (ASC) 158, 242
Atherton Mills 58-59, 65
Auman, Dorothy Cole 246-247
Auman, Walter Shoten 246-247
Austin American-Statesman 13
Australia 140
Avery, Isaac Ervin 59

Baathist regime 111
Baath party 112
Baghdad 111, 117
Bakker, Jim 59, 195-196, 197-200
Bakker, Tammy Faye 199
Bank of America 63, 233
Baptist 11, 34, 42, 43, 46, 47, 160, 193-195, 202
Barnett, E.G. "Hop" (sheriff) 33, 34
Barnett, O.H. (judge) 33
Barnett, Ross 47-48
Baruch, Joseph 59
basketball 250, 252-254, 255-256, 257
Bastille Day 25
Battle of Charlotte 50
Beck, Frederick 39
Beethoven, Ludwig van 236
Belk brothers 59, 61
Belk, John (mayor) 61, 69-70
Belk, John Montgomery 61
Belk, William Henry 60-61
Bender, Harold 155

Berman, Lanny 175
Betts, Jack 141, 142
Bible Belt 199
Bible Crusaders of America 42
Bilbo, Theodore 18
Bill of Rights 55-56, 57-58, 170
bin Laden, Osama 106, 202
Bissell, Marilyn 81
Bloch, Milton 247
Bloomberg, Michael 78
blue-collar 183
Blue Devil 252, 255
Blumenthal Performing Arts Center 5, 242-243, 244
Blumenthal, Sidney 104
Boggan, Henry 9-10
bootlegger 31-35
Bonaparte, Napoleon 26
Bono 134
Bosch, Hieronymus 239
Bosnia 97, 118
Boston University 64
Bowden, Mark 113
Boy Scouts of America 161-162
Brady, Tom 38-40
Branch, Joseph 154
Brazil 114
Brinkley, Christie 9
Britain 25, 26, 27 (see also Great Britain)
Brooke, Hardin 43
Brooks, John 184
brown lung 2, 186-188 (also see byssinosis)
Bryan, William Jennings 41, 76
Buckley, William 10
Buckner, Jennie 270
Bullock, C.L. 44, 45
Bureau of Alcohol, Tobacco and Firearms 173
Burlington Industries 187-188
Burns, John 112
Burr, Aaron 73-75
Burt, A.W. (Rack) 31-34
Bush, George W. 10, 12, 13, 82-84, 105-117
Bush, George H.W. 82, 83, 86-92, 93, 109, 113, 137
Bush,Tom 159
Butterfield, G.K. 120
byssinosis 187

Caldwell, J.P. 65, 76, 143
Caldwell, Joseph 144
Cambridge 212
Canada 25, 133, 259, 260
Cannon, Joe 58
capitalism 179-180
Carden, Michael 182
Carolina Brown Lung Association 187
Carolina Panthers 54

Carsh, Harry 255
Carson, Johnny 129, 130
Carson, Philip 256
Carter, Asa Earl "Ace" 245 (see also Carter, Forrest)
Carter, Betty 18
Carter, Forrest 245 (see also Carter, Asa Earl "Ace")
Carter, Hodding, III vi, 16-18, 269
Carter, Hodding, Jr. 16
Carter, Jimmy 17, 79, 126, 269
Carter, Joel 159-160
Cash, Sleepy 35-37
Cash, W.J. vi
Castro, Fidel 28
Catawba River 59
Catfish Row 17
Catholics 8, 46, 105, 160
Caulkins, Ann 270
censure 102-103
center-city 6, 24, 56
Chalabi, Ahmed 117
Chambers, Julius L. 60
Charlotte College 61
Charlotte Central City Partners 56
Charlotte Hornets 6, 54
Charlotte Knights stadium 186
Charlotte-Mecklenburg Library 240
Charlotte-Mecklenburg schools 58, 61, 67, 146, 147-148, 173, 221-225, 233-234
Charlotte Observer, founding of 53, 65, 142-143
Charlotte Repertory Theatre 242
Chase, Chevy 225
Cheney, Dick 77-78, 109, 110
Cheney, Lynne 78
Chicago 39, 57-58
Chicagoans 57-58
child labor 137
Cho, Seung-Hui 173
Christmas 202-204, 208, 215, 256
CIA 27, 28, 101, 117
Civic Center 70
civil rights 34, 38, 61, 76, 77, 140, 141, 160
Civil War 18, 48, 231
Clausewitz, Karl von 88
Clayton, Hugh N. 39
Cleghorn, Reese vi, 269
Cleghorn, Sarah Norcliffe 178
Clemson 62, 148
Clinton, Bill vi, 7, 83, 93-104, 108, 113,
Clinton, Hillary 7, 101, 118
Coach K 255
Cobb, James C. 184
Coburn, Tom 119
Cohn, David 17-18
Cold War 27, 79, 93, 119
Columbia University 119

Columbine 174, 191
Colvard, Dean 68-69
"Concerned Charlotteans" 161
Cone, Bonnie 54, 61-62
Congress 10, 22, 53, 55, 64, 82, 83,
  84, 95, 97, 99, 103, 120, 167,
  191-192, 240
Conroy, Pat 15
Constitution 55, 57, 74, 99, 100-101,
  102, 157, 171
Convention Center 5
Cook, Philip J. 175
Cornwallis, Lord (Gen.) 25, 50, 52
counter-terror 28
Cowley, Malcolm 229
Craig, Locke (Gov.) 65
Crawford, John 140
Crum, Dick 256-257
Crutchfield, Charles 66-68
Cuba 28, 134, 259, 260

Daisy Red Ryder BB gun 174
Dalton, Harry 247-248
Dalton, Mary 248
Dannelly, Charlie 165
Darrow, Clarence 41
Darwin 41, 44, 46, 64
David, Maria 270
Davidson, Chalmers 65-66
Davidson College vii, 63, 65-66,
  70, 233
Davis, Martin 240-241, 244
Dearman, Stanley 33
death penalty 79, 149-156
Death Row 149-150
DeCastrique, Mark 15
Declaration of Independence 22, 23,
  52, 53, 114, 121
Declaration of Rights 55
Defense of Marriage Act 167
DeGaulle, Charles 26
DeGeneres, Ellen 167
DeLay, Tom 117
Delta Democrat-Times vi, 16, 31
Demon Deacon 252
Department of Education 175
Depression 232
Derian, Patricia 269
Desert Storm 88-92
Dilworth 54, 58, 63
Dilworth Elementary School 221
Dionne, E.J., Jr. 82
Discovery Place 5
Dixiecrats 76
Dodd, John 134
Dole, Bob 96-97, 98, 99
Douglas, Ben E. 62
Douglass, Frederick 21
Duke, Ben 59
Duke, James B. 59
Duke University 141, 175, 233, 243,

  244, 255, 258-259
Dulles, Allen 27

Easley, Mike 12
Eastland, James O. 40
Edmonston Gin Co. 208
Edmonstons 207
Eichner, Maxine 164
Eisenhower, Dwight 26, 75, 76
Ellis, Tom 80
Ellmers, Renee 163
Elon University 167, 168
ERA 79
Ericsson Stadium 56
Ervin, Sam 131-132
Ethridge, Mark, III 15
European Union (EU) 114
Evans, Martha 64
Evers, Charles 38
Evers, Medgar 38
Exum, James 154

Family Choice Plan 148
Faubus, Orval 48
Faulkner, William 141, 143, 229-230
FBI 101
First Baptist Church (Charlotte) 194
First Union 54
Flono, Fannie 148
Flowers, Gennifer 99
Flynn, Erroll 237
Focus on the Family 158
Foote, Shelby 18, 231
Fordham, Christopher 256
Foreign Relations Committee 119
Forrester, Jim 165-166
Foster, Jodie 242
Foster, Vince 107
France 21, 25, 26, 73, 74, 107, 110,
  114, 117
Franklin, Benjamin 25
French Revolution 73
Friday, Bill 68
Friede, Julie 245
Froehling, Beth 164
Frye, Henry 154
Fusion movement 142

Gantt, Harvey 60, 62, 64, 120, 148
Gardner, Jim 4
Gastonia Cotton Yarn Co. 247
gay rights 77-78, 157-169
General Agreement on Tariffs and
  Trade 97
George III (King) 22, 51
Georgia 157, 158
Genocide Treaty 131
Germany 107
Gingrich, Newt 98
gold rush 53, 59
Goodman, Ellen 10, 173

Gorbachev, Mikhail 94
Gore, Al 82, 95, 102
Gore, Ney 41, 43-45
Graham, Billy 59, 195-196, 235
Graham, Frank Porter 125, 251-252
Graham, Franklin 166, 200-202
Great Britain 23 (see also Britain)
Great Trading Path 52
Great Wagon Road 58
Greater Charlotte Chamber of
  Commerce 181, 183
Griffin, Will 81
Grundy, Pam 148
Guatemala 27
Guatemala City 28
Guevara, Che 28
Guiliani, Rudolph 78
gun control 79
gun rights 170-176
Guthrie, Woody 15

Haiti 97, 145
Halifax Resolves 53
Hall, B.B. 42
Hamer, Bill 36
Hamer, Fannie Lou 40
Hamilton, Alexander 24, 74-75
Hamlet, NC 183-185
Hanchett, Tom 14
Harris, Mark 194
Harvard University vi, 65, 119,
  171, 212
Heaton, George 193
Helms, Jesse v, 14, 77, 80-81,
  123-134, 239-240
Helms, Parks 240
Hemings, Sally 73
Henley, William 39
Heritage Village (Heritage USA)
  198-200
Herrera, Leonel 152
Higgins, George 159
Hill, Bonnie 154-155
Hill, Randy 154-156
Hill, Zane 154-156
Hines, Lewis 178
HIV 203
Hoffa, Jimmy 180-182
Hokies 173
Holmes, Oliver Wendell, Jr. 170
Holshouser, Jim (Gov.) 77, 150
Holtz, Lou 129
Hood, John 163
Hook, C.C. 63
Hoover, Herbert 93
Hornersville High School 207
Hornersville, Missouri v, 208
Hornets (NBA team) 6, 54
hornets' nest of rebellion 50
Horton, George Moses 144
Horton, William 144

House Bill 49 41
Humphrey, Hubert H. 76-77
Humvees 116
Hunt, Jim (Gov.) 94, 155-156
Hurt, Henry 230-231 (see also Paine, Hank)
Hunter Manufacturing Co. 247
Hussein, Saddam 12, 87-91, 93-94, 107-113, 115, 116, 117, 118

Imperial Food Products 184
Independence Day 25
India 114
Ingram, John 125-127
Iran 27, 114
Iraq 11, 83, 87-91, 94, 107-117, 118
Iredell, James 55
Ireland 21
IRS 101, 198, 235
Islam 200-202
Israel 89-91, 113, 115
Israeli-Palestinian 115
Italy 21

Jackson, Andrew 103, 132
Jackson, Jesse 118
Jaguar 140
James, Bill 159
Jarrette, Henry 149
Jaycees 137
J.C. Penney 167, 203
Jefferson Pilot Broadcasting 67
Jefferson, Thomas 24, 26, 52, 53, 73-75, 248
Jesse Helms Center 128, 134
Jesus 9, 11, 192, 194, 196, 197, 203, 204 (see also: Saviour)
Jews 160
Jim Crow-law 180-181
John Birch Society 47
John Locke Foundation 163
Johnson, Lyndon 79, 99
Johnson, Paul 26
Jordan, Michael 58, 253
Jordan, Vernon 104
Junior League 263

Keohane, Nan 258-259
Kendall, David 32, 34
Kennedy, John (JFK) v, 47, 99
Kennedy, Teddy 47
Kennedy, Anthony 157
Kenya 120
Key, V.O. 76
Robert Khayat 231
Khomeini (Ayatollah) 27
King, Martin Luther, Jr. (Dr.) 58, 133
Kleinschmidt, Mark 168
Klopman, William 187-188
Knesset 115
Kornegay, Byron 30, 32, 33

Kremlin 94
Kristol, William 109
Krzyzewski, Mike 255, 256, 259-260 (see also Coach K)
Kudzu 14
Ku Klux Klan 17, 35, 126, 136, 245
Kuralt, Charles 59, 236
Kurds 111, 112
Kushner, Tony 242
Kuwait 87, 89-92, 94, 107, 113, 115

Lafayette, Marquis de 25
Latin America 28
Latta, E.D. 53-54, 58, 63
Latta Park 54
Lavitan, Gladys 236
Lawrence, David 196, 270
Lee, Richard Henry 22
Lee, Robert E. 102
Lee, William States 59
Lewinsky, Monica 100-101, 104
Liberia 145
Liberty Bell Award vii
Lincoln, Abraham 23, 102
Locke, Pat 81
Lomax, Sonny 208
Long, Betty Jane 44-45
Long, Huey 18
Louis XVI (King) 25
Louisiana 17, 18
Lowder, Ephraim 188
Luebke, Paul 6
Lugar, Richard 119
Lumumba, Patrice 28

Madison, James 55, 73
Mapplethorpe, Robert 129-130
Marlette, Doug 7, 12, 13, 14-16, 75, 90, 116, 138, 151, 159, 195-197, 198, 201, 217, 255, 270
Marlette, Melinda Hartley 270
Marshall, John (Chief Justice) 75
Martin, Harry 153-154
Martin, Hoyle 159
Martin, Jim (Gov., Congressman) 77, 80-81
Martin, Joan 233
Martin, Joe 233-234
Martin, T.T. 42-43
Mashburn, L.R. 31
Masterson, Dorothy 236
Mathis, Carolyn 81
McColl, Hugh, Jr. 59, 63-64, 233
McCullough, W.T. 44
McCrory, Pat 242
McDonald's 186
McDougall, Walter A. 24
McGovern, George 77, 81
McLaughlin, Virginia 221
McMillan, James (U.S. Judge) 67, 146
Meadows, Joseph 39

Mecklenburg Baptist Association 193
Mecklenburg County 49-70
Mecklenburg County Bar Association vii
Mecklenburg County commissioners 158-160
Mecklenburg Declaration of Independence (Meck Dec) 51-52, 53
Mecklenburg League of Women Voters 65
Mecklenburg Resolves 51
Medicare 97, 133
Meek, Walter (Buck) 45
Memorial Hospital 212
Memphis 17, 36, 207
Mencken, H.L. 94
Mercedes-Benz 140
Meredith, James v, 37, 48
Mexico 97
Mexico City 35
Michelangelo 239
Middle East 106, 107
Mideast 28, 87-92
Millay, Edna St. Vincent 16
Miller Brewing Co. 183
Minnery, Tom 158
Minnich, Elizabeth Kamarck 270
Minor, Bill 231
Minor, Wilson F. 270
Mint Museum 53, 238, 246
Mint Theatre Guild 236
Mississippi v, vi, 16-18, 26, 29-48, 164, 232, 269
Mississippi Freedom Democratic Party 40
Mississippi Freelance vi
Mississippi, Greenville v, 16, 18
Mississippi, Newton County 32
Mississippi State University 46, 68
Mississippian v, vi, 45, 48, 230
Missouri 36, 207
Moeser, James 258-259
Morgan Guaranty Savings and Loan 101
Monroe, James 73
Moore, Richard 120
Moore, Russel 38
Morrison, Cameron 64
Moss, J.G. 45
Mossadegh, Mohammad 27
Muhleman, Max 54
Murphy, Eddie 139
Museum of the New South 14, 23
Myers Park Baptist Church 112, 190, 193-195, 203, 233
Myers Park High School 222
Myrick, Sue 64

NAACP 60
Naismith, James 252

National Endowment for the Arts (NEA) 131, 239-240
National Public Radio 235
National Rifle Association 171, 191
NationsBank 54
NASCAR 225
NATO 114
Nazis 192
NCAA 250, 254-255, 256
N.C. Baptist State Convention 193-195
N.C. State University 168
NCNB 233
Neill, Rolfe 269-270
Neshoba County vi, 30-33
Neshoba Democrat 33
New Deal 79
New Orleans 26
New Orleans Times-Picayune 231
New South 14, 23, 65, 76, 142
New York Times 67, 110, 245 (see also NY Times)
Niebuhr, Reinhold 106
Nieman Foundation vi
nigger 139-141, 142
Nike 255
Nixon, Richard 47, 67, 75, 76-77, 99
North American Free Trade Agreement (NAFTA) 97, 119
North Calvary Baptist Church 32
North Carolina 4, 12, 14
North Carolina Coalition Against Domestic Violence 164
North Carolina Journalism Hall of Fame vii
North Carolina Literary Hall of Fame 35
Northern Ireland 118
Northside Park 31
Notre Dame 37
nuclear power 107
NY Times 12

Obama, Barack 72, 118-122
Obama, Michelle 167
Oldham, Dorothy 230-231
Ole Miss v, vi, vii, 36, 37, 47, 48, 229-230, 269 (see also University of Mississippi)
Omni Charlotte Hotel 161
Oppel, Rich 2, 129, 270
Orr, Robert 163
Owen, Ben 44
Owen, John 144
Oxford, Mississippi 14, 228, 229

Pahlavi, Mohammed Reza (Shah) 27
Paine, Thomas 23
Paine, Hank 230-231
Palestinians 121
Palin, Sarah 167

Parchman (prison) 47
Parents and Friends of Lesbians and Gays 160
Parker, Kathleen 15
Pataki, George 78
Patrick, Cheri C. 166
Payne, Gene 10
Peabody Hotel 17
Pelosi, Nancy 84
Pentagon 105, 115, 116, 117
Percy, Walker 18
Percy, William Alexander 17
Perry, Marshall 38
Perdue, Bev 120, 165
Perlmutt, David 234
Perry, Antoinette 236
Persian Gulf 89-92
Peters, Mike 12
Philadelphia, Pa. 22, 64, 121, 145
Philadelphia, Miss. 32, 33
Phillips, Jim, Jr., 120
"Playboys" 145
Poole, Samuel 149
Potter, Robert 147, 199
Powell, Colin 78, 98, 109, 110
Powell, Dannye Romine 14, 270
Powell, Lew 270
Powell, Dwane 16
Presbyterian 46-47, 51, 52
Price, Cecil 34
Price, David 120
Princeton 52
pro-life 84
Pulitzer Prize vii, 2, 13, 14, 18, 24
PTL 196, 197-199

Quayle, Dan 95
Queens College 233

Rams Club 257
Rand, Tony 120
Randolph-Macon 230
Rather, Dan 67
Reagan, Ronald 47, 79, 95, 132, 137
Reconstruction 119, 142
Reed, Conrad 53, 59
Reed, Roy 270
Reese, Addison 63
Revolutionary War 24-26, 246
Rice, Condoleezza 78
Ridder, Peter 270
Right to Work 183
Riley, Dick 94-95
Ritchie, Fiona 235
Robinson, William G. 172
Rodin, Auguste 239
Rogers, Will 15
Roosevelt, Franklin (FDR) 79-80, 99, 102
Roth, Jennifer 235
Rowan Oak 228-231

Rubin, Trudy 117
Rumsfeld, Donald 107, 109, 115-117
Rundgren, Todd 132
Russell, Daniel 142
Russia 114

Sabatini, Rafael 237
Saluda Swim and Tennis Club 137
Samaritan's Purse 166, 201
Sandburg, Carl 58
Sanford, Terry 48
Sargent, Ben 13
Saudi Arabia 86, 88, 90
Saviour 42, 196 (see also Jesus)
Scalia, Antonin 152, 158, 170-172
Schlesinger, James 117
Schwarzenegger, Arnold 78
Schweitzer, Albert 193
Scopes trial 41
Scott, Bob 1 87
Seagrove Pottery 246
Seagrove Pottery Musuem 246
Sears, Roebuck & Co. 57-58
segregation v, 17, 18, 48, 61, 147, 245
Sept. 11 (attacks) 201-202
Seven Years' War 26
Shamrock Gardens 148
Sharp, Thurman 32-33
Shields, Walton 43
Shiite Muslims 111
Shinn, George 54
Shinn, Jerry 129-131
Shinseki, Eric (Gen.) 116
Shoemaker, Steve 233
Siers, Kevin 7, 9, 10, 11, 12, 14, 98, 127, 133, 172, 193, 210, 217, 220, 258
Silver, James 34-37, 269
Sir Walter Raleigh Award 14
slavery 22, 36, 144-145
Smith, Al 35
Smith, Dean 254, 256
Smith, Eric 147, 224
Snepp, Frank 181
Sobran, Joseph 10
Social Security 975, 133
Solomon, Marcia 160-161
Soucek, Dan 166
South Africa vi, vii
South Africans 121
South Korea 114
Southern Baptist Church 195
Southern Literary Festival 229
Soviet sphere 27
Soviet Union 119
Spain 114
Spangler, Dick 256-257, 264
Spencer, Samuel 55
Spirit Square 5, 159-160
Stam, Paul 164, 168

Starr, Kenneth 100-101
Stennis, John 38
Stern, Howard 7
Storrs, Tom 63
Stroud, Wade 69
Strug, Kerri 97
Sturkey, Don 270
Summers, Lester 39
Supreme Court 22, 38, 44, 61, 64, 77,
    104, 138, 139, 149, 152, 153-154,
    155, 157-158, 161-162, 163, 164,
    170-171, 192
Swann vs. Charlotte-Mecklenburg 61
Switzer, Barry 254
Swofford, John 256

Talbert, Samuel 269
Taliban 202
Tar Heel 252, 256
Tarleton, Banastre (Col.) 42
Teamsters 181
Tennessee National Guard 115
terrorism 89, 105
terrorists 26, 105, 115
Tea Party 163
Ten Commandments 191-192
Texas 13, 152, 157
textile mills 2, 186-188
Thames, Rick 270
"Thistle and Shamrock, The" 235
Thomas, Clarence 157
Thompson, John 256
Thrash, R.C. 32
Thurmond, Strom 76-77
Tillett, Gladys Avery 64-65
Tillis, Thom 167
Tin Fulton Walker & Owen 168
tobacco companies 185-186
Tompkins, D.A. 53, 58, 65, 76, 142-
    143
Tougaloo 229-230
Trujillo, Rafael 28
TownPark Players 236
Truman, Harry 79
Tsongas, Paul 79
Tulsa World 14, 15
Turkey 111
Turner, James Harvey 44
Tyson, Timothy 141

unions (labor) 182-185
United Fruit Co. 27
United Nations (U.N.) 83, 87, 88, 90,
    91, 107, 108, 109-110, 112, 113,
    118, 134
United Way 162
University of Minnesota 233
University of Mississippi 14, 35, 215
    (see also Ole Miss)
University of North Carolina (UNC) 63,

68, 120, 125, 133, 134, 144-145,
    146, 164, 168, 235, 250, 251, 253,
    255, 256-257, 258, 264
University of North Carolina-Charlotte
    (UNCC) 54, 61-62, 68-69
University of North Carolina-
    Greensboro 64
US Airways 6
U.S. Army 179, 215, 269
U.S. Mint 59

Vanderbilt 35
Vicksburg 17
Vietnam 15, 26, 87, 89-91
Vinroot, Richard 77, 163
Virginia 22, 230
Virginia Tech 173, 174-175
Vitale, Dick 253

Wachovia 63
Wad's 15
Wainwright, Loudon, III 132
Wake Forest 35
Waldron, Ann 17
Walker, Alice 231
Walker, Percy 237
Wallace, George 38, 48
Wallace, Gerald 245
Waller, Bill 40
Walsh, Rob 56
War Production Board 248
Warren, Robert Penn 229
Washburn, George 41-42, 248
Washington, George 25, 59, 73, 74
Watt, Mel 120
WBT 9, 66-67
WBTV 67
weapons of mass destruction 107-108,
    112-113, 118
Welty, Eudora 229, 213-233
West Germany 21
Weyhe, Arthur 238
WFAE 235
whiskey 32, 34
white supremacy 141, 143
Whitewater Development Co. 101
Whitfield, Gov. 43
Whitman, Walt 242
Wicker, Tom 10
Wilkenses 207
Wilkie, Curtis 270
Williams, John Bell 34
Williams, Carl 206, 214-215, 269
Williams Gro. and Mkt. 207
Williams, Jonathan 211-212, 216-218,
    221, 222
Williams, Marylyn Lentine 207, 208,
    209-210, 211-212, 215, 216-218,
    221
Williams, Roy 250

Williams, Vina 206, 214-216, 269
Williamses 207
Wilson, Thomas 115
Wilson, Tina N. 4
Windham, Eck 17
Windham, E.K. 42
Winston-Salem 7, 63
Winston-Salem Sentinel 247
Winter, W.A. 43
Witherspoon, John 52
Wolfowitz, Paul 109, 116, 117
Wood, Jack 56
Works Progress Administration 232
World Trade Center 105, 107
World War I 26, 62, 247
World War II 26, 45, 61, 102, 117, 146,
    248
WRAL 168
Wrenn, Carter 80
Wright, Jeremiah 121-122
Wylie, Walker Gill 59
Winfrey, Oprah 167
Wynn, W.T. 42

Yates, Sidney 240
Yawer, Ghazi al 116
Yorktown 25
Young Men's Christian Association
    252